Wine Guide

2014

By Mary  Edward Nalley

WINE GUIDE 2014

editor in chief **DANA COWIN**
executive wine editor **RAY ISLE**
deputy editor **CHRISTINE QUINLAN**
design director **PATRICIA SANCHEZ**
volume editor **WENDY G. RAMUNNO**
contributing editors **KRISTEN WOLFE BIELER, TARA Q. THOMAS**
copy editor **ELZY KOLB**
research chief **JANICE HUANG**
researchers **NANCY FANN-IM, ELLEN MCCURTIN, PAOLA SINGER**
digital coordinator **JOHN KERN**

design concept **PLEASURE / KEVIN BRAINARD & RAUL AGUILA**

cover photography **JONNY VALIANT**
prop stylist **SUZIE MYERS**
"Blossom" wineglass by Rogaska

produced for FOOD & WINE magazine by
gonzalez defino, ny / gonzalezdefino.com
principals **JOSEPH GONZALEZ, PERRI DEFINO**

AMERICAN EXPRESS PUBLISHING CORPORATION

president/ceo **ED KELLY**
chief marketing officer/president, digital media **MARK V. STANICH**
senior vice president/chief financial officer **PAUL B. FRANCIS**
vice presidents/general managers **FRANK BLAND, KEITH STROHMEIER**

vice president, books & products/publisher **MARSHALL COREY**
director, book programs **BRUCE SPANIER**
senior marketing manager, branded books **ERIC LUCIE**
associate marketing manager **STACY MALLIS**
director of fulfillment & premium value **PHILIP BLACK**
manager of customer service & product fulfillment **BETSY WILSON**
director of finance **THOMAS NOONAN**
associate business manager **UMA MAHABIR**
operations director (prepress) **ROSALIE ABATEMARCO SAMAT**
operations director (manufacturing) **ANTHONY WHITE**

ISSN 1522-001X
Manufactured in the United States of America.

FOOD&WINE
BOOKS
American Express Publishing Corporation, New York

Wine
Guide

2014

FRANCE ITALY SPAIN PORTUGAL GERMANY AUSTRIA GREECE UNITED STATES AUSTRALIA NEW ZEALAND ARGENTINA CHILE SOUTH AFRICA

Contents

Wine Guide

OLD WORLD

2014

Foreword

In the Tasting Room at FOOD & WINE, we try more than 2,000 wines each year, at every price level, from every wine-producing region in the world. This work is essential for the magazine—not only does it help us suggest pairings for recipes, it gives us a comprehensive sense of what the wine talents of the world are doing. That knowledge is crucial for this book, our yearly guide to the most trustworthy wine producers in the world. We've chosen the 500 we feel are the best of the best, so that you can pick a great bottle no matter what store or restaurant you happen to be in, and no matter how much you want to spend. (And, for that matter, no matter what you might be cooking or eating.) This year, to make the guide even more helpful, we've changed the format slightly: Rather than recommending specific vintages, we simply highlight one or two of each producer's signature bottlings, wines that have proven to be reliably great year in and year out. Our goal is to simplify the sometimes daunting process of buying wine; we hope you feel we've succeeded.

Dana Cowin
Dana Cowin
Editor in Chief
FOOD & WINE

Ray Isle
Ray Isle
Executive Wine Editor
FOOD & WINE

KEY TO SYMBOLS

TYPE OF WINE
- ● RED
- ● ROSÉ
- ○ WHITE

PRICE
- $$$$ OVER $60
- $$$ $30+ TO $60
- $$ $15+ TO $30
- $ $15 AND UNDER

FOR MORE EXPERT WINE-BUYING ADVICE

Join the F&W community at *foodandwine.com*

Follow us *@fandw*

Become a fan at *facebook.com/foodandwine*

Wine / Terms

You won't find much fussy wine jargon in this guide, but some of the terms commonly used to describe the taste of wine might be unfamiliar or used in an unfamiliar way. References to flavors and textures other than "grape" are meant to serve as analogies: All the wines in this guide are made from grapes, but grapes have the ability to suggest the flavors of other fruits, herbs or minerals. Here's a mini glossary to help you become comfortable with the language of wine.

ACIDITY The tart, tangy or zesty sensations in wine. Ideally, acidity brightens a wine's flavors as a squeeze of lemon brightens fish. Wines lacking acidity taste "flabby."

APPELLATION An officially designated winegrowing region. The term is used mostly in France and the U.S. In Europe, a wine's appellation usually reflects not only where it's from but also aspects of how it's made, such as vineyard yields and aging.

BALANCE The harmony between acidity, tannin, alcohol and sweetness in a wine.

BIODYNAMICS An organic, sustainable approach to farming that takes into account a farm's total environment, including surrounding ecosystems and astronomical considerations, such as the phases of the moon.

BODY How heavy or thick a wine feels in the mouth. Full-bodied or heavy wines are often described as "big."

CORKED Wines that taste like wet cork or newspaper are said to be corked. The cause is trichloroanisole (TCA), a contaminant sometimes transmitted by cork.

CRISP A term used to describe wines that are high in acidity.

CRU In France, a grade of vineyard (such as *grand cru* or *premier cru*), winery (such as Bordeaux's *cru bourgeois*) or village (in Beaujolais). Also used unofficially in Italy's Piedmont region to refer to top Barolo vineyards.

CUVÉE A batch of wine. A cuvée can be from a single barrel or tank (*cuve* in French), or a blend of different lots of wine. A Champagne house's top bottling is called a *tête de cuvée*.

DRY A wine without perceptible sweetness. A dry wine, however, can have powerful fruit flavors. *Off-dry* describes a wine that has a touch of sweetness.

EARTHY An earthy wine evokes flavors such as mushrooms, leather, damp straw or even manure.

FILTER/FINE Processes used to remove sediment or particulates from a wine to enhance its clarity.

FINISH The length of time a wine's flavors linger on the palate. A long finish is the hallmark of a more complex wine.

FRUITY A wine with an abundance of fruit flavors is described as fruity. Such wines may give the impression of sweetness, even though they're not actually sweet.

HERBACEOUS Calling a wine herbaceous or herbal can be positive or negative. Wines that evoke herb flavors can be delicious. Wines with green pepper flavors are less than ideal, and are also referred to as "vegetal."

LEES The sediment (including dead yeast cells) left over after a wine's fermentation. Aging a wine on its lees (*sur lie* in French) gives wine nutty flavors and a creamy texture.

MINERAL Flavors that (theoretically) reflect the minerals found in the soil in which the grapes were grown. The terms *steely, flinty* and *chalky* are also used to describe these flavors.

NÉGOCIANT In wine terms, a *négociant* (French for "merchant") is someone who buys grapes, grape juice or finished wines in order to blend, bottle and sell wine under his or her own label.

NOSE How a wine smells; its bouquet or aroma.

OAKY Wines that transmit the flavors of the oak barrels in which they were aged. Some oak can impart toast flavors.

OXIDIZED Wines that have a tarnished quality due to exposure to air are said to be oxidized. When intended, as in the case of sherry (see p. 291), oxidation can add fascinating dimensions to a wine. Otherwise, it can make a wine taste unappealing.

PALATE The flavors, textures and other sensations a wine gives in the mouth. The term *mid-palate* refers to the way these characteristics evolve with time in the mouth.

POWERFUL Wine that is full of flavor, tannin and/or alcohol.

RUSTIC Wine that is a bit rough, though often charming.

TANNIN A component of grape skins, seeds and stems, tannin is most commonly found in red wines. It imparts a puckery sensation similar to oversteeped tea. Tannin also gives a wine its structure and enables some wines to age well.

TERROIR A French term that refers to the particular attributes a wine acquires from the specific environment of a vineyard— i.e., the climate, soil type, elevation and aspect.

Wine
Buying Guide

Knowing where and how to shop for wine makes discovering great wines easy and even fun, no matter where you live or what your budget. Take advantage of these tips to shop smarter.

IN SHOPS

SCOPE OUT THE SHOPS Visit local wine shops and determine which ones have the most helpful salespeople, the best selection and the lowest prices. Ask about case discounts, and whether mixing and matching a case is allowed. Expect at least a 10 percent discount; some stores will offer more. These days, many retailers are increasing their discounts and offering one-liter bottles and three-liter wine boxes that deliver more wine for the money. Finally, pay attention to store temperature: The warmer the store, the more likely the wines are to have problems.

ASK QUESTIONS Most wine-savvy salespeople are eager to share their knowledge and recommend some of their favorite wines. Let them know your likes, your budget and anything else that might help them select a wine you'll love.

BECOME A REGULAR The better the store's salespeople know you, the better they can suggest wines that will please you. Take the time to report back on wines they've suggested—it will pay off in future recommendations.

GET ON THE LIST Top wine shops often alert interested customers to special sales, hard-to-find wines or great deals in advance. Ask to get on their e-mail lists.

ONLINE

KNOW YOUR OPTIONS Take advantage of the Internet to easily find the wine you want and get the best price on it. The two most common ways to buy wine online are via online retailers or directly from wineries. Retailers may offer bulk discounts if you buy a case and shipping discounts if you spend a certain amount. Wineries don't often discount, but their wines can be impossible to find elsewhere. A great advantage of online shopping is price comparison: Websites like Wine-Searcher.com allow you to compare prices at retailers around the world.

BE WILLING TO ACT FAST Some of the steepest discounts on prestigious or hard-to-find wines are offered via so-called "flash sales" at sites such as WineAccess.com, WinesTilSoldOut.com and Lot18.com. Announced by e-mail, sales typically last just a day or two, and the best deals might sell out in under an hour.

KNOW THE RULES The difference between browsing for wine online and actually purchasing it has everything to do with where you live and how "liberal" your state is about interstate wine shipments. The laws governing direct-to-consumer inter-state shipments differ from state to state. If you're considering buying wine from an out-of-state vendor, find out first whether it can ship to your state.

KNOW THE WEATHER If you're ordering wine online when it's hot outside, it's worth paying for express delivery: A week spent roasting in the back of a delivery truck risks turning your prized case of Pinot into plonk. Some retailers and wineries offer free storage during the summer months; they'll hold purchased wine until the weather cools and you give the OK to ship.

IN RESTAURANTS
CHECK OUT THE LIST Many restaurants post their wine list online or are happy to e-mail it upon request. Scoping out the wine menu in advance dramatically increases your odds of picking the right wine for your meal. For starters, if the selection looks poor, you can ask about the restaurant's corkage policy and perhaps bring your own bottle instead. A mediocre list

might be limited in selection, have a disproportionate number of wines from one producer, fail to specify vintages or carry old vintages of wines meant to be drunk young and fresh. When faced with a bad wine list, order the least expensive bottle that you recognize as being reasonably good.

On the other hand, if the list is comprehensive, you can spend all the time you like perusing it in advance, rather than boring your dining companions while you pore over it at the table. You'll have plenty of time to spot bargains (or overpriced bottles) and to set an ordering strategy based on the list's strengths and your own preferences.

ASK QUESTIONS Treat the wine list as you would a food menu. You should ask how the Bordeaux tastes in comparison to the California Cabernet as readily as you'd ask about the difference between two fish dishes. Ask to speak to the wine director, if there is one. Then, tell that person the type of wine you're looking for—the price range, the flavor profile—as well as the dishes you will be having. If you want to indicate a price range without announcing the amount to the table, point to a bottle on the list that costs about what you want to spend and explain that you are considering something like it. And if you're unsure how to describe the flavors you're looking for, name a favorite producer who makes wine in a style you like. With this information, the wine director should be able to recommend several options.

TASTE THE WINE When the bottle arrives, make sure it's exactly what you ordered—check the vintage, the producer and the blend or variety. If it's not, speak up. You may be presented with the cork. Ignore it. Instead, sniff the wine in your glass. If it smells like sulfur, cabbage or skunk, tell your server that you think the wine might be flawed and request a second opinion from the wine director or the manager. If there's something truly wrong, they should offer you a new bottle or a new choice.

OLD WOR

France/
Italy/
Spain/
Portugal/
Germany/
Austria/
Greece/

66
ITALY

134
GERMANY

LD

16
FRANCE

104
SPAIN

126
PORTUGAL

144
AUSTRIA

154
GREECE

France

Wine Region

"Burgundy makes you think of silly things, Bordeaux makes you speak of them and Champagne makes you do them." That's a quote from the 18th-century French epicure Jean Anthelme Brillat-Savarin, wittily dispensing with France's three most famous wine regions. Of course, if Brillat-Savarin had tried to cover all of France's wine regions, he would have found himself rambling on for hours. France is the most significant country in the world when it comes to wine. It's the birthplace of most of the grapes we know best, and it bottles more than a billion gallons of wine every year—everything from utterly nondescript plonk to the greatest wines in the world. There's no way around it: If you want to learn about wine, you have to learn about France.

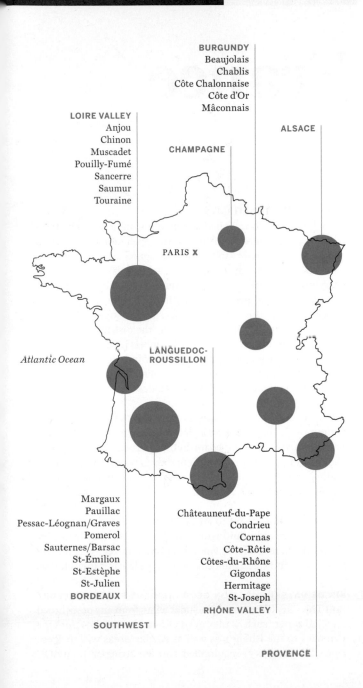

BURGUNDY
Beaujolais
Chablis
Côte Chalonnaise
Côte d'Or
Mâconnais

LOIRE VALLEY
Anjou
Chinon
Muscadet
Pouilly-Fumé
Sancerre
Saumur
Touraine

ALSACE

CHAMPAGNE

PARIS **X**

Atlantic Ocean

LANGUEDOC-ROUSSILLON

Margaux
Pauillac
Pessac-Léognan/Graves
Pomerol
Sauternes/Barsac
St-Émilion
St-Estèphe
St-Julien
BORDEAUX

Châteauneuf-du-Pape
Condrieu
Cornas
Côte-Rôtie
Côtes-du-Rhône
Gigondas
Hermitage
St-Joseph
RHÔNE VALLEY

SOUTHWEST

PROVENCE

France/

WINE TERMINOLOGY

French wine regions, called appellations, indicate more than where a wine comes from. To use an appellation on a label, a producer is required to follow rules designed to ensure that the wine reflects a certain style and quality. Regulations can cover everything from permitted grape varieties and harvest dates to aging periods and production methods. The most prestigious appellations are tiny sub-appellations within larger regions: In general, the smaller and more specific the district, the stricter its rules. Although most French wine labels list an appellation, few indicate the grape used to make the wine. (Alsace labels are an important exception; see opposite.) From bottom to top, the hierarchy of quality designations includes:

VIN DE TABLE *Vin de table* labels are not permitted to mention vintages or grapes or to give a place of origin more specific than France. Most of these wines are dull, but certain iconoclasts have chosen to ignore some AOC demands (see opposite) and are making great wines labeled *vin de table*. The category is being phased out and incorporated into the *vin de France* category.

VIN DE FRANCE Meant to attract drinkers more interested in grape variety and brand name than origin, this new category allows vintners to blend wines from different regions and still list vintage and variety information on the labels if they choose.

VIN DE PAYS/INDICATION GÉOGRAPHIQUE PROTÉGÉE (VDP/ IGP) The VdP/IGP category includes wines from any of six broad regional zones (such as the Pays d'Oc, which stretches from the Pyrenees to the Rhône), as well as smaller areas within these zones. The category's requirements are less stringent than AOC regulations, allowing for higher yields and greater freedom in choosing grape varieties. Winemakers may also label VdP/IGP wines with the grape variety. The category is appealing to those who wish to produce large quantities of commercial wines, but there are also vintners who take advantage of the designation's relative freedom to put out quirky, high-quality bottlings.

APPELLATION D'ORIGINE CONTRÔLÉE/APPELLATION D'ORIGINE PROTÉGÉE (AOC/AOP) The AOC (controlled region of origin) category encompasses most French wines exported to the U.S. Standards vary by region and typically spell out permitted grapes, winemaking practices, minimum alcohol levels and harvest size (overly large harvests tend to yield dilute wines). There are AOC regions within larger AOC regions as well; generally, the more specific the subregion, the higher the standards (and, often, the price). A new, optional designation for AOC wines is AOP (protected region of origin), which EU regulators hope all member countries will soon be using; it maintains basically the same requirements as AOC and could provide consistency from country to country.

ALSACE

CLAIM TO FAME

Alsace produces some of the world's finest Rieslings and Gewurztraminers, two Germanic grapes that reflect the bicultural heritage of this eastern border region. Blocked from cool, wet Atlantic weather by the Vosges Mountains, the sunny Alsace climate creates wines that are lusher and more powerful than the German versions. Their combination of zesty acidity, minerality and, often, a hint of sweetness makes them incredibly food-friendly, while their reasonable prices offer terrific value. Alsace wines are also refreshingly easy to identify and understand: Bottled in skinny, tapered green glass, they carry the name of the grape variety (or type of blend) on the label.

🍇 KEY GRAPES: WHITE

GEWURZTRAMINER Often made in an off-dry (i.e., slightly sweet) style, spicy Alsace Gewurztraminers (*gewürz* means "spice" in German) display flamboyant lychee and floral aromas.

MUSCAT Alsace Muscat can be made from three different Muscat varieties: Muscat Blanc à Petit Grains, Rosé à Petit Grains and Ottonel. The wines tend to be delicate, lightly floral and dry, although some sweet late-harvest versions are made.

PINOT BLANC Alsace wines labeled *Pinot Blanc* often contain a second, similar variety called Auxerrois; winemakers are also allowed to add Pinot Gris and/or Pinot Noir that has been vinified as white wine. Regardless, Pinot Blanc–labeled wines tend to be broad and full-bodied, with musky apple and floral tones, and sometimes a touch of sweetness.

PINOT GRIS Pinot Gris is the same grape as Italy's Pinot Grigio, yet the wines are very different: Alsace Pinot Gris tends to be creamier and richer than its light, crisp Italian counterparts.

RIESLING The region's most widely planted grape is also arguably its greatest, yielding medium-bodied wines whose stony flavors reflect the minerally soils. Styles range from bone-dry to sweet, though most Alsace Rieslings are dry. There's no uniform labeling requirement to indicate sugar levels.

SYLVANER, AUXERROIS & CHASSELAS These unexceptional varieties don't generally make great wines on their own and are nearly always blended with more powerful, distinctive types such as Riesling, Gewurztraminer, Muscat and Pinot Gris.

 KEY GRAPES: RED
PINOT NOIR The region's only red grape makes light red and rosé wines defined by their crisp berry character, as well as the rare sparkling Blanc de Noirs of Crémant d'Alsace.

WINE TERMINOLOGY
ALSACE The basic Alsace designation includes nearly all of the region's still wines. Quality standards that these wines must meet include a limit on vineyard yields (lower yields generally mean higher quality) and minimum ripeness levels for grapes.

CRÉMANT D'ALSACE These sparkling wines are usually based chiefly on the Pinot Blanc grape and feature perky acidity and fresh, fruity flavors.

EDELZWICKER This term is used to denote blends made from Alsace's best varieties (*edel* means "noble" in German). It's now a catchall category for white blends, typically simple, zesty wines that taste best when consumed within a year or so of release.

GENTIL Generally of a higher quality than *edelzwicker* blends (see above), *gentil* wines are made to AOC standards. These multivariety blends must contain at least 50 percent of some combination of Riesling, Gewurztraminer and Muscat.

GRAND CRU Wines from 51 vineyards may use this relatively recent designation, which comes with limits on vineyard yields. Most of the vineyards are recognized as outstanding, but some producers have protested the inclusion of a handful of controversial sites and don't use the term *grand cru* on their wines.

RÉSERVE Producers use this term to indicate a higher-quality wine, though its exact meaning is not regulated.

VENDANGES TARDIVES/SÉLECTION DE GRAINS NOBLES These sweet whites are made from very ripe, late-harvested grapes (see p. 298).

Producers/ Alsace

ALBERT BOXLER

Most of the vineyards at this small estate west of Colmar lie in *grand cru* territory, which partly accounts for the quality of its wines. Another factor is continuity: Jean and Sylvie Boxler live in the same sturdy farmhouse in which Jean's ancestors made their wines for the past three centuries. The fame of Boxler's whites rests on dense, racy Rieslings from Brand and Sommerberg, two of Alsace's greatest sites. Easier to find, and likewise superb, are Boxler's brilliant Pinot Gris and Gewurztraminer.

BOTTLES TO TRY

○ **Pinot Gris / $$**
○ **Sommerberg Grand Cru Riesling / $$$**

ANDRÉ KIENTZLER

Crumbling castles top the vine-latticed hills around Ribeauvillé, the medieval village of movie-set picturesqueness where Thierry Kientzler fashions his coveted white wines. Sourced from a trio of exalted *grand cru* vineyards—Geisberg, Kirchberg de Ribeauvillé and Osterberg—the estate's top cuvées have made their maker into Alsace's most unassuming star. Not given to brashness, Kientzler leaves the dazzle to his wines, from stony Osterberg Rieslings to powerful, taut Gewurztraminers. The entry-level wines offer textbook purity at compelling prices.

BOTTLES TO TRY

○ **Gewurztraminer / $$**
○ **Osterberg Grand Cru Riesling / $$$**

DOMAINES SCHLUMBERGER

Most midsize and large wineries in Alsace buy grapes and unfinished wine from small growers to complement their estate-grown fruit. But family-owned Schlumberger owns the largest domaine in Alsace—some 300 acres—giving it remarkable control over quality for its size. Its *grand cru* sites yield benchmark Gewurztraminer and Riesling, while entry-level wines—named for the prince-abbots who once owned much of the estate—are now more consistent. Its signature style combines lushness with crisp acidity in wines that are intense but not heavy.

BOTTLES TO TRY

○ **Les Princes Abbés Riesling / $$**
○ **Kitterlé Gewurztraminer / $$$**

DOMAINE WEINBACH

The walled Clos des Capucins vineyard lies at the heart of this ancient estate, known as Weinbach (wine creek) when the Capuchin monks arrived in 1612. It's one of a handful of renowned sites that the Faller family draws on for its sumptuous white wines; others include the Schlossberg, Furstentum and Altenbourg vineyards, all farmed biodynamically. Winemaker Laurence Faller zeroes in on micro-plots of vines to create as many as 20 to 30 different cuvées in a single vintage, including luscious, powerful Rieslings and Gewurztraminers.

BOTTLES TO TRY

○ **Réserve Personnelle Gewurztraminer / $$**
○ **Cuvée Ste. Catherine Riesling / $$$**

DOMAINE ZIND-HUMBRECHT

Olivier Humbrecht turned his family's estate into one of France's most influential wineries—not by modernizing it but by going back to radically traditional winemaking. Working with fruit from a magnificent collection of vineyards assembled by his parents, Léonard and Ginette, the erudite Humbrecht eschews fining, filtration, added yeasts and almost any kind of modern manipulation of grape juice. In recent years, his sumptuous, saturated wines—already among the best in Alsace—have shown even greater precision and purity, a change Humbrecht attributes to biodynamic farming.

BOTTLES TO TRY
- Gewurztraminer / $$
- Grand Cru Brand Riesling / $$$$

HUGEL ET FILS

It's not surprising that Hugel's wines are so consistent: The family has been turning out some of Alsace's best bottlings for some 375 years. Passed down from fathers to sons for 12 generations, Hugel offers wines in three tiers. Entry-level bottlings are dry, crisp and food-friendly; Tradition cuvées are a step up in complexity; the finest, labeled Jubilee, come from family-owned vineyards, including superb *grand cru* sites. Easiest to find is Hugel's affordable Gentil, a lightly floral blend of five varieties.

BOTTLES TO TRY
- Gentil / $
- Pinot Gris / $$
- Jubilee Riesling / $$$

JOSMEYER

Proprietor Jean Meyer spent a decade converting Josmeyer to an all-estate-grown, biodynamically farmed domaine, a move that cut production in half and boosted quality. Now in a background role, Meyer leaves the winemaking to his daughter Isabelle and vineyard management to his former son-in-law Christophe Ehrhart, who spearheaded the move to eco-friendly farming. Despite the changes, the Josmeyer house style—elegant, with clean-cut fruit and mineral flavors—remains intact.

BOTTLES TO TRY
- Pinot Blanc / $$
- Le Dragon Riesling / $$$

KUENTZ-BAS

Alsace fans have cheered the revitalization of Kuentz-Bas, a venerable estate set in Husseren-Les-Châteaux, a village with a bird's-eye view of the Rhine Valley. Fourteenth-generation Alsace vintner Jean-Baptiste Adam acquired the property from Kuentz-Bas cousins in 2004 and promptly slashed yields, converted to organic and biodynamic farming and installed Samuel Tottoli as winemaker. The results have been dramatic: Even the least expensive wine, a crisp, four-variety white blend (known simply as the Blanc), is multifaceted and delicious.

BOTTLES TO TRY

○ **Kuentz-Bas Blanc** ∕ **$**
○ **Trois Châteaux Pfersigberg Riesling** ∕ **$$$**

TRIMBACH

Trimbach's bracing, mineral-rich wines include some of Alsace's most reliable bargains as well as some of its most iconic whites, such as the collectible, coveted Clos Ste. Hune Riesling. Made since 1626 by the Trimbach family, the wines are uncompromisingly dry, steely and fresh. Trimbach doesn't recognize *grand cru* designations for most vineyards; look instead for white or gold labels, reserved for its best wines.

BOTTLES TO TRY

○ **Réserve Pinot Gris** ∕ **$$**
○ **Cuvée Frédéric Emile Riesling** ∕ **$$$**
○ **Clos Ste. Hune Riesling** ∕ **$$$$**

BORDEAUX

CLAIM TO FAME

Bordeaux's stratospherically priced premier red wines—with names like Lafite, Latour and Pétrus—set the standard by which other Cabernet Sauvignon– and Merlot-based bottlings produced around the world are judged. Unfortunately, the Bordeaux stars also overshadow the millions of bottles of affordable and frequently delicious wines that this vast Atlantic region produces. Its perfect combination of maritime climate (warm days, cool nights) and wine-friendly soils (gravel and clay) are suited to dry and sweet whites, too, though reds make up about 90 percent of Bordeaux's output today.

REGIONS TO KNOW

LEFT BANK The gravelly soils deposited on the Gironde Estuary's left (western) bank are ideal for growing Cabernet Sauvignon, especially in the Médoc plain, which fans north and seaward from the city of Bordeaux. The left bank's most famous subregions—**MARGAUX, PAUILLAC, ST-JULIEN** and **ST-ESTÈPHE**—produce firmly tannic, cassis- and cedar-inflected reds of impressive structure and longevity. Less-famous left bank appellations such as **HAUT-MÉDOC, MOULIS** and **LISTRAC** are also worth paying attention to, as they can produce terrific values.

GRAVES South and inland of Bordeaux proper, the Graves sub-zone is known for three things: tart, dry whites based on Sémillon and Sauvignon Blanc; relatively light good-value reds from Merlot, Cabernet Sauvignon and Cabernet Franc; and, most famously, the prestigious sub-appellation of **PESSAC-LÉOGNAN,** home to exalted châteaus such as Haut-Brion.

RIGHT BANK Clay soil mixes with gravel on the right (eastern) bank of the Gironde and its Dordogne tributary, making this Merlot country, with wines that are plusher and less tannic than those from the left bank. The **POMEROL** and **ST-ÉMILION** sub-districts are the right bank's most prestigious; regions such as **FRONSAC, LUSSAC-ST-ÉMILION, LALANDE-DE-POMEROL** and **CÔTES DE BLAYE** offer similarly styled wines at far gentler prices.

ENTRE-DEUX-MERS This sprawling area between the Dordogne and Garonne rivers (its name means "between two seas") produces the bulk of Bordeaux's white wines. Most are crisp, affordable bottlings with straightforward citrus and herb flavors.

CÔTES DE BORDEAUX This new umbrella appellation groups four low-profile subregions occupying hilly slopes (*côtes*) on the right banks of the Gironde and the Garonne and Dordogne rivers, where a growing number of producers are offering high-quality, value-priced wines.

❧ KEY GRAPES: WHITE

SAUVIGNON BLANC This grape is responsible for the hallmark citrus- and herb-driven aromas and zippy acidity in Bordeaux whites. It is usually blended with Sémillon.

SÉMILLON Rounder than Sauvignon Blanc, Sémillon is marked by its smooth, rich texture and minerally fruit, and gives Bordeaux's best dry whites their ability to age. Traditionally blended with Sauvignon Blanc, it yields medium-bodied, citrusy wines. Sémillon is also the primary grape used to make the sweet wines of Sauternes (see p. 297).

♣ KEY GRAPES: RED

CABERNET FRANC Lighter in color and body than Cabernet Sauvignon, Cabernet Franc typically plays a supporting role in Bordeaux's reds, to which it lends its signature sweet tobacco and herb aromas. There are, however, a handful of mostly famous exceptions, such as the wines of Château Cheval Blanc and Château Ausone, in which Cabernet Franc takes center stage.

CABERNET SAUVIGNON Grown around the world, the Cabernet Sauvignon grape comes into its own in Bordeaux—specifically, on the left (western) bank of the Gironde Estuary, where the Médoc subzone turns out wines of peerless finesse and power. In contrast to the vast majority of California Cabernets, Bordeaux examples display more austere, less fruity flavors, with herb-inflected cassis notes and sharper acidity. Nearly all Bordeaux Cabernet gets blended with Merlot to soften its firm tannins and add fruitiness.

MERLOT The most widely planted grape in Bordeaux, Merlot is at its best on the right (eastern) bank of the Gironde and the Dordogne River. Less sweetly ripe than Merlot bottlings from the world's warmer regions, Bordeaux versions showcase the grape's characteristically supple tannins and rich plum and black cherry flavors, along with herb and spice notes.

PETIT VERDOT & MALBEC Thick-skinned, darkly colored and tannic, these red varieties are only small players in Bordeaux wines today, even though both grapes are native to the region.

WINE TERMINOLOGY
Bordeaux's most basic wines are labeled simply *Bordeaux*. Bordeaux Supérieur wines are made to slightly higher standards. Wines with district designations—such as Médoc, Graves and St-Émilion—are required to meet higher standards than those

labeled *Bordeaux* or *Bordeaux Supérieur.* Within the districts are communes, such as St-Estèphe and Margaux (both in Médoc); wines with communal designation must meet still more stringent requirements. The more specific its regional designation, the higher the standards a wine must meet.

BORDEAUX This entry-level category can include wines made anywhere in Bordeaux. Most wines in this category are simple; many are whites from Entre-Deux-Mers.

BORDEAUX SUPÉRIEUR A step up from the basic Bordeaux category, these wines are required to be higher in alcohol, which implies that they were made from riper grapes—historically a measure of higher quality.

CLARET Not legally defined, this is a primarily British term for red Bordeaux wines. It tends to be used to denote a lighter, simpler Bordeaux.

CRU BOURGEOIS This category includes Médoc châteaus that didn't make the cut for *cru classé* (see below) but are still considered good. For various bureaucratic reasons, it is viewed as a stamp of approval rather than a true classification.

CRU CLASSÉ Bordeaux's system for ranking wines, established in 1855, created a hierarchy of wineries (or châteaus) considered superior based on the prices their wines commanded. It applies only to châteaus in Médoc and Sauternes and a single château in Graves. The ranking grouped 61 superior wineries by *cru* (growth), from first (*premier cru*) to fifth. In 1955 a similar system was set up for the St-Émilion district, using just three rankings: *grand cru, grand cru classé* and, at the top, *premier grand cru classé.* It is subject to revision (and inevitable appeal) every 10 years or so. Pay attention to the *classé* on the end—plain old *grand cru* applies to most estate-bottled St-Émilion wine. The famed red wines of Pomerol are not ranked.

MIS EN BOUTEILLE AU CHÂTEAU Only estate-bottled wines made from estate-grown grapes can use this term, meaning "bottled at the winery." Theoretically, these wines are better because of the greater control the producer has over both fruit and wine.

Producers/ Bordeaux

CHÂTEAU CANON

Created in the 1700s by Jacques Kanon, a privateer (i.e., a state-approved pirate) for Louis XV, this St-Émilion property is gorgeous—a limestone château with a walled vineyard running right up to the town itself. Now owned by the Chanel fashion house and managed by John Kolasa (ex–Château Latour director), the château puts out a stylish, Merlot-based flagship red, as well as a lively, juicy second wine called Clos Canon.

BOTTLES TO TRY
- Clos Canon ⁄ $$$
- Château Canon ⁄ $$$$

CHÂTEAU D'AIGUILHE

This ancient estate is located in the Côtes de Castillon, a low-profile region near St-Émilion that has become a source of some of Bordeaux's best value reds. Well-known producer Stephan von Neipperg acquired the château in 1998 and, working with esteemed consultant Stéphane Derenoncourt, soon turned it into one of the district's stars. His suavely styled red is among the most terrific wines in the region (and a great value, too).

BOTTLE TO TRY
- Château d'Aiguilhe ⁄ $$$

CHÂTEAU DE FIEUZAL

Located in Pessac-Léognan, the Graves district's top dry-wine appellation, Fieuzal is one of only 13 Graves châteaus entitled to make *grand cru* red wines; its whites carry just the Pessac-Léognan appellation. After Irish banker Lochlann Quinn bought the estate in 2001, the white wines quickly improved; the flagship white is now considered one of the region's best. The reds are reaching new heights, too, thanks to winemaker Stéphen Carrier and consultant Hubert de Boüard, owner of Château Angélus.

BOTTLES TO TRY
- ○ Château de Fieuzal ⁄ $$$
- Château de Fieuzal ⁄ $$$

CHÂTEAU DE PEZ

The claim to fame of Château de Pez, founded in 1452, used to be that it was one of the oldest estates in St-Estèphe. But since being acquired by the Rouzaud family of Roederer Champagne in 1995, this *cru bourgeois* (see p. 27) has been attracting equal fame for the pristine quality of its wine. While most St-Estèphe estates rely chiefly on Cabernet Sauvignon, de Pez's flagship bottling typically contains a substantial portion of Merlot, which helps soften the wine's muscular structure. Compared with *crus classés*, it's a value buy.

BOTTLE TO TRY
● Château de Pez ∕ $$$

CHÂTEAU D'ISSAN

Château d'Issan's wine was served at Eleanor of Aquitaine's wedding in 1152, and the winery's exalted motto translates roughly as "For kings' tables and gods' altars." In recent history, the estate's grounds, complete with a moat-enclosed castle and gliding swans, lived up to this fairy-tale image, even if the wines did not. But in 1998, Emmanuel Cruse took over the Margaux estate from his father and began a massive renovation: regrafting vines, building a new cellar and bringing in winemaking guru Jacques Boissenot to consult. These days Château d'Issan is once again making wines worthy of its glorious heritage.

BOTTLES TO TRY
● Blason d'Issan ∕ $$$
● Château d'Issan ∕ $$$$

CHÂTEAU FOMBRAUGE

The largest wine estate in St-Émilion, Château Fombrauge fell into good hands when a Bordeaux mogul, Bernard Magrez, purchased it in 1999. Magrez diligently enhanced the vineyards and the winery—something he has done repeatedly with other châteaus he owns, including Pape Clément and La Tour Carnet. Made under the direction of renowned consultant Michel Rolland, the estate's red has become one of the best values in St-Émilion. Magrez and Rolland's success gained official recognition in 2012, when Fombrauge earned a deserved promotion to *grand cru classé*.

BOTTLE TO TRY
● Château Fombrauge ∕ $$$

CHÂTEAU GLORIA

Although its vineyards consist partly of land that once belonged solely to famous classified growths, this St-Julien estate was not included in Bordeaux's 1855 classification—because it didn't exist. It wasn't until the early 1940s that founder Henri Martin began assembling the more than 120 acres that make up Château Gloria, now run by his son-in-law. The estate's combination of top vineyards and lack of classification means that its wines are usually fantastic buys, offering a structure and complexity comparable to those of its prestigious neighbors at a price that's much easier to swallow.

BOTTLE TO TRY
● Château Gloria ╱ $$$

CHÂTEAU JEAN FAUX

Pascal and Chrystel Collotte fell in love with this centuries-old wine estate in the Bordeaux Supérieur region and purchased it in 2002, complete with a millhouse, pond, orchard, pasture and gardens. At the time, Pascal worked in the cooperage business, selling barrels. While mastering the running of the rambling farm (pigs and chickens included), the couple rehabilitated the vineyards and brought in superstar consultant Stéphane Derenoncourt. They work the vines organically and produce one red wine, a polished, layered blend of Merlot and Cabernet Franc.

BOTTLE TO TRY
● Château Jean Faux Bordeaux Supérieur ╱ $$

CHÂTEAU LAROSE-TRINTAUDON

Affordable, dependable and widely available, Château Larose-Trintaudon's substantial production makes it one of Bordeaux's largest *crus bourgeois*. Although the estate has been around since 1719, its modern history began with a Spanish family, the Forners. Founders of Rioja's Marqués de Cáceres winery, the Forners purchased Larose-Trintaudon in 1963 and replanted its vineyards. (They eventually sold the winery to French insurance company Allianz in 1986.) Usually a 60-40 blend of Cabernet Sauvignon and Merlot, the estate wine is made in a consistent style, with plump, medium-bodied fruit and toast flavors built for near-term drinking.

BOTTLE TO TRY
● Château Larose-Trintaudon ╱ $$

CHÂTEAU LÉOVILLE BARTON

There are lots of reasons to love this St-Julien estate, starting, of course, with its wine. Léoville Barton produces archetypal St-Julien—a refined red that's known for its muscular combination of power and elegance. Another reason is Anthony Barton, its affable, quotable proprietor. Barton descends from an Irish ancestor who created a hugely successful *négociant* business after settling in Bordeaux in 1722; his family has owned Léoville Barton since 1826. Barton's fair pricing and insistence on classically styled reds have earned him respect; they also make his wines savvy picks for long-term cellaring.

BOTTLE TO TRY

● Château Léoville Barton / $$$$

CHÂTEAU PALMER

Named for a British major general who acquired the estate in 1814, spent a fortune on it and ran it into the ground, Château Palmer today is among the stars of Margaux. It's now owned by the Sichel and Mähler-Besse families, who have kept the long-lived *grand vin* on a steady course while introducing a second wine, Alter Ego, which delivers plenty of class and structure at about a quarter of the price of the flagship red. Both wines stand out for having a higher-than-typical percentage of Merlot (sometimes even equal to or more than the Cabernet), which gives them a certain generosity of texture.

BOTTLES TO TRY

● Alter Ego / $$$$
● Château Palmer / $$$$

CHÂTEAU PHÉLAN SÉGUR

For anyone looking to spend around $50 on a bottle of Bordeaux, Phélan Ségur is a go-to choice. Although not a classified growth, the château has been turning out wines of similar quality in recent years. Businessman Xavier Gardinier sold two Champagne houses (Pommery and Lanson) and then acquired this St-Estèphe estate in 1985. His investments, and now the work of his sons, have boosted quality. Another huge influence has been superstar consultant Michel Rolland, who lends an assist with the wines—hence their rich, potent fruit character.

BOTTLE TO TRY

● Château Phélan Ségur / $$$

CHÂTEAU PONTET-CANET

In 2010 Château Pontet-Canet in Pauillac became the first major Bordeaux wine producer to earn the official Agence Bio (AB) organic certification. Two years later, owner Alfred Tesseron installed clay amphorae in the winery's cellars to use in aging its acclaimed reds. It's a method increasingly favored by naturalist winemakers all over the world but nearly unheard of in tradition-bound Bordeaux. These latest developments in Tesseron's passionate, 20-year quest to refine Pontet-Canet's already acclaimed wines may seem risky, but his earlier tweaks and innovations have paid consistent dividends, with wines that rank among the best in all of Bordeaux.

BOTTLE TO TRY
● Château Pontet-Canet / $$$$

CHÂTEAU RAUZAN-SÉGLA

The Wertheimer brothers, owners of the Chanel fashion house, bought this 350-year-old Margaux *grand cru* and Château Canon (see p. 28) in the mid-'90s and tapped former Latour director John Kolasa to manage both properties. After a full renovation that restored the current château (built in 1903) and its grounds to their former splendor, the estate is in top shape today. Its Cabernet-driven blend, made with moderate amounts of new oak, exhibits classic Margaux grace and is a credit to Kolasa's keen sense of restraint. A generous portion of Merlot accounts for the wine's soft, velvety tannins.

BOTTLE TO TRY
● Château Rauzan-Ségla / $$$$

CHÂTEAU TROTANOY

Pomerol does not officially rank its châteaus, but if it did, Trotanoy no doubt would place at the top. Owned by the Moueix family (*négociants* and château owners who helped bring Pomerol to prominence in the 1960s), Trotanoy is, like most Pomerol estates, quite small. And like all Pomerol wineries, it's focused on Merlot. From 18 acres of vineyards, it turns out just 2,000 or so cases of the *grand vin* each year. That scarcity—and the wine's typically superb quality—are reflected in its breathtaking price.

BOTTLE TO TRY
● Château Trotanoy / $$$$

BURGUNDY

CLAIM TO FAME

Burgundy's inconsistent weather means that vintages can vary wildly in quality from year to year, and its patchwork of regions (and subregions, and sub-sub-subregions) takes effort to grasp. Why bother? Because no place on Earth can match Burgundy for the alluring grace of its best wines. In great vintages its ethereal, smoky reds and majestic whites offer both polish and power.

REGIONS TO KNOW

CHABLIS This cool northern subregion is geologically more similar to Champagne than it is to the rest of Burgundy, giving its wines—all made with Chardonnay—a stony austerity. Unlike other white Burgundies, most Chablis wines are unoaked, resulting in fresh whites with steely crispness. The region's best bottles are labeled with *grand* or *premier cru* vineyard names, followed by the Chablis appellation; lesser wines are labeled simply *Chablis*. Petit Chablis wines are from less prestigious subregions.

CÔTE CHALONNAISE Though much red is made here, affordable Chardonnay has long been the hallmark of this region located on the Côte d'Or's southern border. While values can still be had, prices have crept up, and wines from its four top villages—**GIVRY, MERCUREY, MONTAGNY** and **RULLY**—are the most expensive. Mercurey and Givry also make worthwhile reds.

CÔTE D'OR This high-rent region is split in two. The northern **CÔTE DE NUITS** specializes in Pinot Noir and contains most of Burgundy's red *grands crus,* including those in legendary villages like **CHAMBOLLE-MUSIGNY** and **GEVREY-CHAMBERTIN.** To the south, the **CÔTE DE BEAUNE** produces some of the planet's most compelling Chardonnays, from villages such as **MEURSAULT** and **PULIGNY-MONTRACHET,** and a single *grand cru* red, **CORTON.**

MÂCONNAIS At Burgundy's southern extreme, the Mâconnais is a go-to source of affordable, largely reliable whites. Though much entry-level wine is made here, a growing number of ambitious, small-scale producers are pushing quality to new levels. The region's top offerings come from **POUILLY-FUISSÉ.**

♣ KEY GRAPES: WHITE

CHARDONNAY Most Burgundy white wines are made from Chardonnay, though styles differ greatly among the various subregions. Burgundy Chardonnays range from the flinty, high-acid whites of Chablis in the north to the rich, oak-aged offerings of the Côte d'Or, and reflect varying climates and soils as much as different winemaking traditions.

SAUVIGNON BLANC & ALIGOTÉ Small amounts of these grapes grow in a few spots around Burgundy: Sauvignon in the northern village of St-Bris, and Aligoté in the Côte Chalonnaise.

♣ KEY GRAPES: RED

PINOT NOIR With its silky texture, effortless depth and aromas of violet, cherry and earth, good red Burgundy is the ultimate in Pinot Noir. Unfortunately, bad red Burgundy can be just as expensive as the good, so choosing bottles wisely is key. Pinot Noir vines planted in well-drained limestone soil on sunny slopes tend to produce the most powerful, long-lived wines.

WINE TERMINOLOGY

Burgundy ranks wines by the vineyards from which they originate, not by the producer who made them (as in Bordeaux). Burgundy labels list the region; some also list the subregion, and the most prestigious include a vineyard name. Generally, the more specific the locality on a label, the finer the wine, but vintage is also very important when assessing quality.

BOURGOGNE Burgundy's most basic wines are labeled with just the name of the region, Bourgogne, and occasionally with the grape. Quality ranges from so-so to solid.

DISTRICT A district appellation (such as Chablis or Mâconnais) is the next step up in quality after AOC Bourgogne. The grapes must be grown exclusively in the named district.

VILLAGE A wine may take the name of a specific village if all of its grapes have been grown within that village's boundaries—for instance, Meursault or Nuits-St-Georges. These are more prestigious than district-wide appellations but not necessarily better. Those from multiple villages within a larger region can append

"Villages" to that region, as in Côte de Nuits–Villages (used for reds and a bit of white) and Côte de Beaune–Villages (always red). Terrific introductory wines, Côte de Nuits–Villages offer the best values in this pricey slice of Burgundy.

PREMIER CRU With the second-highest distinction, *premier cru* vineyards have a lengthy history of producing superior wines. These wines must be made only with grapes grown in the designated vineyards, whose names are typically noted right after the village name (e.g., Meursault *Premier Cru* Genevrières).

GRAND CRU Vineyards designated as *grand cru*, the highest classification in Burgundy, are so elite that some, like Montrachet, don't include the *grand cru* title on their wine labels. To capitalize on their prestige, some villages added the name of the local *grand cru* vineyard to their own names. (For example, the wines from the town of Chassagne became Chassagne-Montrachet. While many are superb, they're not true Montrachet.)

NÉGOCIANTS Merchants who buy wine, grapes or must (freshly pressed juice) from small growers and/or producers and create wines under their own names.

Producers/ Burgundy

BOUCHARD PÈRE & FILS

Although it's known as one of Burgundy's most prominent *négociants*, Bouchard is also the largest vineyard owner in the Côte d'Or. The Henriot family, which bought Bouchard in 1995, added to their already remarkable collection of estates, then invested in a new winery to boost quality further. Its velvety Vigne de l'Enfant Jésus comes from a Beaune vineyard that Bouchard purchased in 1791, but the village and regional bottlings are also top-notch (and far less expensive).

BOTTLES TO TRY
- Beaune du Château Premier Cru / $$$
- Vigne de l'Enfant Jésus Beaune Premier Cru Grèves / $$$$

CHÂTEAU-FUISSÉ

Antoine Vincent turns out serious Mâconnais whites at this ancient, underrated estate owned by the Vincent family since the 1860s. Most of its vineyards are in Pouilly-Fuissé, the Mâconnais's top subzone, which helps explain the wines' consistent quality. Château-Fuissé's most interesting wines may be its single-vineyard cuvées: Le Clos, Les Brûlés and Les Combettes. Each one brilliantly highlights vineyard-driven differences in flavors. Its JJ Vincent *négociant* bottlings, on the other hand, are crisp, straightforward blends meant for drinking, not thinking.

BOTTLES TO TRY
- JJ Vincent Bourgogne Blanc / $
- Le Clos Pouilly-Fuissé / $$$
- Vieilles Vignes Pouilly-Fuissé / $$$

DOMAINE BARRAUD

Fifth-generation winemaker Julien Barraud and his parents, Daniel and Martine Barraud, take a high-touch, low-tech approach (organic farming and handpicked grapes, for starters) to their Mâconnais vineyards. The result is revelatory whites like the En Buland Vieilles Vignes; made from 80-year-old vines, it compares favorably with wines from pricier Côte d'Or appellations. The Barrauds keep crop yields low to create more intense wines, then age them in barrel to give them a silky richness.

BOTTLES TO TRY
- Alliance Vergisson Pouilly-Fuissé / $$$
- En Buland Vieilles Vignes Pouilly-Fuissé / $$$

DOMAINE BRUNO CLAIR

Although he's based in Marsannay, a northern district known for rustic, straightforward reds, Bruno Clair owns parcels of some of the Côte d'Or's best vineyards. These include a plot in Chambertin Clos-de-Bèze, a legendary *grand cru*, as well as some of the best *premiers crus* in Gevrey-Chambertin and Savigny. For value hunters, it's hard to beat Clair's Marsannay reds, which show off the appellation's refined side. His serious, silky rosé is a Marsannay specialty pioneered by his grandfather.

BOTTLES TO TRY
- Marsannay Rosé / $$
- Les Longeroies Marsannay / $$$
- Chambertin Clos-de-Bèze Grand Cru / $$$$

DOMAINE CHRISTIAN MOREAU PÈRE & FILS

The Moreau name goes a long way back in Chablis—a barrel-making ancestor first got into the wine business two centuries ago. But in 1985 the family sold its J. Moreau et Fils *négociant* company. Fortunately, it held on to a few stellar vineyards, some of them now farmed by Christian Moreau and his winemaker son Fabien. These include part of Les Clos, arguably Chablis's greatest *cru*. Moreau's basic Chablis is reliably terrific, especially given its reasonable price.

BOTTLES TO TRY
- Chablis / $$
- Les Clos Chablis Grand Cru / $$$$

DOMAINE DANIEL DAMPT ET FILS

Vivid, zesty whites are the hallmark of this terrific Chablis estate, which turns out wines of textbook purity from a barrel-free cellar. Daniel Dampt's sons, Vincent and Sébastien, clearly picked up their father's know-how and have stayed true to their family's house style. They start with top-quality grapes from estate-owned vineyards (including famous *premiers crus* such as Vaillons and Fourchaume), then keep the wines' flavors bright and true to their *terroirs* by aging them in tanks. The result is cuvées that offer amazing value across a range of prices. Both brothers also bottle wines under their own names, from their own small parcels of vines.

BOTTLES TO TRY
- Chablis / $$
- Les Vaillons Chablis Premier Cru / $$$

DOMAINE DENIS MORTET

This Gevrey-Chambertin domaine became one of Burgundy's brightest stars in the 1990s under Denis Mortet, who fashioned dazzling, full-bodied reds from some of the Côte de Nuits' finest *crus*. Son Arnaud has maintained the quality and bold style of Mortet wines while dialing back his father's enthusiastic use of new oak. Like his father, Arnaud lavishes even his basic village wines and Marsannay bottlings with the kind of care many vintners reserve for their splurge-worthy *grands crus*.

BOTTLES TO TRY
- Cuvée de Noble Souche Bourgogne / $$$
- Vieilles Vignes Gevrey-Chambertin / $$$$

DOMAINE FAIVELEY

Following in the footsteps of six generations might intimidate even the most self-assured 25-year-old, but Erwan Faiveley wasn't afraid to make big changes when he took over his family's domaine in 2007. His bold moves have paid off: Recent vintages have been the best in years. Known for its elegant, ageworthy reds, the winery owns one of the Côte d'Or's largest portfolios of top vineyards.

BOTTLES TO TRY

○ **Joseph Faiveley Bourgogne** ∕ **$$**

● **Nuits-Saint-Georges** ∕ **$$$**

● **Chambertin Clos-de-Bèze Grand Cru** ∕ **$$$$**

DOMAINE JACQUES-FRÉDÉRIC MUGNIER

Freddy Mugnier discovered a genius for winemaking after giving up a career as an oil engineer in the mid-1980s. Drawing on some of Chambolle-Musigny's best vineyards, parcels of which had been owned by his family but rented out for decades, Mugnier was soon producing extraordinary wines. Though he makes three refined cuvées from Nuits-Saint-George, it's his definitive Chambolle-Musignys that have earned cult status. Their delicate, silky grace and pure fruit and mineral tones make them some of the most captivating expressions of Pinot Noir in the world.

BOTTLES TO TRY

● **Chambolle-Musigny** ∕ **$$$$**

● **Les Amoureuses Chambolle-Musigny Premier Cru** ∕ **$$$$**

DOMAINE JEAN-MARC BOILLOT

With assorted cousins and siblings making wine up and down Burgundy's storied slopes, the Boillots can be hard to keep straight. Jean-Marc Boillot is a family star: In 1984, he famously walked out of his family's estate in protest of its so-so wines. A few he made under his own label impressed his grandfather Etienne Sauzet (see p. 40) enough that Sauzet bequeathed Boillot one-third of his vineyards—which Boillot parlayed into a larger, much-admired domaine of his own. Signature bottlings include lavish whites from Puligny-Montrachet and sleek, full-flavored reds from Pommard.

BOTTLES TO TRY

○ **Montagny Premier Cru** ∕ **$$**

● **Jarollières Pommard Premier Cru** ∕ **$$$$**

RARITIES & COLLECTIBLES

DOMAINE D'AUVENAY/DOMAINE LEROY The brilliant owner of these two estates, Lalou Bize-Leroy, turns out tiny quantities of profound wines matched in reputation only by those of Domaine de la Romanée-Conti—where she was co-director until 1992.

DOMAINE DE LA ROMANÉE-CONTI Known by wine geeks simply as DRC, this iconic estate produces eight of the world's most expensive, coveted and collectible wines. A bottle of the 2009 flagship *grand cru* can have a five-figure price tag.

DOMAINE DU COMTE LIGER-BELAIR For much of the last century, the Liger-Belairs let others make wine from their astounding Côte de Nuits vineyards. Now the 40-year-old scion Louis-Michel Liger-Belair has revived the family's estate, crafting sought-after cuvées from legendary *crus* like La Romanée.

DOMAINE LEFLAIVE

This domaine in Puligny-Montrachet makes legendary white Burgundy. Winemaker Anne-Claude Leflaive (whose grandfather Joseph Leflaive began the winery in 1920) and cellarmaster Eric Rémy craft biodynamically grown whites in tiny quantities from some of the world's most famous vineyards. For a taste of Leflaive's refined style at a gentler price, look for its Mâcon bottling, which comes from 23 acres near the village of Verzé.

BOTTLES TO TRY

○ Mâcon-Verzé / $$$
○ Puligny-Montrachet / $$$$

DOMAINE MÉO-CAMUZET

Méo-Camuzet is one of the most admired estates in Vosne-Romanée, the prestigious Côte d'Or subzone that's Burgundy's equivalent of Park Avenue. Its collection of *grand* and *premier cru* vineyards spans some of the most storied vines in the world, and its wines command eye-watering sums. Happily, Jean-Nicolas Méo, an heir to the domaine, created the Frère & Soeurs *négociant* line. Its wines provide a taste of Méo-Camuzet's sumptuous, velvety style without the second-mortgage prices.

BOTTLES TO TRY

● Frère & Soeurs Marsannay / $$$
● Aux Brûlées Vosne-Romanée Premier Cru / $$$$
● Frère & Soeurs Chambolle-Musigny / $$$$

DOMAINE RAMONET

Ramonet's brilliant Chassagne-Montrachet wines set the standard for this prestigious subzone in the Côte de Beaune. Run by brothers and third-generation vintners Noël and Jean-Claude Ramonet, the 42-acre domaine produces a little red wine, but its outstanding whites have made its reputation. Fashioned in an exuberant and intense style, the grapes are sourced chiefly from vineyards in and around the towns of Chassagne-Montrachet and Puligny-Montrachet, including legendary sites such as Le Montrachet, Bienvenues and Bâtard.

BOTTLES TO TRY

○ **Chassagne-Montrachet** ∕ **$$$**
○ **Les Ruchottes Chassagne-Montrachet Premier Cru** ∕ **$$$$**

DOMINIQUE CORNIN

There's a lot of simple, ordinary wine coming out of the Mâconnais, Burgundy's most affordable district. But there are also superb, quality-conscious artisan grower–winemakers, like Dominique Cornin, the fourth generation in his family to tend vines. He and his 20-something son Romain farm dozens of small parcels in and around the village of Fuissé, where the limestone-rich soils make for particularly structured, mineral-driven white wines. Farming organically and employing only minimal oak, the Cornins fashion intense, stony whites that emphasize fruit flavors.

BOTTLES TO TRY

○ **Domaine de Lalande Mâcon-Chaintré** ∕ **$$**
○ **Pouilly-Fuissé** ∕ **$$**

ETIENNE SAUZET

Sauzet is one of the top estates in Puligny-Montrachet, itself one of the world's best addresses for white wine. Etienne Sauzet began bottling his own wines back in the 1950s, when the vast majority of Burgundy growers sold their wines by the barrel to large *négociants*. His son-in-law, Gérard Boudot, expanded on Sauzet's success. Today, helped by Boudot's daughter Emilie and her husband, Benôit Riffault, the domaine produces powerful, nuanced whites, nearly all from *grands* and *premiers crus*.

BOTTLES TO TRY

○ **Bourgogne Blanc** ∕ **$$$**
○ **Les Combettes Puligny-Montrachet Premier Cru** ∕ **$$$$**

JEAN-MARC BROCARD

It's possible to explore the full range of Chablis's extensive *crus* just by tasting the wines of Jean-Marc Brocard. From Petit Chablis to village wines, *grands crus* and even the obscure Sauvignons of nearby St. Bris, Brocard offers bottles that demonstrate just how diverse the region is. Jean-Marc's son Julien is converting the estate to biodynamic farming; look for ladybugs or moons on the labels of wines from environmentally green sites. One constant, though, is style: Brocard's wines are invariably bright, unoaked and crisp.

BOTTLES TO TRY
- ○ **Domaine Sainte Claire Chablis** / **$$**
- ○ **Montmains Chablis Premier Cru** / **$$**

LA CHABLISIÈNNE

La Chablisiènne is part of a tiny, elite group of the world's cooperative wineries that are known for turning out wines of quality as well as quantity. Farming roughly a quarter of Chablis's vineyards, La Chablisiènne's members contribute fruit from a comprehensive cross section of the region. That its winemakers are capable of crafting deliciously fresh, direct Petit Chablis and Chablis isn't surprising; but that its top bottles, including the brilliant *grand cru* Château Grenouilles, rank alongside those from tiny boutique growers is remarkable.

BOTTLES TO TRY
- ○ **La Pierrelée Chablis** / **$$**
- ○ **Château Grenouilles Chablis Grand Cru** / **$$$**

MAISON JOSEPH DROUHIN

Though best known for its wines from legendary Côte d'Or enclaves such as Musigny and Vosne-Romanée, this family-owned *négociant* owns top Chablis vineyards, too. Estate fruit, all organically farmed, makes up more than half of Drouhin's supply, meaning that this large producer maintains an impressive grip on quality. Wines from Beaujolais, the Mâconnais and the Côte Chalonnaise, on the other hand, come mostly from purchased grapes and represent Drouhin's best values.

BOTTLES TO TRY
- ○ **Domaine de Vaudon Chablis** / **$$**
- ○ **Meursault** / **$$$**
- ● **Clos des Mouches Beaune Premier Cru** / **$$$$**

MAISON LOUIS JADOT

It's relatively easy to produce tiny amounts of amazing wine from world-class vineyards but far harder to fashion vast amounts of consistently tasty, value-packed everyday bottlings. Jadot achieves both with astonishing regularity, along with midrange wines that regularly outclass their peers. With holdings in Beaujolais, the Mâconnais and Pouilly-Fuissé, Jadot offers a range of wines whose breadth, depth and inarguable quality make it one of Burgundy's elite *négociants*.

BOTTLES TO TRY
- ○ **Mâcon-Villages** / $
- ○ **Folatières Puligny-Montrachet Premier Cru** / $$$$
- ● **Gevrey-Chambertin** / $$$

OLIVIER LEFLAIVE

Born into a prominent wine family, Olivier Leflaive began his own label in 1984, using purchased grapes. He later left his family's legendary domaine (see p. 39) to concentrate on his eponymous wine venture (plus a hotel and restaurant in the center of Puligny-Montrachet). Gifted winemaker Franck Grux crafts Leflaive's vibrant, beautifully layered wines, most of which are white.

BOTTLES TO TRY
- ○ **Les Sétilles Bourgogne** / $$
- ○ **Meursault** / $$$

VINCENT DAUVISSAT

The wines of Vincent Dauvissat are virtually unmatched in Chablis for prestige and price. Even so, the superstar estate's best bottles still cost a mere fraction of what their counterparts in the great *crus* of Côte d'Or command. Sourced from some of Chablis's finest sites, including three *premier* and two *grand cru* vineyards, and light in the oak department, Vincent Dauvissat wines offer stony purity and fresh, minerally acidity. These qualities can make the wines seem somewhat austere when young; even the humble Petit Chablis usually tastes better with a little bottle age.

BOTTLES TO TRY
- ○ **Chablis** / $$$
- ○ **Petit Chablis** / $$$
- ○ **Les Clos Chablis Grand Cru** / $$$$

WILLIAM FÈVRE

This remarkable Chablis estate has hit its stride. No other producer owns vineyards in as many Chablis *grand cru* vineyards as William Fèvre, but for years the wines mostly failed to live up to their exalted origins. Now, under the ownership of the Henriot Champagne company and the direction of winemaker Didier Séguier, Fèvre is creating minerally, multifaceted whites—chiefly from *premier* and *grand cru* sites—that rank with Chablis's best.

BOTTLES TO TRY
- **Champs Royaux Chablis** / **$$**
- **Montmains Chablis Premier Cru** / **$$$**
- **Valmur Chablis Grand Cru** / **$$$$**

BURGUNDY

BEAUJOLAIS

CLAIM TO FAME

Although it's considered part of Burgundy, Beaujolais has a profile all its own, with a different climate (warmer) and a different soil (granite, schist and sandstone) from the rest of the region. It also features a different signature grape: Gamay. Responsible for tanker-loads of the grapey, simple red called Beaujolais Nouveau, Gamay also yields the deeply lush, floral-edged reds of Beaujolais's 10 *crus*, which are some of the most underrated wines on the planet.

KEY GRAPES: RED

GAMAY Supple tannins and juicy, exuberant fruit define this easy-to-love variety. Lighter wines from cooler vintages showcase tangy cranberry and strawberry tones; riper, more concentrated grapes yield medium-bodied, graceful red wines loaded with mouth-filling raspberry and cherry flavors.

WINE TERMINOLOGY

BEAUJOLAIS NOUVEAU Designed to be consumed within weeks of harvest, Beaujolais Nouveau is as light-bodied and simple as red wine gets. By French law, it is released the third Thursday of every November, conveniently coinciding with the start of the U.S. holiday season.

BEAUJOLAIS Basic Beaujolais accounts for nearly half of the region's wine output. Quality varies considerably, but in general, wines labeled simply *Beaujolais* tend to offer slightly more substance than Beaujolais Nouveau, with fruity berry flavors and succulent acidity.

BEAUJOLAIS-VILLAGES Only wines made with grapes sourced from 38 villages occupying gentle hills at the center of the region can be designated Beaujolais-Villages. Typically produced with more care and precision than basic Beaujolais, these wines exhibit bright, red-berry flavors as well as an added depth of mineral and spice.

CRU BEAUJOLAIS The region's finest wines come from 10 hillside villages in the northern part of Beaujolais, where granite and schist soils and sunny slopes yield riper, more concentrated wines. Deep flavors and ample tannins give the best bottles the ability to age, unlike other Beaujolais. Cru Beaujolais labels often list only the village name: Brouilly, Chénas, Chiroubles, Côte de Brouilly, Fleurie, Juliénas, Morgon, Moulin-à-Vent, Régnié or St-Amour.

Producers/
Beaujolais

CHÂTEAU DES JACQUES

One of Beaujolais's most respected names, Château des Jacques has vineyards that span six Beaujolais subregions. Its flagship offerings come from its home appellation of Moulin-à-Vent, where its holdings include five ancient, walled vineyards. Just a few barrels' worth of the winery's single-vineyard Moulin-à-Vent *crus* are imported to the U.S. each year, but its basic Moulin-à-Vent bottling, which blends grapes from all five sites, is comparatively easy to find and consistently great, as is the richly fruity Morgon.

BOTTLES TO TRY
- Morgon / $$
- Moulin-à-Vent / $$

DANIEL BOULAND

Anyone who thinks that top Beaujolais can't stand up to Burgundy should seek out the wines of Daniel Bouland. This small-scale vintner in the Morgon hamlet of Corcelette creates seductively deep, velvety reds of rare complexity, though the techniques he uses are elemental. A protégé of the late, great naturalist winemaker Marcel Lapierre, Bouland relies on very old vines and a lot of hard labor (handpicking grapes, farming organically) to achieve concentrated fruit.

BOTTLES TO TRY
- **Corcelette Vieilles Vignes Morgon** / **$$**
- **Delys Morgon** / **$$**

DOMAINE DES TERRES DORÉES/
JEAN-PAUL BRUN

Beaujolais's best wines have traditionally come from vines planted in granite. Naturalist winemaker Jean-Paul Brun defies conventional wisdom by turning out incredible cuvées from limestone soils. Instead of aiming for maximally ripe wines high in alcohol and toasty oak, Brun favors lighter, subtler notes. He relies on wild yeasts, and uses techniques to extract more flavors and create longer-lived reds. The result is ethereal wines that are both deeply flavored and delicately styled.

BOTTLES TO TRY
- **L'Ancien Vieilles Vignes Beaujolais** / **$$**
- **Moulin-à-Vent** / **$$**

LOIRE VALLEY

CLAIM TO FAME

White wines star in this meandering river valley, the longest (and probably most château-dotted) in France. In fact, the Loire Valley produces more whites than any other French region. They range from the flinty, citrusy Sauvignon Blancs of Sancerre and Pouilly-Fumé to complex Chenin Blancs in Vouvray to brisk, oyster-friendly bottlings at the coast, where the Loire River meets the cold Atlantic just past Muscadet. But don't overlook Loire reds, whether the Cabernet Francs of Chinon, the Pinot Noirs of Sancerre or other rarer pleasures. Thanks to the valley's cooler climate, its reds are refreshingly crisp and food-friendly.

REGIONS TO KNOW

ANJOU & SAUMUR For quality wine production, Chenin Blanc is the most important grape in these central Loire regions. In Anjou it is often made into well-respected sweet wines. **SAVENNIÈRES,** a small Anjou subzone, uses Chenin Blanc to create incredibly concentrated dry (as well as sweet) whites that are among the greatest examples of the grape. Red and rosé wines from Anjou and Saumur highlight the fresh side of Loire Cabernet Franc with bright acidity and green-herb notes. **SAUMUR-CHAMPIGNY** is exclusively a red wine region.

MUSCADET The largest white wine appellation in France, Muscadet relies entirely on the Melon de Bourgogne variety, which thrives in the region's relatively cool, coastal climate and sandy soil—conditions that would prove disastrous for most grapes. However, the best Muscadet bottlings come from grapes grown on rocky soil, not sand, and in 2011, three new designations based on soil types, called *crus communaux*, were created (see Wine Terminology, opposite).

SANCERRE & POUILLY-FUMÉ Benchmark whites made from Sauvignon Blanc are the calling card of these sister appellations in the upper Loire. Sancerres tend to be lighter and more perfumed, while Pouilly-Fumés are often fuller-bodied, with smoky mineral, herb and citrus tones. For Sauvignon Blanc made in a similar style at a more affordable price, look to the satellite regions of **MENETOU-SALON, QUINCY** and **REUILLY.** Though famous for white wines, Sancerre produces small amounts of rosé and red wine from Pinot Noir.

TOURAINE This large region centered on the midvalley town of Tours grows a dizzying array of red and white grapes, including Sauvignon Blanc, Gamay, Pinot Noir, Cabernet Sauvignon, Malbec (known locally as Côt) and a local specialty, Pineau d'Aunis. But none of the wines made from them compare to the legendary Chenin Blanc–based white wines of the premier subregion, **VOUVRAY.** Whether bone-dry or sweet, sparkling or still, they're among the world's most enthralling (and long-lived) whites. Touraine is also responsible for the Loire Valley's best red wines (in the subregions of **CHINON** and **BOURGUEIL**), smoky renditions of Cabernet Franc.

❧ KEY GRAPES: WHITE

CHENIN BLANC Is there a grape more versatile than Chenin Blanc? Its wines veer from light and mouth-puckeringly tart to sweet, full and rich, and come in sparkling, still and dessert bottlings. Their common thread: bright acidity, which gives the best Chenin Blancs amazing longevity.

MELON DE BOURGOGNE Coastal Muscadet's signature grape yields light-bodied, fairly neutral and refreshing whites with light citrus flavors and a hint of salty sea spray. A few select producers buck the norm, making top-notch small-lot cuvées from old vines that offer intense, chalky minerality and richer fruit. The best examples even age well, making this category a bargain for budding collectors.

SAUVIGNON BLANC In contrast to more exuberantly tropical and herbaceous Sauvignon Blancs from elsewhere in the world, Loire examples combine the grape's refreshing acidity and trademark citrus tones with smoky mineral and chalk aromas.

❧ KEY GRAPES: RED

CABERNET FRANC The Loire's most distinctive red variety turns out wines with red-fruit, herb and pepper notes typical of cool-climate reds, and, often, a smoky tobacco edge. Their high acidity and sometimes astringent tannins mean they're built for food.

WINE TERMINOLOGY

CRUS COMMUNAUX Specific to Muscadet's largest and best-known subregion, Sèvre et Maine, this new designation identifies that zone's top *terroirs* and sets production standards governing yields (lower), ripeness levels (higher) and time spent aging on lees (longer). Three *crus communaux*—Clisson, Gorges and Le Pallet—were approved in 2011; more are expected.

SEC Meaning "dry," this term indicates a wine with little to no residual sugar—although Chenin Blanc, with its hallmark honey notes, can give the impression of sweetness even when sec.

DEMI-SEC Though this term translates as "half-dry," a demi-sec wine is more accurately described as falling halfway between dry (sec) and sweet.

SUR LIE Appearing on Muscadet's better bottles, this term (pronounced *soor LEE*) indicates that a wine has been aged on its lees, the sediments left over after a wine's fermentation. The dead yeasts give a wine a creamier texture and a slight nutty edge.

VIN DE PAYS DU VAL DE LOIRE Much of the Loire's everyday wine is produced under this region-wide designation, which is also an umbrella term for many smaller *vin de pays* designations within it. These wines list a grape variety as well as a vintage.

Producers/ Loire Valley

ALPHONSE MELLOT
DOMAINE DE LA MOUSSIÈRE

The history at this Sancerre estate is impressive, as are the wallet-thinning prices its top wines command. Founded in 1513 and handed down from one Alphonse Mellot to another ever since, Domaine de la Moussière is run by the energetic Alphonse No. 19. He cut crop yields, converted to biodynamic farming and created two of the Loire's most expensive red wines. The stalwart offering, though, is the entry-level La Moussière white. Named for the vineyard from which it's sourced, it is reliably zesty, chalky and fragrant—in other words, textbook Sancerre.

BOTTLE TO TRY

○ La Moussière Sancerre ∕ $$$

CLOS ROUGEARD

In the 1970s, while their neighbors were exchanging oak barrels for steel tanks, wild yeasts for packaged versions and organic fertilizers for industrial chemicals, the Foucault family kept making wine using the same low-tech, minimalist techniques. Now their "naturalist" Clos Rougeard offerings are considered cutting-edge. Brothers Charly and Nady Foucault fashion three culty, long-lived reds (plus a single, very rare white) that set the standard for Saumur-Champigny and, arguably, the entire Loire.

BOTTLE TO TRY

● Saumur-Champigny ∕ $$$$

COULY-DUTHEIL

A Chinon appellation star, Couly-Dutheil turns out some of the Loire's best Cabernet Franc–based wines. Its flagship reds come from Clos de l'Echo, an ancient walled vineyard that, according to local legend, was once owned by the family of François Rabelais, the 16th-century satirist. Meaty and ripe, these wines are as serious and ageworthy as Chinon gets. In recent years, Arnaud Couly and his father, Jacques, have improved the quality of the estate's basic wines, including its fresh, earthy rosé.

BOTTLES TO TRY
- **René Couly Rosé** / **$**
- **Baronnie Madeleine** / **$$**
- **Clos de l'Echo** / **$$**

DOMAINE DES AUBUISIÈRES

There are few better examples of the ridiculously good values to be found in Loire wine than in Bernard Fouquet's Vouvrays. Just two of the still wines from his family estate, Domaine des Aubuisières, are reliably imported into the U.S.: the tank aged Silex bottling, which is his freshest and offers the kind of purity you'd expect from a Chenin-based white named for flint rocks; and the weightier and lightly sweet single-vineyard Les Girardières, one of the rare affordable whites that can generally improve with a few years of age.

BOTTLES TO TRY
- ○ **Cuvée de Silex Vouvray** / **$**
- ○ **Les Girardières Vouvray** / **$$**

DOMAINE DES BAUMARD

Depth and concentration are not the qualities that first come to mind with Loire Valley Cabernet Franc, but Anjou vintner Jean Baumard and his son Florent fashion wines of rare complexity with seeming ease. From rivetingly mineral and tart Chenin Blancs to a lush Cabernet Franc and long-lived dessert wines, the Baumards' portfolio is a Loire winemaking tour de force. Their most famous dry cuvée is Clos du Papillon, a profound, chalky Chenin from a butterfly-shaped vineyard above the town of Savennières.

BOTTLES TO TRY
- ○ **Savennières** / **$$**
- ○ **Clos du Papillon Savennières** / **$$$**

DOMAINE DIDIER DAGUENEAU

Didier Dagueneau, the prodigiously bearded wild man of the Loire, made some of the best Pouilly-Fumés and Sancerres ever. He died when his ultralight plane crashed in 2008, but his son, Louis-Benjamin, has kept the estate's wines at the same exalted level. Extremely low vineyard yields, biodynamic farming and, unusually, aging in oak barrels result in some of the planet's greatest Sauvignon Blancs. Marked by stony minerality (the Silex bottling is actually named after the flinty soil in which its grapes are grown), a silken texture and crystalline purity, these are truly ravishing whites, with prices to match.

BOTTLES TO TRY
- Blanc Fumé de Pouilly / $$$$
- Silex / $$$$

DOMAINE DU CLOS NAUDIN

Vintner Philippe Foreau does little to promote the wines of Clos Naudin: As one of Vouvray's elite estates, with a small production and an exalted reputation, the winery's output essentially sells itself. Harvested by hand and aged in cellars tunneled out of limestone rock beneath the small winery, the minerally whites showcase the complex, ageworthy side of the Chenin Blanc grape, in dry (sec), off-dry (demi-sec) and sweet (*moelleux*) versions, in both still and sparkling cuvées.

BOTTLES TO TRY
- Demi-Sec Vouvray / $$
- Sec Vouvray / $$

DOMAINE HUET

Domaine Huet's reputation as one of Vouvray's finest estates was forged by Gaston Huet, a.k.a. "the pope of Vouvray," a World War II hero and town mayor for more than 40 years. When not politicking, Huet was creating definitive Vouvray. His son-in-law Noël Pinguet, who joined the estate in the 1970s, continued the tradition while converting the vineyards—including legendary sites such as Clos du Bourg, Le Mont and Le Haut Lieu—to biodynamic farming. Cellarmaster Jean-Bernard Berthomé became head winemaker upon Pinguet's retirement in 2012.

BOTTLES TO TRY
- Le Mont Sec Vouvray / $$
- Le Haut Lieu Demi Sec / $$$

DOMAINE LUCIEN CROCHET

"Soil" is a misnomer for the carpet of whitish rocks that crunch underfoot in the Crochet family's Le Chêne vineyard. The estate's 94 vineyard acres in Sancerre include prized limestone-studded holdings such as Le Chêne and La Croix du Roy, plus a clutch of top sites on south-facing hillsides. The extra sun exposure translates to especially ripe grapes, which means that even the reds crafted by winemaker Gilles Crochet are lush. White wines, meanwhile, are racy, fresh and intense.

BOTTLES TO TRY
- ○ **Sancerre** ⁄ **$$**
- ○ **Le Chêne Sancerre** ⁄ **$$$**

DOMAINE PASCAL JOLIVET

Pascal Jolivet comes from a winemaking family, but he started his own wine business from scratch in the 1980s, purchasing grapes from all over Sancerre and Pouilly-Fumé. Today he's one of the largest exporters of wine from both regions, and instead of buying most of the fruit he needs, Jolivet is able to obtain about half of his grapes from vineyards he owns himself—many of them in top sites. That control over farming helps Jolivet keep a firm grip on quality.

BOTTLES TO TRY
- ○ **Pouilly-Fumé** ⁄ **$$**
- ○ **Sancerre Blanc** ⁄ **$$**
- ◐ **Attitude Rosé** ⁄ **$$**

DOMAINE VACHERON

This Sancerre estate is best known for its reds—not because its whites aren't terrific (they are), but because few Sancerre domaines offer Pinot Noirs of such silky finesse. Winemaking cousins Jean-Laurent and Jean-Dominique Vacheron inherited their grandfather's obsession with the variety—Jean-Laurent even worked at Burgundy's iconic Domaine de la Romanée-Conti. The Vacherons show a zeal for meticulous winemaking and biodynamic farming—two factors that have made this estate a rising star.

BOTTLES TO TRY
- ○ **Sancerre** ⁄ **$$**
- ◐ **Sancerre Rosé** ⁄ **$$**
- ● **Sancerre Rouge** ⁄ **$$**

NICOLAS JOLY

Nicolas Joly's business card reads "Nature Assistant," which is how this Savennières winemaker prefers to describe his role. Joly is France's most visible evangelist for biodynamics, a radically holistic, organic farming philosophy. The Clos de la Coulée de Serrant, one of three impressive Joly cuvées, hails from a legendary Chenin Blanc vineyard and is one of the Loire's most famous wines. Joly's daughter Virginie has brought more consistency to recent vintages, which offer Savennières's trademark qualities: tart acidity, a silky, rich texture and alluring notes that range from citrus to minerals, flowers and honey.

BOTTLES TO TRY

○ **Les Clos Sacrés** ⁄ **$$$**

○ **Clos de la Coulée de Serrant Savennières** ⁄ **$$$$**

RHÔNE VALLEY

CLAIM TO FAME

From the exalted, powerful reds of the tiny Hermitage appellation in the north to the southern Rhône's suppler, berry-rich red blends, the Rhône offers some of the best quality for price in all of France. Northern Rhône reds get their spice and brooding dark-fruit flavors from the Syrah grape; in contrast, southern Rhône reds are multivariety blends based chiefly on Grenache. The region's often-overshadowed whites can be terrific values.

REGIONS TO KNOW

NORTHERN RHÔNE A narrow stretch of steep and often-terraced hills, the northern Rhône occupies a transitional zone between cooler-climate Burgundy to the north and sunnier Mediterranean climes to the south—a position that's reflected in its wines' alluring mix of finesse and robust flavor. Though responsible for less than 5 percent of the Rhône's total production, the northern Rhône is the source of many of its most celebrated wines. Its top subregions for reds include **CÔTE-RÔTIE** ("roasted slope," for its sunny exposure), **CORNAS** and **HERMITAGE**. The tiny **CONDRIEU** appellation produces coveted, voluptuous white wines from Viognier. The northern Rhône's largest subzone, **CROZES-HERMITAGE,** is responsible for about half of the region's wine. Much of it is ordinary, but values abound.

SOUTHERN RHÔNE Some 35 miles south of the northern Rhône's Hermitage hill, the sunnier southern Rhône begins. Many grapes are permitted in its various subregions, most selected for their ability to withstand the hotter Mediterranean climate—in prestigious **CHÂTEAUNEUF-DU-PAPE,** 13 varieties are allowed. The **GIGONDAS** and **VACQUEYRAS** appellations produce mostly red wines similar to (but less profound and costly than) those of Châteauneuf-du-Pape. Across the river, the **LIRAC** and **TAVEL** districts are best known for outstanding rosés and, increasingly, some reds. Farther afield, the satellite regions of **VENTOUX, LUBERON** and **COSTIÈRES DE NÎMES** make wines similar to basic Côtes-du-Rhône (see p. 54).

❦ KEY GRAPES: WHITE

GRENACHE BLANC, CLAIRETTE & BOURBOULENC Used only in the southern part of the Rhône Valley, these plump grape varieties typically get blended with Marsanne, Roussanne and Viognier to create the region's medium-bodied, white peach– and citrus-inflected wines.

MARSANNE & ROUSSANNE These fragrant varieties are usually blended to make the northern Rhône's full-bodied, nutty, pear-scented white wines. In the southern Rhône, they are frequently used to complement Viognier. Though not high in acidity, the resulting wines often have the ability to age for a decade or more.

VIOGNIER Lush and fragrant, the honeysuckle-scented Viognier is responsible for the celebrated whites of the northern Rhône's Condrieu appellation.

❦ KEY GRAPES: RED

GRENACHE The southern Rhône's darkly fruity, full-bodied red wines are made primarily with Grenache, which gets bolstered with a combination of Cinsaut, Syrah, Mourvèdre and/or Carignane in a typical blend.

SYRAH The only red grape permitted in northern Rhône red wines, Syrah can achieve great power and complexity, expressing a mix of dark fruit accented by black pepper and meat flavors. Most northern Rhône red wines are allowed to include regional white grapes, except in Cornas, where Syrah must stand alone.

WINE TERMINOLOGY

CÔTES-DU-RHÔNE Côtes-du-Rhône is the Rhône's most basic category, representing the vast majority of its wines, both red and white. Most Côtes-du-Rhône wines come from the south, although the entire valley is permitted to use the designation. Very little basic Côtes-du-Rhône wine comes from the north; most northern Rhône bottlings meet higher standards and are entitled to label their wines with one of the region's eight *crus*.

CÔTES-DU-RHÔNE VILLAGES This designation identifies wines made from grapes grown in the dozens of southern Rhône villages that satisfy stricter quality requirements than those for the basic Côtes-du-Rhône designation. Of these villages, 18 have earned the right to append their name to the wine label—for example, Côtes-du-Rhône Villages Cairanne. All reds and rosés with the villages designation must be at least 50 percent Grenache; whites are based on Grenache Blanc, Clairette, Marsanne, Roussanne, Bourboulenc and Viognier.

Producers/ Rhône Valley

ALAIN GRAILLOT

Alain Graillot established his winery in 1985, and within a few years rocked the Rhône wine scene with two Crozes-Hermitage wines that astonished critics: Complex and powerful, they proved that the region's wines could compete with bottlings from the Rhône's more prestigious zones. Despite a background in the agro-chemicals industry, Graillot is pro-organic farming, working his vines without pesticides or chemical fertilizers. The entry-level Crozes beats wines costing twice its price, and La Guiraude (a selection of the year's best barrels) sets the standard for the region.

WINE INTEL
While cycling in Morocco, Graillot discovered a Syrah vineyard. Now he and Bordeaux winemaker Jacques Poulain produce a Moroccan Syrah, Syrocco, with a bicycle featured on its label.

BOTTLES TO TRY
- Crozes-Hermitage / $$
- La Guiraude Crozes-Hermitage / $$$

CHÂTEAU DE BEAUCASTEL

Château de Beaucastel produces definitive Châteauneuf-du-Pape—savory, fragrant, deep yet buoyant blends that have made this southern Rhône subregion one of the world's most admired wine zones. A pair of flagship red and white Châteauneufs anchor the portfolio; they're complemented by two even rarer cuvées—a white made from ancient Roussanne vines and the monumental, Mourvèdre-based Hommage à Jacques Perrin. Wallet-savvy Rhône fans stock up on Coudoulet de Beaucastel, the estate's overachieving red and white Côtes-du-Rhônes.

BOTTLES TO TRY
- **Coudoulet de Beaucastel Côtes-du-Rhône** ∕ **$$**
- **Châteauneuf-du-Pape** ∕ **$$$$**

CHÂTEAU LA NERTHE

What to do if you want to buy a winery but haven't got the money? If you're Alain Dugas, you convince someone else to invest in one and let you run it. Teaming up with the Richard family, Dugas took over the management of this historic Châteauneuf estate in 1985 and, along with his protégé, Christian Voeux, returned it to the region's front ranks. Since Dugas's retirement in 2008, Voeux has stepped into his shoes; he keeps turning out gorgeously polished, ageworthy reds and some of the best whites in Châteauneuf.

BOTTLES TO TRY
- ○ **Châteauneuf-du-Pape** ∕ **$$$**
- **Châteauneuf-du-Pape** ∕ **$$$**

CLOS DES PAPES

The Avril family has resisted the trend of culling the best barrels of a vintage to create an ultra-luxury, prestige cuvée. Instead, all of the best wine goes into the single, stellar red and white Châteauneuf-du-Papes that the Avrils have fashioned for more than a century. Small quantities and high demand mean that both wines can be hard to find. Happily, any red juice that's not good enough for the acclaimed flagship bottling goes into Le Petit Vin d'Avril, a humble, nonvintage blend. Supple, juicy and compulsively delicious, it's the perfect house red.

BOTTLES TO TRY
- **Le Petit Vin d'Avril** ∕ **$$**
- **Châteauneuf-du-Pape** ∕ **$$$$**

DELAS FRÈRES

An all-star team of winemaking talent plus an infusion of cash from corporate parent Louis Roederer has taken this historic *négociant*'s wines from solid to often spectacular. With a home base close to St-Joseph, Delas offers wines from both northern and southern Rhône regions. Under managing director Fabrice Rosset and enologists Jacques Grange and Jean-François Farinet, Delas is living up to the potential of its superb vineyards at the top end and delivering terrific value in everyday bottlings.

BOTTLES TO TRY

- Côtes-du-Rhône Saint-Esprit / $
- Le Clos Crozes-Hermitage / $$$
- Les Bessards Hermitage / $$$$

DOMAINE CLUSEL-ROCH

Gilbert Clusel and Brigitte Roch and their son Guillaume collaborate on brilliant Côte-Rôties and a rare Condrieu, all made at a tiny winery attached to their house in Vérenay, a hamlet at the foot of the Côte-Rôtie's northern slopes. They grow only a cousin of Syrah called Serine in their small collection of Côte-Rôtie vineyards. Short-lived and low-yielding, Serine is hard to farm but produces complex, expressive reds. The top cuvée, Les Grandes Places, comes from a single plot of ancient vines.

BOTTLES TO TRY

- Côte-Rôtie / $$$
- Les Grandes Places Côte-Rôtie / $$$$

DOMAINE DE LA JANASSE

Domaine de la Janasse's rise to the elite ranks of Châteauneuf-du-Pape producers began in 1991, when 19-year-old Christophe Sabon took over winemaking from his father, Aimé. The latter stepped aside to focus on the organically farmed vineyards, leaving Christophe free to vinify some of the Rhône's most layered and sought-after Grenache-based reds. Sabon's small-lot prestige cuvées, like the Cuvée Chaupin and *vieilles vignes* (old vines) Châteauneuf-du-Papes, command high prices; two affordable Côtes-du-Rhônes give a taste of Janasse's rich, structured style.

BOTTLES TO TRY

- Réserve Côtes-du-Rhône / $$
- Les Garrigues Côtes-du-Rhône / $$$
- Chaupin Châteauneuf-du-Pape / $$$$

DOMAINE DE LA MORDORÉE

The Tavel-based brothers Christophe and Fabrice Delorme sold their high-tech enterprises in 1986 to get back to their family's roots as winegrowers. In an amazingly short time, Christophe's Lirac and Tavel bottlings became known as some of the region's best. But it was La Mordorée's pure, intense Châteauneuf-du-Papes that vaulted the young domaine to stardom. It's hard to go wrong with anything in the Delormes' lineup, from fresh, fragrant rosés to rich Lirac blends (including a terrific white) and two Côtes-du-Rhônes (one red, one rosé).

BOTTLES TO TRY

- ○ **La Reine des Bois Lirac** / **$$**
- ◐ **La Dame Rousse Tavel** / **$$**
- ● **La Reine des Bois Châteauneuf-du-Pape** / **$$$$**

DOMAINE DU PÉGAU

In 1987, when she was barely out of university, Laurence Féraud convinced her parents to let her take charge of the cellar at their modest Châteauneuf estate. Within a few years, Pégau was selling out every vintage and the wines had become an emblem of seductive, richly layered Châteauneuf-du-Pape. Féraud's *négociant* selections are as polished as her old-vine, estate-grown cuvées, which include offerings from a new 100-acre Côtes-du-Rhône property named Château Pégau.

BOTTLES TO TRY

- ● **Sélection Laurence Féraud Côtes-du-Rhône** / **$**
- ● **Plan Pégau** / **$$**
- ● **Châteauneuf-du-Pape** / **$$$$**

DOMAINE RENÉ ROSTAING

Most of the fruit from René Rostaing's Côte-Rôtie vineyards go into a basic cuvée, though this powerful, famously refined Syrah is anything but. Now called Ampodium, it has the largest production of Rostaing's three brilliant Côte-Rôties but still is made in small quantities. It's worth tracking down as an ideal introduction to the region's smoky, structured reds. A baby brother bottling, Les Lézardes Syrah, is about half the price and comes from old vines just outside the Côte-Rôtie district.

BOTTLES TO TRY

- ● **Les Lézardes Syrah** / **$$$**
- ● **Ampodium Côte-Rôtie** / **$$$$**

DOMAINE ROGER SABON

Even by French standards the Sabon winemaking family ranks as ancient: Its first recorded vineyard in Châteauneuf-du-Pape dates to 1540. Today, the domaine is a three-generation affair, with Roger Sabon's three sons and two of his grandchildren involved. Grenache is at the heart of the reds, including the famous Le Secret des Sabon bottling. Produced from centenarian vines, it's among the region's benchmark wines but is tough to find Stateside. Instead, look for the terrific Châteauneuf-du-Pape, Côtes-du-Rhône and Lirac bottlings.

BOTTLES TO TRY
- ● **Rhône by Roger Sabon Côtes-du-Rhône** ⁄ **$$**
- ● **Réserve Châteauneuf-du-Pape** ⁄ **$$$**

E. GUIGAL

Guigal is the northern Rhône's preeminent producer, turning out magisterial reds in minuscule quantities from estate vineyards in Côte-Rôtie and Condrieu as well as widely available, affordable wines from across the Rhône Valley. The former include three breathtakingly pricey Côte-Rôtie wines from the La Turque, La Mouline and La Landonne vineyards (famously nicknamed "the La Las"), while the latter offer a tour of every key Rhône appellation.

BOTTLES TO TRY
- ○ **Côtes-du-Rhône** ⁄ **$**
- ● **Gigondas** ⁄ **$$**
- ● **Hermitage** ⁄ **$$$$**

JEAN-LUC COLOMBO

Nothing about Jean-Luc Colombo's Rhône career is traditional. For starters, the Marseille-born consultant first made his name in a laboratory, not a vineyard, advising winegrowers in the then-obscure Cornas region during the 1980s. But Colombo's gift for transforming Cornas's rustic, earthy Syrahs into polished, powerful reds elevated the entire appellation. The four prestigious, estate-grown Cornas wines he makes at the winery he established in 1994 cap a portfolio built on reliably tasty, modern-style *négociant* bottlings.

BOTTLES TO TRY
- ○ **Les Abeilles Côtes-du-Rhône** ⁄ **$**
- ● **Les Ruchets Cornas** ⁄ **$$$$**

RARITIES & COLLECTIBLES

DOMAINE ALAIN VOGE This Cornas domaine is the source of one of the world's greatest Syrahs, Les Vieilles Fontaines, a powerfully built red made in only great vintages from a handful of 80-year-old vines rooted in granite soil.

DOMAINE AUGUSTE CLAPE As traditional as Cornas gets, Clape's ageworthy cuvées are as rare as they are coveted. They come from vines farmed by generations of the Clape family, including patriarch Auguste ("the King of Cornas"), son Pierre-Marie and grandson Olivier.

THIERRY ALLEMAND Thierry Allemand supported himself as an electrician and cellar hand for 15 years until he could afford to focus solely on his own tiny Cornas estate. The two resulting reds, Reynard and Chaillot, are magisterial.

M. CHAPOUTIER

Michel Chapoutier's progressive views make him an anomaly in tradition-minded France. After turning around his family's wine business in the early 1990s, he was among the first in the Rhône to adopt all-biodynamic farming. And in this blend-dominated region, Chapoutier champions vineyard-specific and single-variety wines. These cuvées fill out a portfolio that ranges from culty Hermitages to terrific value bottlings.

BOTTLES TO TRY

- ○ **La Bernardine Châteauneuf-du-Pape** / **$$$**
- ● **Belleruche Côtes-du-Rhône** / **$**
- ● **Les Granits St-Joseph** / **$$$**

PAUL JABOULET AÎNÉ

It took a Swiss financier, his Champagne-born wife and their precociously talented winemaker daughter to bring this iconic Rhône producer back to glory. Maker of one the world's greatest reds, Hermitage La Chapelle, as well as a wide *négociant* range, Jaboulet has been transformed under the Frey family, who bought the winery in 2006. They've slashed production, built a sleek new winery and put this 180-year-old estate back on top.

BOTTLES TO TRY

- ○ **Mule Blanche Crozes-Hermitage** / **$$$**
- ● **Parallèle 45 Côtes-du-Rhône** / **$**
- ● **Cornas** / **$$$**

PERRIN & FILS

The Perrin family is responsible for some of the Rhône's greatest reds and whites from the vineyards of Château de Beaucastel (see p. 55), but they also purchase fruit to produce fabulous wines made for everyday drinking. This *négociant* arm turns out consistent values that spotlight the Rhône's less prestigious corners, such as the juicy, easy-drinking bottlings from Luberon and Ventoux under the Vieille Ferme label.

BOTTLES TO TRY

○ La Vieille Ferme Luberon / $
● Réserve Côtes-du-Rhône / $
● Les Cornuds Vinsobres / $$

TARDIEU-LAURENT

Michel Tardieu worked as a chauffeur for 16 years before jumping into the wine business. He still does plenty of driving, though: Tardieu owns no vines, and spends much of his time seeking out extraordinary vineyards (and then convincing their owners to sell him their grapes). He teamed up with the extremely talented consultant Philippe Cambie to make a handful of ravishing wines, focused on old-vine grapes from the Rhône's most prestigious *crus*, mostly in southern appellations.

BOTTLES TO TRY

● Les Becs Fins Côtes-du-Rhône / $$
● Vieilles Vignes Rasteau / $$$
● Vieilles Vignes Châteauneuf-du-Pape / $$$$

VIDAL-FLEURY

Under winemaker Guy Sarton-de-Joncquey, this historic *négociant* has boosted the quality of its wines, which include a trio of popular Côtes-du-Rhônes (red, white and pink). Based in the northern Rhône, Vidal-Fleury has been producing wine continuously for more than two centuries, making it the Rhône's oldest estate. (Thomas Jefferson even visited, in 1787.) It's also one of its most competitively priced, an aspect that's especially appreciated in its high-end, estate-grown wines, like the elegantly styled La Chatillonne Côte-Rôtie.

BOTTLES TO TRY

● Tavel / $$
● Côtes-du-Rhône / $
● La Chatillonne Côte-Rôtie / $$$$

SOUTHERN FRANCE

CLAIM TO FAME

France's Mediterranean coast and southwest regions were long known for the quantity, not the quality, of their wines. But global demand for affordable wines spurred a dramatic change. While southern France still churns out uninteresting bulk wine, it's also a source of exciting cuvées made from ancient, rediscovered vineyards and ambitious new ones. Its vast reach and varied geography mean that nearly any grape can thrive here.

REGIONS TO KNOW

LANGUEDOC-ROUSSILLON France's Mediterranean coast produces vast amounts of mostly red wine, including many terrific values. Both the Roussillon (closer to Spain) and the Languedoc (at the center of the coastal arc) are turning out increasingly complex wines at prices that don't carry the prestige tax of their northern neighbors. Unlike most parts of France, the Languedoc grows a range of grapes—some native to the region, others from different French regions. Look to subregions like **CORBIÈRES, CÔTES DU ROUSSILLON, FAUGÈRES** and **FITOU** for great red blends, often based on old-vine Carignane and Grenache.

PROVENCE Known for its herb-edged dry rosés, especially those from **BANDOL** (**CÔTES DE PROVENCE** and **COTEAUX D'AIX-EN-PROVENCE** rosés can be excellent, too), Provence is also an overlooked source of bold reds. Go-to regions include Bandol, **LES BAUX DE PROVENCE** and Coteaux d'Aix-en-Provence. Whites are citrusy and soft; the best are from **CASSIS.**

THE SOUTHWEST Outshone by those of neighboring Bordeaux, the wines of France's southwest are little known in the U.S., but that is changing. **BERGERAC** reds are made with the same grapes as Bordeaux—Cabernet, Merlot, Malbec and Cabernet Franc—and can exhibit a similar finesse. Vintners in **CAHORS** craft reds of massive power from the Malbec grape. In **MADIRAN,** winemakers produce dark, full-bodied and tannic wines. The Basque Country's hearty wines are made from a blend of local grapes; **JURANÇON,** for example, is a full-bodied white wine produced from Petit and Gros Manseng grapes in dry and sweet styles.

🍇 KEY GRAPES: WHITE

CHARDONNAY Much of southern France is too warm for fine Chardonnay, though straightforward value versions abound.

GRENACHE BLANC One of the Languedoc's most widely planted white grapes, this fairly neutral variety is usually bottled as part of a blend, contributing softness and mouth-filling body.

MACCABÉO This medium-bodied, floral-edged grape is known as Viura in Spain's Rioja, where it stars, but it's also common in Roussillon and the Languedoc.

MARSANNE, ROUSSANNE & VIOGNIER Best known as Rhône varieties, these grapes do well in the warm regions farther south, producing round, lush and sometimes spicy whites.

PICPOUL BLANC This minerally grape (whose name means "lip-stinger") is behind some of the Languedoc's incredibly refreshing, zesty whites, especially those grown near the town of Pinet.

ROLLE, BOURBOULENC, CLAIRETTE, SÉMILLON & UGNI BLANC Along with Grenache Blanc and Marsanne and a few others, these local grapes create Provence's white blends. Rolle is also common in the Roussillon, where it yields zesty whites similar to Italy's Vermentino (they are thought to be the same grape).

🍇 KEY GRAPES: RED

AUXERROIS Known elsewhere as Malbec or Côt, this smoky red (not to be confused with a white variety of the same name) stars in the southwest's Cahors region. Unlike the fruity, supple Malbecs of Argentina, Cahors reds are spicy, earthy and tannic.

CABERNET SAUVIGNON & MERLOT This duo is mostly used for inexpensive wines destined for export. While a few regions (such as parts of Provence) and a few top producers succeed with more ambitious versions, most of these wines are fruity and simple.

CARIGNANE This widely planted red dominates France's southernmost territory, especially the Roussillon. While much Carignane wine is simple and rustic, it can make great fruity, spicy reds. The best come from old vines in Languedoc's Corbières.

CINSAUT Native to Provence (and eaten locally as a table grape), Cinsaut is the signature variety of the region's fresh, fruity rosés. In the Languedoc it's often blended with Carignane to add perfume to the reds of Minervois, Corbières and Fitou.

GRENACHE & SYRAH Fruity Grenache and firm, tannic Syrah are blended throughout the south. In both the Languedoc and the Roussillon they are combined with Mourvèdre to create hearty, fruity reds, such as the blends of Minervois and Fitou. In Provence they're responsible for noted rosé and red wines.

MOURVÈDRE The calling-card grape of Provence's prestigious Bandol region (and the same as Spain's Monastrell), Mourvèdre yields spicy, rich reds and robust rosés on its own. Elsewhere it is often blended with Grenache and Syrah.

TANNAT Widely planted in the southwest, this tough, tannic grape does best in the Madiran subregion. It's also blended with Cabernet Franc and/or Cabernet Sauvignon for the dark, meaty reds of Irouléguy in the Basque region of France.

Producers/ Southern France

CHÂTEAU LAGRÉZETTE

Luxury-marketing mogul Alain Dominique Perrin acquired this ancient estate outside the town of Cahors in 1980. Perrin poured cash into rehabilitating its abandoned vineyards and a turreted 15th-century castle, then hired superstar consultant Michel Rolland to mastermind the wines. The resulting Malbec-based reds have made Lagrézette into Cahors's most prominent label. Its powerhouse top cuvée, Le Pigeonnier, spends more than two years in new barrels and is expensive, but a range of wines made from purchased grapes offer a taste of Lagrézette's intense, fruity style at more accessible prices.

BOTTLES TO TRY
- **Château Lagrézette** ⁄ $$
- **Le Pigeonnier** ⁄ $$$$

CHÂTEAU MONTUS

In 1980, Alain Brumont broke with his father, the owner of Madiran's Château Bouscassé, and borrowed every franc he could to create a rival estate, Château Montus, in the same southwestern appellation. Right from the start, Montus blew away critics accustomed to the region's rustic red wines, which are based on the tough and tannic Tannat variety. The winery quickly became Madiran's benchmark estate; eventually, Brumont took over Château Bouscassé as well. Combining Tannat with a bit of Cabernet, Montus's Tannat–Cabernet Sauvignon blend is an essential introduction to Madiran's powerful, black-fruited red wines.

BOTTLE TO TRY
- Château Montus ∕ $$$

COMMANDERIE DE LA BARGEMONE

The footprints of the Knights Templar are all over Provence, starting at Commanderie de la Bargemone. The once-powerful estate was established as a regional headquarters for the secretive military order in the 1200s, but today it is far more famous for its fabulous wines than for its medieval history. Rejuvenated by industrialist Jean-Pierre Rozan in the 1970s and managed by the Garin family since 2006, its vineyards lie within Coteaux d'Aix. Bargemone's crisp, strawberry-scented rosé is its flagship wine and a consistent Provençal standout.

BOTTLE TO TRY
- Commanderie de la Bargemone ∕ $

DOMAINE TEMPIER

Domaine Tempier has been setting standards in Bandol, Provence's most prestigious region, for more than half a century. Its best-known bottling is a silky, salmon-colored rosé that's as complex and multifaceted as rosé wines get. Like all of Tempier's bottlings (save for one white) and, indeed, all Bandol reds and rosés, it is based on the Mourvèdre grape. That variety's spicy, powerful side is showcased in Tempier's superb collection of inky, estate-grown reds.

BOTTLES TO TRY
- Domaine Tempier ∕ $$$
- Cabassaou ∕ $$$$
- La Tourtine ∕ $$$$

MAS AMIEL

When he purchased Mas Amiel in 1999, Paris businessman Olivier Decelle joined a trickle of increasingly prominent outsiders who have discovered the Maury area. Long known as an under-the-radar source of terrific red dessert wines, this slice of Roussillon has become one of the region's most promising zones for powerful dry blends based on Grenache. Decelle converted the estate's 420 acres of gnarly old vines to biodynamic farming and hired well-known consultants Stéphane Derenoncourt and Claude Bourguignon. The team's plush, darkly fruity blends come in sweet, dry (sec) and rosé versions.

BOTTLE TO TRY
● Notre Terre / $$

MAS DE DAUMAS GASSAC

This breakout producer pioneered fine wine from the Languedoc region in the 1970s—a time when most experts considered "fine Languedoc wine" to be the punch line to a joke. But encouraged by celebrated enologist Émile Peynaud, owners Aimé and Véronique Guibert persevered, turning out ambitious reds and whites made in a traditional Bordeaux style from 124 acres of vines near Montpellier. Fame followed swiftly; today the Guiberts produce four respected estate cuvées and a well-priced *négociant* line called Moulin de Gassac.

BOTTLES TO TRY
● Moulin de Gassac Guilhem / $
● Mas de Daumas Gassac / $$$

Italy

Wine Region

It is nearly impossible to think of Italian wines without thinking of food. Imagine a great Bordeaux from France, for instance, and the picture that comes to mind is a château surrounded by vineyards. Conjure up a great Chianti Classico, and instead of an austere building you get a vision of pasta with Bolognese sauce; think of a Barolo, and clouds of white truffle shavings start falling through your mind's eye. Associations like these are one great reason to learn about Italian wines; another is that Italian wine is far more varied than many people think. There are more than 300 official wine regions, and over 2,000 native grape varieties, not to mention a history of making wine that stretches back more than 3,000 years. Only a dedicated scholar would study every aspect, but with Italian wine, even the smallest amount of knowledge— like the smallest amount of white truffle— can be immensely rewarding.

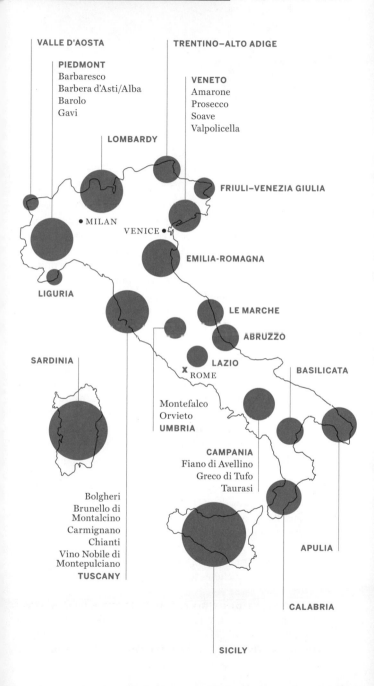

VALLE D'AOSTA

TRENTINO—ALTO ADIGE

PIEDMONT
Barbaresco
Barbera d'Asti/Alba
Barolo
Gavi

VENETO
Amarone
Prosecco
Soave
Valpolicella

LOMBARDY

FRIULI—VENEZIA GIULIA

• MILAN

VENICE •

EMILIA-ROMAGNA

LIGURIA

LE MARCHE

ABRUZZO

SARDINIA

LAZIO

X ROME

BASILICATA

Montefalco
Orvieto
UMBRIA

CAMPANIA
Fiano di Avellino
Greco di Tufo
Taurasi

Bolgheri
Brunello di
Montalcino
Carmignano
Chianti
Vino Nobile di
Montepulciano
TUSCANY

APULIA

CALABRIA

SICILY

Italy

WINE TERMINOLOGY

Italy's official wine regions fall into four main quality categories: DOC, DOCG, IGT and VdT. These categories dictate standards for growing and making wines, including which grape varieties may be used, where the grapes must come from and how much a vineyard can yield (smaller crops generally result in more-concentrated, higher-quality wines), as well as a finished wine's alcohol content. Most Italian wines are labeled by region; some list the grape if it defines a region, such as Montepulciano d'Abruzzo, made from the Montepulciano grape in Abruzzo.

VINO DA TAVOLA (VDT) Most wines designated *vino da tavola* (table wine) are cheap jug blends designed for immediate drinking. VdT wines may come from anywhere in Italy and don't identify their vintage (year of harvest). Some vintners buck traditional DOC/G rules to make ambitious, experimental bottlings under the VdT label, but today most of these high-quality offerings fall into the IGT category.

INDICAZIONE GEOGRAFICA TIPICA (IGT) A big step up in quality from most VdT wines, the IGT category identifies region-specific wines that don't qualify as DOC or DOCG. Often, IGT wines are made using unorthodox grapes or production methods.

DENOMINAZIONE DI ORIGINE CONTROLLATA (DOC) This more regulated category includes the majority of Italy's quality wine.

DENOMINAZIONE DI ORIGINE CONTROLLATA E GARANTITA (DOCG) This, the strictest classification, includes Italy's most prestigious wines. DOCG wines must pass a blind taste test by a panel of experts appointed by Italy's Ministry of Agriculture.

CLASSICO A prestigious subregion, often the original and oldest part of a region whose boundaries were later enlarged.

RISERVA This term indicates a wine that has been aged for a longer period than basic wines of the same designation. Exact requirements differ by region.

SUPERIORE Denotes a wine with a higher alcohol content and greater concentration. *Superiore* wines are made from grapes grown in a top subzone.

PIEDMONT

CLAIM TO FAME
Piedmont's most sought-after reds, Barolo and Barbaresco, are revered for their ageworthy structure and complex aromatics. But don't overlook Barbera and Dolcetto, the food-friendly, supple red wines that the Piedmontese drink every day.

REGIONS TO KNOW
BAROLO & BARBARESCO Sourced from a small number of prized vineyards in the hills around the town of Alba, Nebbiolo-based reds from these two zones have steep price tags reflecting their scarcity. Barolos must be aged three years, two in barrel, before release; Barbarescos must be aged two years, one in barrel. Many of these bottlings don't reach their prime until after a decade or more of age.

DOGLIANI & ALBA Both are sources of top Dolcettos; Alba is also known for good values in Nebbiolo.

GAVI Gavi's melony whites are lively enough to serve as an aperitif and substantial enough to accompany a wide range of foods.

LANGHE, GATTINARA & GHEMME Go-to zones for Nebbiolo-based reds that offer a taste of this compelling grape at a lower price than Barolo and Barbaresco.

ROERO This subregion's zesty, minerally, Arneis-based whites are becoming easier to find in the U.S.

☙ KEY GRAPES: WHITE

ARNEIS The almond-flavored Arneis grape has come back from near extinction; its best wines are from the Roero subregion.

CHARDONNAY Many prominent Piedmont vintners produce worthwhile Chardonnays; they tend to be rich, fruity and fresh.

CORTESE A specialty of southeast Piedmont, Cortese yields tart, citrusy and mostly inexpensive whites. The best come from hillside vines in Gavi, where riper grapes yield fruitier wines.

☙ KEY GRAPES: RED

BARBERA & DOLCETTO Two of Piedmont's most popular wines, these reds offer soft tannins, berry flavors and juicy acidity.

NEBBIOLO The grape behind the bold, majestic wines of Barolo and Barbaresco, Nebbiolo has substantial tannins and firm acidity, which make these wines difficult to drink when young. With savory, floral aromatics (think tar and roses), it's crafted in a range of styles, from traditional (firm, austere and earthy) to modern (smoother and fruitier).

Producers/ Piedmont

ANTONIOLO

Antoniolo shows just how good the wines of the tiny, under-the-radar Gattinara district can be. Located in Piedmont's northern Alpine foothills, Gattinara produces reds that are made from the same grape variety used in Langhe's famous Barolos and Barbarescos—Nebbiolo, known locally as Spanna—but that are lighter-bodied, more delicate and higher in acidity. Antoniolo's single-*cru* Nebbiolos offer complexity comparable to great Langhe examples, while its multivineyard blend makes a fabulous intro to Gattinara's pure, aromatic reds.

BOTTLES TO TRY
- Gattinara / $$$
- Osso San Grato / $$$$

BROVIA

Giacinto Brovia can't help himself: Although he officially passed the reins of this Langhe estate to his daughters, Elena and Cristina, years ago, he still keeps an eye on its wines and vines. That continuity shows in Brovia's traditional Barolos, which are aged in Slavonian and French oak. And although the classic style of Brovia's wines hasn't changed, quality has jumped. Thanks to Cristina's tweaks in the vineyards and Elena's hand in the cellar, Brovia's wines compare to Langhe's best—though they're not nearly as well known, making them an insider favorite.

BOTTLES TO TRY

● **Ca'Mia Barolo** ⁄ **$$$$**
● **Rocche dei Brovia Barolo** ⁄ **$$$$**

CERETTO

Despite its relatively large size, Ceretto maintains a meticulous grip on quality by working from four boutique wineries, each tailored to specific cuvées. Its modernist, single-site Barolos, for example, come from an outpost perched over the legendary Bricco Rocche vineyard, while a tiny cellar in Asili yields two Barbarescos. Coveted by collectors, Ceretto's vineyard-specific reds are pricey and generally hard to find. Fortunately, wine-maker Alessandro Ceretto crafts more-affordable, multilot blends, like the licorice-scented Zonchera Barolo and a citrusy, compulsively delicious Arneis.

BOTTLES TO TRY

○ **Blangè Arneis** ⁄ **$$**
● **Zonchera Barolo** ⁄ **$$$**

COMM. G.B. BURLOTTO

If it weren't for Fabio Alessandria, this distinguished Barolo estate might be a relic of the past. Instead, Alessandria has revived the winery by making stunning Barolos, as did his great-great-uncle, the founder and legendary vintner Giovan Battista Burlotto. The flagship Monvigliero Barolo defines the house style, with intense, perfumed aromas and an elegant structure. Amazingly, grapes for the Barolos are crushed by foot, which accounts for their uncommonly refined texture.

BOTTLES TO TRY

● **Acclivi Barolo** ⁄ **$$$**
● **Monvigliero Barolo** ⁄ **$$$$**

ELVIO COGNO

It's debatable what this tiny producer does best: Elvio Cogno's Barolos, Barbarescos, Dolcettos and Barberas are all consistently great. Cogno himself was the winemaker at the legendary Barolo producer Marcarini until he set up his Novello estate in 1990. His daughter Nadia and her husband, Valter Fissore, run the winery today according to the template established by Cogno. Their powerful, elegant wines balance modern, fruit-focused approachability with earthy, tannic tradition.

BOTTLES TO TRY

- **Vigna del Mandorlo Dolcetto d'Alba** / **$$**
- **Bordini Barbaresco** / **$$$**
- **Vigna Elena Barolo** / **$$$$**

FONTANAFREDDA

Once the hunting grounds of Italy's first king and more recently known best as a producer of sparkling wines, Fontanafredda has been reinvented again under gastronomy guru and Eataly food-market entrepreneur Oscar Farinetti, who bought the vast estate with a partner in 2008. Together with winemaker Danilo Drocco, they have improved quality and spun off two top Barolo *crus* to sister winery Mirafiore. The ripe, juicy Briccotondo Barbera has become a perennial overachiever, whereas the Serralunga d'Alba Barolo showcases muscular, dark fruit.

BOTTLES TO TRY

- **Briccotondo Barbera** / **$**
- **Barolo Serralunga d'Alba** / **$$$**

GAJA

Angelo Gaja became famous (or, to traditionalists, notorious) for planting Cabernet in Piedmont—just one of his radical moves in the 1970s. Gaja pioneered the practice of using French oak barrels to age Nebbiolo, and, just as shockingly, cut crop yields to increase intensity. His lofty reputation rests on his profound Barbaresco and single-vineyard Nebbiolos, which include coveted bottlings such as Sorì Tildìn and Sorì San Lorenzo. Rarity and prestige—not to mention extraordinary quality—make Gaja's red wines breathtakingly expensive.

BOTTLES TO TRY

- **Barbaresco** / **$$$$**
- **Sorì Tildìn** / **$$$$**

RARITIES & COLLECTIBLES

PAOLO SCAVINO A modernist master whose single-vineyard Barolos make a smart addition to any cellar, Enrico Scavino (Paolo's son) created the estate's first *cru* Barolo in 1978 from the Bric dël Fiasc vineyard, still the source of his most coveted cuvée.

PODERI ALDO CONTERNO Aldo Conterno, who died in 2012, helped propel Barolo to prominence in the 1970s with majestic wines that straddle the modernist/retro style divide. His three sons continue his work, with cuvées such as Granbussia Riserva, a legendary multivineyard blend made only in great years.

ROBERTO VOERZIO Voerzio could make much more of his prized Barolos, which come from top La Morra vineyards. Instead, the vintner keeps his crop yields very low. The result is rich, flashy—and incredibly rare—Barolos of impressive balance.

GIACOMO BORGOGNO & FIGLI

Traditionalists held their breath when the Farinetti family (of Eataly food-market fame) purchased this Piedmont stalwart in 2008. The Borgogno family had been making their legendary Barolos in much the same way since the 1700s, a practice that, happily for fans, has continued under the Farinettis. Borgogno is known for traditionally styled Barolos, but the stealth choice here is the alluring, cherry-scented Barbera.

BOTTLES TO TRY
- Barbera d'Alba / $$
- Barolo / $$$$
- Barolo Riserva / $$$$

MARCHESI DI GRÉSY

Although the di Grésy family started their own wine label just 40 years ago, it quickly became one of Barbaresco's best. That's because they already owned one of the area's greatest vineyards, Martinenga, an amphitheater-shaped hillside site that has belonged to the marquis of Grésy since 1797. The three prestigious Barbarescos made from these vines each year are di Grésy's calling card and share an elegant, filigreed style. The family's everyday wines get less attention but are made with similar care.

BOTTLES TO TRY
- Martinenga Nebbiolo / $$
- Martinenga Barbaresco / $$$

MARZIANO ABBONA

It's no surprise that Marziano Abbona's Dolcettos are so phenomenal: "Dolcetto King" Beppe Caviola consults on their winemaking, and Abbona's estate is located in Dogliani, a top subzone for the variety. What's less expected is that Abbona's high-end wines are great, too. Its trio of taut, powerful Barolos as well as one richly styled Barbaresco compete with better-known (and pricier) labels. But the winery's signature pour is still remarkably lush, intense Dolcetto, best sampled in the flagship Papà Celso bottling.

BOTTLES TO TRY
- Papà Celso Dolcetto di Dogliani / $$
- Terlo Ravera Barolo / $$$$

MICHELE CHIARLO

Michele Chiarlo's collectible single-*cru* Barolos have earned this Asti-based estate its place among Piedmont's elite. But Chiarlo is also one of Piedmont's best Barbera houses, having helped to create the ripe, oak-aged style that's worlds away from thinner versions of decades past. That focus on quality shows across the portfolio, including in Tortoniano, a consistently good multi-*cru* Barolo that's less expensive than the rare single-vineyard offerings.

WINE INTEL
Chiarlo has turned a tiny village into a Barolo-obsessed luxury retreat, Palas Cerequio. Its nine suites are named for Barolo *crus;* guests can sample a stunning array of wines from the region's greatest names.

BOTTLES TO TRY
- Le Orme Barbera d'Asti / $
- Tortoniano Barolo / $$$

PIO CESARE

It takes confidence to make bold, expensive changes to your father-in-law's winery, but that's exactly what Giuseppe Boffa did when he took over Pio Cesare in the 1940s. Boffa slashed production and began creating ambitious wines, including stunning Barolos. When Boffa's son, Pio, later took over, he added new cuvées but preserved the wines' firmly structured style. Boffa's entry-level Barolo is a relative steal for its price.

BOTTLES TO TRY
- Dolcetto d'Alba / $$
- Barolo / $$$$
- Ornato Barolo / $$$$

PODERI LUIGI EINAUDI

Founded in 1897 by Luigi Einaudi, a future president of the Italian Republic, this estate is near Dogliani, a town famous for remarkably concentrated, full-bodied Dolcetto. Einaudi's versions are some of the finest, thanks to superb vineyards and the help of top consultant Beppe Caviola. Lush, rich and silky, they're serious wines that show just how complex Dolcetto can be. Caviola's influence has brought new attention to Einaudi's three modern-styled Barolos, too, which feature earthy, ripe fruit flavors and firm tannins.

BOTTLES TO TRY
- Dogliani Vigna Tecc / $$
- Dolcetto di Dogliani / $$

PRODUTTORI DEL BARBARESCO

The famous single-vineyard Barbarescos from this outstanding cooperative illustrate just how transparently the Nebbiolo grape reflects the conditions where it is grown, its *terroir*. Winemaker Aldo Vacca ages Barbaresco only in traditional casks, not small French oak barrels, a choice that imparts less wood flavor to the wines (think smoky, toasty notes) and preserves their distinctiveness and freshness. The sole multivineyard blend—called simply Barbaresco—is a great bargain, with layers of fragrant cherry fruit.

BOTTLES TO TRY
- Barbaresco / $$$
- Rabajà Riserva Barbaresco / $$$$

PRUNOTTO

Tuscany's famous Antinori dynasty (see p. 84) bought this famous Alba estate in 1994 and has poured resources into it. Today it's a Piedmont stalwart, turning out (among other wines) terrific examples of Piedmont's killer Bs: Barolo, Barbaresco and Barbera. Albiera Antinori's moves to acquire prime vineyards for the estate, such as Barbera's Costamiole and a piece of famed Barolo *cru* Bussia, have been key to the winery's success. In the glass, the wines combine a modern penchant for deep fruit and a classic structure.

BOTTLES TO TRY
- Fiulot Barbera d'Asti / $
- Barbaresco / $$$

TENIMENTI CA' BIANCA

While most notable Piedmont estates source fruit from a patchwork of vineyards, Ca' Bianca relies on a single, spectacular site for much of its red grapes. Shaped like an amphitheater and spread across 96 acres in Alto Monferrato, the site is planted chiefly to Barbera, the variety that's been Ca' Bianca's specialty since its founding in the 1950s. Now owned by the Gruppo Italiano Vini, Ca' Bianca produces three distinct Barberas, all vinified in a ripe, modern style. Beyond Barbera, its minerally, almond-edged Gavi stands out.

BOTTLES TO TRY

○ Gavi / $$
● Antè Barbera d'Asti / $$
● Chersì Barbera d'Asti Superiore / $$

VIETTI

One of the great names in Piedmont, Vietti owns vineyards in all nine villages of the Barolo region. Grapes harvested from the best sites go into three stunning single-vineyard Barolos that are as scarce as they are coveted. But the less obvious choice in the uniformly terrific portfolio—which covers all of Piedmont's major bases—is Vietti's Arneis, a gorgeous, citrusy white made from the native grape variety that the winery rescued from near extinction in the 1960s.

BOTTLES TO TRY

○ Arneis / $$
● Tre Vigne Barbera d'Asti / $$
● Rocche Barolo / $$$$

OTHER NORTHERN ITALY

REGIONS TO KNOW

FRIULI–VENEZIA GIULIA The hill country of northern Friuli is dominated by small, high-quality wineries that produce vivid, mineral-laden white wines—many crafted from obscure native grapes—plus a few interesting reds, including the violet-hued Refosco. **COLLIO** and **COLLI ORIENTALI DEL FRIULI** are the premier subregions. The gravelly plains in the warmer southern subregions grow most of Friuli–Venezia Giulia's Merlot and Cabernet Sauvignon, which show a crisp, finessed character.

LOMBARDY Surrounding Milan in north-central Italy, Lombardy derives its reputation for quality wine primarily from the Franciacorta region, which makes superb sparklers (see p. 282). The **OLTREPÒ PAVESE** region, a longtime bulk district, is also starting to make fine wine, including reds from the spicy Bonarda grape.

TRENTINO—ALTO ADIGE Although the names of these adjacent Alpine provinces are typically hyphenated, they make distinctly different wines. Trentino is known for its fresh, fruity reds made from native grapes, whereas the mostly German-speaking Alto Adige produces terrific whites, including crisp Gewürztraminers and compelling Pinot Grigios and Pinot Biancos.

VENETO In addition to sparkling **PROSECCO** (see p. 283), the Veneto offers three signature wines: **AMARONE, VALPOLICELLA** and **SOAVE**. Made from sweet, partially dried grapes, Amarones are high-alcohol reds with luscious depth and body. Based on the same grapes, Valpolicella is a younger, drier version of Amarone. Top vintners often infuse their Valpolicellas with leftover grapes from making Amarone—a process known as *ripasso*—to create wines that are among Italy's great underrated reds. Soave's Garganega-based whites are often bland, yet those made in small amounts from low-yielding, well-situated vineyards (especially in the original *classico* subregion) can be zippy and delicious.

❀ KEY GRAPES: WHITE

CHARDONNAY Northern Italy's Chardonnays display crisp acidity, thanks to shorter summers and cooler temperatures.

FRIULANO, RIBOLLA GIALLA, MALVASIA ISTRIANA & PICOLIT These aromatic natives are Friuli–Venezia Giulia specialties.

GARGANEGA Veneto's Soave wines get their lemon and almond flavors from this indigenous variety.

GLERA Formerly called Prosecco, this grape is the basis for the sparkling wines of the Prosecco region.

MÜLLER-THURGAU, SYLVANER, RIESLING & GEWÜRZTRAMINER The prevalence of these German grapes in Trentino–Alto Adige reflects the region's proximity to Austria and Switzerland.

PINOT GRIGIO, PINOT BIANCO & SAUVIGNON (BLANC) These international varieties thrive in northern Italy, where they yield whites with intense minerality and a crisp, Alpine freshness.

♣ KEY GRAPES: RED

CORVINA, MOLINARA & RONDINELLA This trio of indigenous red varieties provides the basis for three very different Veneto wines: bold, complex Amarone; juicy, medium-bodied Valpolicella; and lighter Bardolino. Using partially raisined grapes for fermentation creates Amarone's sweet-tart flavor and full body.

PINOT NERO Northern Italian Pinot Noir (Pinot Nero) is typically racy and light. Top regions for the grape include Lombardy's Oltrepò Pavese and Alto Adige.

REFOSCO Friuli–Venezia Giulia's best-known red grape yields plummy, dry wines that range from medium- to full-bodied.

SCHIAVA, LAGREIN & TEROLDEGO These Alto Adige varieties are well adapted to the region's short summers. Schiavas are often light and simple; Lagrein and Teroldego offer more tannins and body plus crisp acidity.

Producers/ Other Northern Italy

ABBAZIA DI NOVACELLA

Augustinian monks established this grand monastery and winery in the remote Isarco Valley in 1142. Perhaps competitive pricing has helped keep Novacella in business for nearly nine centuries— the wines are terrific bargains. In addition to racy, minerally examples of all of Alto Adige's go-to varietals (such as Pinot Grigio and Müller-Thurgau), it turns out some of the region's best examples of Kerner, an obscure, incredibly fragrant, fruity white. Novacella's rare Praepositus cuvées can age beautifully.

BOTTLES TO TRY
○ Kerner / $$
○ Müller-Thurgau / $$

ALLEGRINI

Following in the footsteps of his father, who reinvented Valpolicella at a time when most examples were thin, charmless and
mass-produced, Franco Allegrini crafts wines that set the standard for the region. Rich, intense and full-bodied, Allegrini's
reds include fruit from some of the best vineyards in the traditional *classico* zone, farmed to maximize quality rather than
quantity. Their concentrated flavors yield definitive, pricey
Amarone and Valpollicella, as well as more-affordable reds
based on native grapes.

BOTTLES TO TRY
- **Valpolicella Classico / $**
- **Palazzo della Torre / $$**
- **Amarone della Valpolicella Classico / $$$$**

ALOIS LAGEDER

Alois Lageder's Alto Adige wines are not only incredibly eco-
friendly, they're some of Italy's best. Made by Lageder's brother-
in-law, Luis von Dellemann, in the region's first carbon-neutral
winery and pressed from biodynamically grown grapes, the
wines include complex, minerally whites and coolly refined reds
that show why Alto Adige is one of the world's great wine regions.

BOTTLES TO TRY
- ○ **Pinot Bianco / $**
- ○ **Porer Pinot Grigio / $$**
- **Tenutæ Lageder Krafuss / $$$**

BASTIANICH

Joe Bastianich is a multitasker extraordinaire: This New York–
based restaurateur, wine writer, gourmet retail guru and reality
cooking show judge has also been a vintner since 1997. That's
when he purchased this Friuli estate with his famous chef mom,
Lidia. Winemaker and Friuli native Emilio Del Medico (with
an assist from star consultant Maurizio Castelli) fashions wines
that compete with Friuli's best. They include an intense, focused
Friulano, and Vespa Bianco, a rich Super-White (a high-quality
blend of French and native Friulian grapes) based on Chardon-
nay, Sauvignon Blanc and Picolit.

BOTTLES TO TRY
- ○ **Adriatico Friulano / $$**
- ○ **Vespa Bianco / $$$**

JERMANN

Born into a winemaking family in Collio, Silvio Jermann pioneered Friuli's Super-Whites—complex, ambitious blends of French grapes and native varieties such as Ribolla Gialla and Picolit. Jermann's rich, creamy flagship cuvée, Vintage Tunina, combines Sauvignon Blanc, Chardonnay and three native varieties to create what is arguably Friuli's most famous Super-White. His other top wines are also multivariety blends, including the fancifully named Were Dreams (based on Chardonnay) and the red Blau & Blau. For more-affordable (and equally delicious) options, look to Jermann's single-variety wines.

BOTTLES TO TRY

○ **Pinot Grigio** ⁄ **$$**

○ **Vintage Tunina** ⁄ **$$$$**

J. HOFSTÄTTER

One of the only midsize, family-owned producers left in Alto Adige (where cooperatives dominate), J. Hofstätter is responsible for two of Alto Adige's most famous and expensive varietal wines: a Pinot Nero from the Barthenau estate and the Kolbenhof estate Gewürztraminer. But there are many everyday, less scarce wines to covet from Hofstätter, too, including the spicy Meczan Pinot Noir (a grape known locally as Pinot Nero or Blauburgunder), an unusually fruity Lagrein and a wide range of zesty whites.

BOTTLES TO TRY

● **Lagrein** ⁄ **$$**

● **Meczan Pinot Nero-Blauburgunder** ⁄ **$$**

LES CRÊTES

Les Crêtes is tucked away in Valle d'Aosta, a tiny Alpine region that shares its polyglot culture with nearby France and Switzerland. Aosta's wines have emerged from obscurity thanks in part to Les Crêtes, the best known of the area's family-owned estates. Owner Costantino Charrère, a former ski instructor, and winemaker Pietro Boffa use international varieties as well as blends of obscure local grapes to create riveting, mountain-grown wines such as the Burgundy-esque Cuvée Bois Chardonnay and the silky Torrette red blend.

BOTTLES TO TRY

○ **Cuvée Bois Chardonnay** ⁄ **$$$$**

● **Torrette** ⁄ **$$**

LIS NERIS

Though it's not a large estate—about 150 planted acres in all—Lis Neris's vineyards straddle two key Friuli wine zones, Collio and Isonzo, not far from the border with Slovenia. Fourth-generation vintner Alvaro Pecorari crafts emblematic Friuli whites in two styles: bright, zesty, steel-fermented examples, such as the Tocai-based Fiore di Campo, and creamier, oak-aged cuvées, including the vibrant, minerally Jurosa Chardonnay.

BOTTLES TO TRY

○ **Fiore di Campo / $$**

○ **Jurosa Chardonnay / $$**

MASI

Masi's voluptuous Amarones are both relatively easy to find and reliably great—a rare accomplishment, especially for a wine that is as labor-intensive as Amarone. That consistency is thanks to sixth-generation scion Sandro Boscaini, who has embraced technical rigor while sticking to labor-intensive methods like *appassimento*—the ancient process of air-drying grapes before crushing them. Masi's velvety, seductively styled Amarones are decidedly modern, emphasizing rich, intense fruit. Easier to drink every day are Masi's excellent Valpolicella and its humbler IGT wines, all made from traditional local grapes.

BOTTLES TO TRY

● **Bonacosta Valpolicella Classico / $**

● **Campofiorin / $$**

● **Costasera Amarone / $$$**

PRÀ

Graziano Prà is a Soave master, so much so that even his least-expensive Soave is routinely better than other producers' top offerings. Prà's vineyards climb the volcanic hills of Monteforte d'Alpone, a small district in the *classico* subzone. Unlike low-land producers that churn out millions of gallons of watery Soave, Prà severely limits his production. By farming organically and pruning vines mercilessly, he creates revelatory whites, like the flagship Monte Grande, a satiny, oak-aged cuvée with almond and citrus flavors.

BOTTLES TO TRY

○ **Monte Grande Soave Classico / $$**

○ **Soave Classico / $$**

SPERI

Speri's Sant'Urbano red is a revelation to anyone used to tart, watery Valpolicella. Laden with fragrant, silky dark fruit and spice, it gets concentration from air-dried grapes that come from a single estate-owned vineyard—a rarity in the Veneto, a region built on industrial wine and purchased grapes. In fact, the Speri family makes wine only from vineyards it owns, which accounts for the consistent quality of Speri's luscious reds. That care shows, too, in the Roverina Valpolicella, a juicy, easygoing blend.

BOTTLES TO TRY
- Vigneto La Roverina Valpolicella Classico Superiore / $$
- Vigneto Sant'Urbano Valpolicella Classico Superiore / $$$

TUSCANY

CLAIM TO FAME

Few wine regions have the instant name recognition of Tuscany's Chianti, first legally defined in 1716 (but recognized as a wine region as early as the 13th century). While the boundaries of that original growing region define today's *classico* subzone, the vastly expanded Chianti territory now includes seven more subregions. Some of Chianti's most acclaimed wines, however, don't carry its name. Only reds based on the Sangiovese grape can be called Chianti. Ambitious, rule-breaking Super-Tuscans, most often based on international grapes such as Cabernet, Merlot and Syrah, carry the humbler IGT Toscana designation.

REGIONS TO KNOW

CHIANTI There has never been a better time to drink Chianti. Spurred by international competition, its vintners have replanted vineyards and adopted new techniques—like aging wines in small French oak barrels instead of giant old vats. Of Chianti's eight subzones, **CHIANTI CLASSICO** is the original and most prestigious. Only **CHIANTI RUFINA** routinely produces wines to rival Chianti Classico's top bottles. Most wineries use only Sangiovese, or blend it with Cabernet, Merlot or native grapes such as Canaiolo and Colorino. (In Chianti Classico, these grapes can make up no more than 20 percent of the wine.) Generic Chianti, with no subzone, is the simplest. *Riserva* Chiantis require at least two years of aging and are more powerful.

MONTALCINO Vintners near the town of Montalcino make Tuscany's greatest wine, **BRUNELLO DI MONTALCINO**, from a local Sangiovese clone, Brunello. Made from the same grape, **ROSSO DI MONTALCINO** reds are younger, lighter versions of Brunellos.

MONTEPULCIANO Though not far from Montalcino, Montepulciano produces lighter wines that can include small amounts of other grapes along with Sangiovese (known locally as Prugnolo Gentile). **VINO NOBILE DI MONTEPULCIANO** wines must be aged two years (three for *riservas*). Like Montalcino, Montepulciano releases younger, baby brother reds under *rosso* designations.

MAREMMA In the coastal Maremma district, pioneering producers broke with tradition to create the original Super-Tuscan wines in the late 1960s. The Maremma's most famous subregions are **BOLGHERI** and the single-estate **BOLGHERI SASSICAIA** DOC.

CORTONA Established in 1999, this DOC is devoted chiefly to international grapes; it has become a source of exciting Syrahs.

CARMIGNANO Vintners in the town of Carmignano have been boosting their Sangiovese-based wines with Cabernet Sauvignon since the 1700s—long before these blends became known as Super-Tuscans. As a result, their reds typically feature lower acidity and firmer tannins than those of Chianti Classico.

SCANSANO The hilly area around the Maremma village of Scansano makes reds based on Sangiovese, known locally as Morellino. Basic **MORELLINO DI SCANSANO** has improved a great deal lately. It's generally aged in tanks, which keeps it vibrant and fresh.

❦ KEY GRAPES: WHITE

TREBBIANO Tuscany's main white grape variety—and the most commonly grown white grape in Italy—makes mostly light, unremarkable wines, though quality is improving.

VERMENTINO Full of minerality and zesty lime, this white grape thrives in milder coastal subregions like the Maremma.

VERNACCIA A specialty of the hilltop town of San Gimignano, this grape yields crisp, full-bodied and nutty whites.

♣ KEY GRAPES: RED

CABERNET, MERLOT & SYRAH These international varieties are popular blending grapes for native Sangiovese.

CANAIOLO, MAMMOLO & COLORINO Vintners typically blend these native red varieties with Sangiovese.

SANGIOVESE Sangiovese is king in Tuscany, where it yields high-acid, cherry- and herb-inflected reds in a range of styles.

Producers/ Tuscany

ALTESINO

Altesino's now-famous Montosoli Brunello was one of the first single-vineyard *crus* from Montalcino when it was introduced in 1975, and it's still one of the region's best reds, thanks largely to winemaker Claudio Basla. Now owned by Elisabetta Gnudi Angelini (also the proprietor of Borgo Scopeto and Caparzo), Altesino offers bold, earthy reds (and one white) that compete with Montalcino's finest—at every price point.

BOTTLES TO TRY
- **Rosso di Altesino** ╱ **$$**
- **Montosoli Brunello di Montalcino** ╱ **$$$$**

ANTINORI

Although Marchese Piero Antinori is the scion of a Tuscan wine dynasty that stretches back six centuries, he still makes his home above the family business. Granted, that home is Florence's 15th-century Palazzo Antinori, and the business is one of Italy's most iconic brands. Though the Antinori empire stretches across Italy and the globe, wines from its vast Tuscan estates are still its best known. Antinori's Santa Cristina Sangiovese remains one of Italy's most consistent red wine bargains; its Tignanello Super-Tuscan is one of its most collectible rarities.

BOTTLES TO TRY
- **Santa Cristina Sangiovese** ╱ **$**
- **Tignanello** ╱ **$$$$**

BADIA A COLTIBUONO

A former monastery, this impressive Chianti Classico estate is devoted now to the secular pursuit of great wine and food. Its present owners, the Stucchi Prinetti family, descend from a Florentine banker who bought the property in 1846. (That the family matriarch is culinary authority Lorenza de' Medici only adds to the glamour.) But forget the wines' aristocratic origins—what's more impressive is their consistent quality. Badia a Coltibuono's Sangiovese-based reds stick to a classic style, with firm acidity and bright, fragrant cherry tones.

BOTTLES TO TRY
- **Chianti Classico ∕ $$**
- **Chianti Classico Riserva ∕ $$$**

BARONE RICASOLI

The Ricasoli family essentially invented Chianti wine as we know it: A famous ancestor pioneered the formula that became the basis for today's Chianti Classico. Now Ricasoli reds again rank among Chianti's best, thanks to the 32nd baron, Francesco Ricasoli, who bought back the family brand from an international conglomerate in 1993. He slashed production, replanted vineyards and restored greatness to Italy's oldest wine estate (some 900 years and counting).

BOTTLES TO TRY
- **Brolio Chianti Classico ∕ $$**
- **Colledilà Chianti Classico ∕ $$$**

BRANCAIA

While vacationing in Chianti in 1981, a Swiss couple, Brigitte and Bruno Widmer, impulsively purchased a run-down farmhouse that came with 21 acres of vineyards. The accidental vintners embraced their new role, buying a second Chianti Classico vineyard in 1989 and, eventually, a sister estate in the Maremma. Daughter Barbara, with an assist from renowned consultant Carlo Ferrini, now directs the cellar. Brancaia's Chianti Classico is superb, but the estate is known best for three Super-Tuscans, including a powerful three-variety blend, Il Blu, and its affordable sibling, Tre.

BOTTLES TO TRY
- **Tre ∕ $$**
- **Il Blu ∕ $$$$**

CAPEZZANA

Though records of winemaking at this Carmignano estate date back 12 centuries, Capezzana is a thoroughly modern winery. Owners Count Ugo and Countess Lisa Contini Bonacossi were among the first to introduce Cabernet Sauvignon in Carmignano in the 1960s and later led the drive to establish the region as a DOCG. Today Capezzana is Carmignano's finest producer, with a lineup ranging from everyday reds—such as the supple, invigorating Barco Reale blend—to a muscular Super-Tuscan, Ghiaie della Furba.

BOTTLES TO TRY
- Barco Reale di Carmignano / $
- Ghiaie della Furba / $$$

CARPINETO

While many of Chianti Classico's go-to *riserva* wines have crept upwards of $30 in recent years, Carpineto's rock-solid version still sells for a little more than $20. Scale is one secret to the winery's success: Carpineto owns a thousand-plus acres of farmland scattered across Tuscany, with a little more than half of it devoted to grape-growing in prime zones like Chianti, Montepulciano and Montalcino. Even more affordable than Carpineto's Chiantis are its clean, fruity Dogajolo wines, which offer modern blends of Tuscan and international grapes.

BOTTLES TO TRY
- Dogajolo Rosato / $
- Chianti Classico Riserva / $$

CASANOVA DI NERI

Like most top Montalcino wineries, Casanova di Neri is young (by Italian standards, at least): Giovanni Neri established his namesake estate in 1971. Neri steadily built the winery's reputation, but it took his son, Giacomo, to launch it to international stardom with a series of outstanding Brunellos in the early 2000s. Made in a flashy, concentrated style, they're among Montalcino's most collectible reds. For a terrific—and more affordable—alternative, look for Neri's Sant'Antimo, a juicy, fruity Sangiovese made to drink now.

BOTTLES TO TRY
- Rosso di Casanova di Neri Sant'Antimo / $$
- Tenuta Nuova Brunello di Montalcino / $$$$

CASTELLO BANFI

U.S. importers John and Harry Mariani weren't content to just sell Italian wine; they wanted to make it. In 1978 they bought a chunk of Montalcino, and now their holdings include an entire hamlet surrounding a medieval fortress they named Castello Banfi. With thousands of acres across Tuscany, Banfi makes a large number of wines spanning a wide range—from everyday bottlings to pricey, prestigious Brunellos. Value bets include the direct, affordable Centine trio and a basic Chianti Classico.

BOTTLES TO TRY

- **Centine Rosso** / $
- **Chianti Classico** / $
- **Brunello di Montalcino** / $$$$

CASTELLO DEI RAMPOLLA

This 13th-century estate is one of Chianti Classico's most progressive. The late Alceo di Napoli created a pioneering Cabernet-based wine, Sammarco, in 1980; his children, Maurizia and Luca, have pushed that radical legacy further. They converted to biodynamic farming (among the first in Chianti to do so) and introduced Alceo, a rare and pricey Cabernet–Petit Verdot blend. Happily, Rampolla's two stunning, classically structured Chiantis sell for a fraction of the price of their Super-Tuscan siblings.

BOTTLES TO TRY

- **Chianti Classico** / $$
- **Sammarco** / $$$$

CASTELLO DI FONTERUTOLI

Brothers Filippo and Francesco Mazzei are the 24th generation to run this Chianti Classico estate, and might be the most dynamic. In recent years, the family has expanded its vineyard holdings, built a cutting-edge winery and hired legendary winemaker Carlo Ferrini. They've also refocused Fonterutoli from Super-Tuscans to Sangioveses; just two nontraditional blends remain, the flagship Siepi and the ridiculously drinkable, affordable Badiola. The result is a choice portfolio of expertly made bottlings, including an elegant, über-reliable Chianti Classico.

BOTTLES TO TRY

- **Mazzei Badiola** / $
- **Fonterutoli Chianti Classico** / $$
- **Siepi** / $$$$

CASTELLO DI MONSANTO

Monsanto owner Fabrizio Bianchi started breaking traditions to make great wines in Chianti back in the 1960s. Bianchi ripped out white grapes from his Chianti vineyards, bottled the first single-vineyard Chianti Classico (Il Poggio Riserva) and made a groundbreaking Sangiovese-only red—all moves considered radical at the time. Today the portfolio meshes modern bottlings made from international grapes, such as the Nemo Cabernet, with traditionally styled Chiantis.

BOTTLES TO TRY
- **Chianti Classico ⁄ $$**
- **Il Poggio Chianti Classico Riserva ⁄ $$$$**

CASTELLO DI VOLPAIA

As newlyweds, Giovanella Stianti and Carlo Mascheroni received an amazing wedding gift: The bride's father bestowed on them an 11th-century village in Chianti Classico, complete with castle, forest, fields and villas. From that hilltop hamlet, Volpaia, the Mascheroni Stiantis run a cooking school with guest accommodations and make extraordinary olive oil, vinegar and, of course, wine. Though it now produces cuvées from the Maremma as well, Castello di Volpaia's strongest offerings are its fragrant, classically structured reds from the organically farmed Volpaia estate.

BOTTLES TO TRY
- **Chianti Classico ⁄ $$**
- **Chianti Classico Riserva ⁄ $$**

FATTORIA LE PUPILLE

Few people outside Tuscany had heard of Morellino di Scansano, a Sangiovese-driven subzone of the Maremma, when Elisabetta Geppetti took over Fattoria Le Pupille in 1985, but the area has since blasted into popular view, thanks in part to the winery. A series of high-profile consultants helped shape its wines from the start, including Giacomo Tachis and superstar winemaker Christian Le Sommer, a veteran of Bordeaux's Château Latour. Portfolio highlights include two terrific Morellinos, a brisk white blend and a lauded Super-Tuscan, Saffredi.

BOTTLES TO TRY
- **Morellino di Scansano ⁄ $$**
- **Poggio Valente Morellino di Scansano Riserva ⁄ $$$**

RARITIES & COLLECTIBLES

MONTEVERTINE Montevertine's single-vineyard red, Le Pergole Torte, helped trigger a Chianti quality revolution. Made from 100 percent Sangiovese (once illegal in Chianti) and first released in the late 1970s, it's a benchmark for the grape and the region.

TENUTA DI TRINORO Andrea Franchetti created this estate in Tuscany's hinterlands in 1992—a minute ago in Tuscan time. Yet today the flagship Tenuta di Trinoro bottling, a lush, powerful blend of Bordeaux varieties, is one of Italy's great reds.

TUA RITA Few Merlots made anywhere rival the Redigaffi bottling from this boutique Maremma producer. Intense and occasionally opulent, Redigaffi is inspired by the great wines of Pomerol but is also, somehow, ineffably Tuscan with its perfume of fruit, mineral and herb notes.

FATTORIA SELVAPIANA

A star consultant (Franco Bernabei), a top subregion (Chianti Rufina) and a focused portfolio (four wines, plus v*in santo*) are just a few reasons Selvapiana's wines stand out from the pack. Rufina's high elevation and cold nights give Selvapiana's grapes their thick skins and higher acidity, which translates into firm, ageworthy reds. The fresh, cherry-driven intro bottling is a textbook example of Rufina's wines, while the single-vineyard Bucerchiale Riserva offers a serious step up in complexity.

BOTTLES TO TRY
- **Chianti Rufina** / **$$**
- **Vigneto Bucerchiale Riserva** / **$$$**

FONTODI

The Manetti family used to make three Chianti Classicos at their Panzano winery, but in the mid-1990s they dropped their Fontodi Riserva and now offer just two, one of which is the single-vineyard Vigna del Sorbo. The move bolstered quality across the board, and freed up juice for Flaccianello, Fontodi's block-buster Sangiovese. Owner Giovanni Manetti and consulting enologist Franco Bernabei also make Syrah and Pinot Noir from Fontodi's organic vineyards.

BOTTLES TO TRY
- **Chianti Classico** / **$$$**
- **Vigna del Sorbo Chianti Classico Riserva** / **$$$$**

GIANNI BRUNELLI

Laura Vacca and her late husband, Gianni Brunelli, established one of Siena's most beloved restaurants, Osteria Le Logge, in the 1970s. Its phenomenal success allowed the couple to repurchase Brunelli's old family vineyard on the north slope of Montalcino, plus a site on the hill's warmer, southern side. Farming biodynamically, and working with local winemaker Paolo Vagaggini, they created a quartet of superb, sought-after reds. The flagship Brunello blends fruit from both vineyards to create a harmonious, concentrated red that's terrific in both warm and cool vintages.

BOTTLE TO TRY
● **Brunello di Montalcino** ⁄ **$$$$**

LE MACCHIOLE

Born and raised in Bolgheri, Eugenio Campolmi watched as his sleepy coastal home became Italy's newest world-class wine region, thanks mostly to wealthy outsiders. Campolmi started Le Macchiole in 1980 with 12 acres of vines next door to Super-Tuscan star Ornellaia (see p. 92); soon, his wines were competing with Bolgheri's best. His widow, Cinzia Merli, and longtime consultant Luca d'Attoma have continued to make superb wines since Campolmi's death in 2002.

BOTTLES TO TRY
● **Bolgheri Rosso** ⁄ **$$$**
● **Messorio** ⁄ **$$$$**

MARCHESI DE' FRESCOBALDI

With five Tuscan estates, the Frescobaldi wine dynasty (now in its 30th generation) is the region's largest vineyard owner—and growing. Yet size doesn't detract from its winemaking precision or taste for innovation: Frescobaldi wines, including traditional regional bottlings from Nipozzano, still win acclaim, and the family has pioneered progressive ventures such as the launch of the Maremma's Tenuta dell'Ammiraglia and Montalcino's Luce della Vite estate. The darkly fruity Castiglioni Toscana blend highlights Frescobaldi's modern side.

BOTTLES TO TRY
● **Tenuta di Castiglioni Toscana** ⁄ **$$**
● **Castello di Nipozzano Montesodi Chianti Rufina Riserva** ⁄ **$$$**
● **Castelgiocondo Brunello di Montalcino** ⁄ **$$$$**

MASTROJANNI

The Illy family, of espresso fame, converted some of its coffee fortune into wine by purchasing this boutique Montalcino estate in 2008. Francesco Illy and his brother Riccardo, grandsons of Illy's founder, kept the talented team of general manager Andrea Machetti and winemaker Maurizio Castelli and haven't changed the muscular, classic style of Mastrojanni's Brunellos. But their investment in new equipment and great attention to detail (sorting tables, for example, are used to pluck out imperfect fruit at harvest, grape by grape) have boosted the wines' already high quality.

BOTTLES TO TRY
- **Rosso di Montalcino / $$**
- **Brunello di Montalcino / $$$**

PETROLO

Artist Luca Sanjust's family winery in the unheralded Aretini hills produced light, ordinary Chianti for decades—until Sanjust's mother replanted the estate and asked him to manage it. That was in 1993; new vintages have since vaulted Petrolo out of obscurity and, improbably, into Tuscany's elite. Its reputation rests on Galatrona, a velvety, powerful Merlot produced in small quantities. Easier to find is Torrione, an elegant red that shows just how good Sangiovese from Aretini can be.

BOTTLES TO TRY
- **Torrione / $$$**
- **Galatrona / $$$$**

PODERI BOSCARELLI

When the De Ferrari Corradi family bought this small estate in Montepulciano in the early 1960s, the hilltop town's reputation for great wine had faded into history. That Montepulciano's Sangiovese-based reds now live up to their "noble" moniker is due in part to Boscarelli's Vino Nobile reds; the indisputable quality of these wines helped galvanize a generation of vintners who restored Montepulciano to the ranks of Tuscany's top subzones. Bolstered by grapes from the stellar Cervognano vineyard, Boscarelli's reds offer fruity depth and fragrant, polished power.

BOTTLES TO TRY
- **Vino Nobile di Montepulciano / $$$**
- **Vino Nobile di Montepulciano Riserva / $$$**

POLIZIANO

In great vintages, Poliziano owner Federico Carletti will bottle juice from the estate's Asinone vineyard as its own cuvée. The result is one of Montepulciano's best bottlings, but it's hard to find. Making that cuvée only in great years, however, helps ensure that Poliziano's classic Vino Nobile wines benefit from Asinone's top-quality fruit. Carletti has expanded in recent years to vineyards in the Maremma and Cortona with terrific results, though the Montepulciano reds remain Poliziano's calling card.

BOTTLES TO TRY

- **Rosso di Montepulciano / $**
- **Vino Nobile di Montepulcianio / $$**
- **Asinone Vino Nobile di Montepulcianio / $$$**

RUFFINO

Ruffino is synonymous with Chianti. Launched as a *négociant* business in 1877 and hugely successful abroad, it changed the Chianti industry overnight when it began using modern glass bottles in 1975, an instant update to the iconic straw fiascos. Ruffino makes wines across Chianti and beyond, including estate bottlings from farms in Chianti Classico, Montalcino and Montepulciano. The fruity, smooth Santedame is made in a modern style; the easy-to-find Riserva Ducale gets its consistency from the masterful blending of fruit from many sites.

BOTTLES TO TRY

- **Riserva Ducale Chianti Classico Riserva / $$**
- **Tenuta Santedame Chianti Classico / $$**

TENUTA DELL'ORNELLAIA/MASSETO

This iconic Maremma estate produces two of Italy's greatest wines, both based on French grapes: Ornellaia, a Bordeaux-inspired blend, and Masseto, a single-vineyard Merlot. Their princely prices reflect the wines' scarcity and prestige; Le Serre Nuove offers a taste of the Ornellaia style at about a quarter of the cost. Though its first vintage was only in 1985, the property has already belonged to three great wine dynasties: Lodovico Antinori founded the estate, then sold it to California's Mondavi family; today it's owned by the Frescobaldis (see p. 90).

BOTTLES TO TRY

- **Le Serre Nuove / $$$**
- **Ornellaia / $$$$**

OTHER CENTRAL ITALY

REGIONS TO KNOW

ABRUZZO Led by its signature bottling, Montepulciano d'Abruzzo, this mountainous region has become a terrific source of value-priced reds. Often a simple wine with soft, straightforward berry and plum flavors, Montepulciano d'Abruzzo can also be remarkably robust, spicy and tannic. Top vintners are showcasing the grape's polished side at both ends of the style (and price) spectrum. Whites are steadily improving; look for those made from the local Pecorino and Passerina varieties.

EMILIA-ROMAGNA This region's wines are not as famous as its meats and cheeses (e.g., Prosciutto di Parma and Parmigiano-Reggiano) but are worth discovering. Emilia-Romagna's most prominent bottling is Lambrusco, a fizzy, often sweet wine that's usually red but ranges in color from white to deep purple. The best are dry and come from small producers. Quality-focused wineries also turn out fine offerings made from white grapes like Albana, Chardonnay and Malvasia, and reds based on Sangiovese, Barbera, Cabernet Sauvignon and Pinot Nero (Pinot Noir).

LAZIO Located on the outskirts of Rome, the prolific vineyards of Lazio have supplied the city's taverns and trattorias with wine for millennia. The region's defining wine, Frascati, is a ubiquitous, crisp, citrusy white that's often thin and innocuous, but it can deliver complexity when made with care. Authorities approved two new DOCGs, **FRASCATI SUPERIORE** and **CANNELLINO DI FRASCATI,** in 2011, which will, in theory, guarantee higher quality, though it's too early to tell. Reds based on the Cesanese grape have been gaining attention since the **CESANESE DEL PIGLIO** zone was promoted to DOCG status in 2008.

LE MARCHE Le Marche juts out from Italy's eastern coast like the shapely calf in the peninsula's boot. The region's top reds are made from Sangiovese (Tuscany's signature variety) or Montepulciano, a grape that bursts with soft plum and berry flavors. Blends of the two grapes are the specialty of **ROSSO PICENO,** a DOC near the port city of Ancona; **ROSSO CORNERO** is a bold, smoky red made chiefly from Montepulciano. Le Marche's top white is the zesty, mouth-filling Verdicchio; the best versions come from the hilltop **VERDICCHIO DEI CASTELLI DI JESI CLASSICO** subzone. Wines made from little-known native white grapes such as Pecorino and Passerina are turning up more often in the U.S.

UMBRIA The green hills of landlocked Umbria are home to **ORVIETO,** a light-bodied, usually inexpensive white made from a blend of local grapes. Mass-produced bottlings, made chiefly with the Trebbiano grape, are generally forgettable; look instead for versions sourced from old Grechetto vines grown in the soft volcanic rock of Orvieto's *classico* subzone, which can be fantastic. Umbria's best-known reds are forceful, bold examples of the Sagrantino grape.

❦ KEY GRAPES: WHITE

GRECHETTO A white variety presumed to be native to Greece (hence its name), Grechetto is grown chiefly in Umbria and yields refreshing lime- and peach-flavored bottlings.

PASSERINA & PECORINO Found mainly in Abruzzo and Le Marche, the appley Passerina and mineral-driven Pecorino are increasingly bottled on their own to make some of central Italy's most appealing whites.

TREBBIANO A handful of quality-driven vintners (mostly in Abruzzo) are proving that the Trebbiano grape, widely used for characterless bulk wines, can indeed yield whites of distinction.

VERDICCHIO Once bottled chiefly in amphora-shaped bottles, Verdicchio-based wines are typically almond-scented, crisp and citrusy; they're among the world's most seafood-friendly whites.

❦ KEY GRAPES: RED

MONTEPULCIANO Not to be confused with the Tuscan town of the same name, where the wines are made from Sangiovese (see p. 83), the plummy, spicy Montepulciano grape is behind some of central Italy's best reds.

SAGRANTINO A native of Umbria, this grape yields powerful, tannic and long-lived reds. Full of spice, earth and plum notes, Sagrantino thrives around the Umbrian village of Montefalco.

Producers/ Other Central Italy

ARNALDO CAPRAI

In 1989, at the age of 21, Marco Caprai took charge of his family's Umbrian estate and set about making the spicy, plummy and utterly obscure Sagrantino grape famous. Working with the University of Milan, Caprai showed that the variety contains more flavor compounds than any other grape; he also created benchmark Sagrantinos such as 25 Anni and Collepiano. His Montefalco Rosso blend incorporates Sagrantino seamlessly.

BOTTLES TO TRY

- **Montefalco Rosso** / **$$**
- **Collepiano Sagrantino di Montefalco** / **$$$**

CANTINE GIORGIO LUNGAROTTI

It's unlikely that Umbrian wine would be as admired today if it weren't for Giorgio Lungarotti, who founded this winery in the early 1960s. Lungarotti pioneered the planting of international grapes in Umbria and proved that they could blend well with local varieties. The fragrant, cherry-edged Vigna Monticchio is one of Umbria's most collectible reds; its baby brother, the Sangiovese-based Rubesco, makes an affordable introduction.

BOTTLES TO TRY

- **Rubesco Rosso di Torgiano** / **$$**
- **Vigna Monticchio Rubesco Riserva** / **$$$**

CASALE DEL GIGLIO

Casale del Giglio's vineyards occupy a slice of Agro Pontino, a region southeast of Rome along the Tyrrhenian Sea. Unusual in Italy, the area has no winemaking history; it was a swamp until Mussolini drained it in the late 1920s. Liberated from tradition, Casale del Giglio's owners, the Santarelli family, experiment constantly. Their new-wave wines include varietal bottlings made from French and Italian grapes as well as innovative blends such as Mater Matuta, which combines Syrah and Petit Verdot.

BOTTLE TO TRY

- **Mater Matuta** / **$$$**

CATALDI MADONNA

One reason this Abruzzo estate produces such fantastic wines is its location. Situated in the highlands of the rugged Aterno River valley, Cataldi Madonna's vineyards yield ripe, thick-skinned grapes that give its wines more structure than is usual in Abruzzo. Vintner and philosophy professor Luigi Cataldi Madonna takes full advantage of the climate to produce some of Abruzzo's most outstanding Montepulcianos and unusually intense whites. Even his basic Trebbiano bursts with vibrant, complex fruit and mineral notes—a far cry from the usually bland and boring renditions of this humble white grape.

BOTTLES TO TRY

○ **Trebbiano d'Abruzzo** ⁄ **$**

● **Montepulciano d'Abruzzo** ⁄ **$$**

MONASTERO SUORE CISTERCENSI

Giampiero Bea, of Umbria's famous, tiny Paolo Bea winery (see below), assists the nuns of this Cistercian monastery north of Rome with producing a pair of white blends every year. Each cuvée combines four local white varieties that the nuns grow organically, with the Rusticum getting an orangish tint from extended contact with the grapes' skins. Captivating minerality, fresh, complex flavors and sane prices have made the sisters' offerings an insider favorite among U.S. wine cognoscenti.

BOTTLES TO TRY

○ **Coenobium** ⁄ **$$**

○ **Coenobium Rusticum** ⁄ **$$**

PAOLO BEA

Cult Umbrian winemaker Giampiero Bea and his father, Paolo, take the kind of high-risk, naturalist approach to winemaking that drives cellar-dwelling control freaks crazy: They eschew any kind of additions to wine (like yeasts or sulfites) or manipulations (such as filtering it or controlling the temperature of a fermentation). If the results weren't so stunning, the Beas would be dismissed as kooks. But the wines are surreally good; their elegant, earthy Sagrantino-based reds are arguably the greatest expressions of this Umbrian grape.

BOTTLES TO TRY

● **Rosso de Véo Umbria IGT** ⁄ **$$$**

● **Montefalco Sagrantino Secco Vigna Pagliaro** ⁄ **$$$$**

SERGIO MOTTURA

When Sergio Mottura isn't making some of Italy's best Grechetto wines, he runs a small hotel, La Tana dell'Istrice, near his vineyards north of Rome. Straddling the regions of Umbria and Lazio, his vines grow in hilly, volcanic soil—sloping land that's harder to farm but yields small, intensely flavored grapes. Mottura showcases the results in a range of whites that include the single-vineyard Poggio della Costa Grechetto as well as two affordable, standard-setting Orvietos.

BOTTLES TO TRY

O **Orvieto Secco** ⁄ **$**
O **Poggio della Costa** ⁄ **$$**

VILLA BUCCI

No winery has mastered the Verdicchio grape like Villa Bucci. Located in Le Marche's prestigious Castelli di Jesi subregion, where Verdicchio is the chief white grape, Villa Bucci produces two benchmark Verdicchios as well as two Rosso Piceno reds (blends of Montepulciano and Sangiovese), all shaped by the legendary Giorgio Grai, the winery's longtime consultant. The rich, creamy Verdicchio Riserva is made only in excellent vintages and is worth snapping up if you can find it. But the regular Verdicchio is better than most wineries' *riservas* in any case.

BOTTLE TO TRY

O **Verdicchio dei Castelli di Jesi Classico Superiore** ⁄ **$$**

SOUTHERN ITALY

CLAIM TO FAME

Once known for its bulk wine, southern Italy is now a source of high-quality bottlings, often made from grapes found nowhere else. There's still a lot of disappointing wine made in this part of the country, but the region's best vintners offer compelling wines that frequently deliver great value.

REGIONS TO KNOW

APULIA This is the home of Primitivo, a plush grape that has gained fame as Zinfandel's Italian twin. Less well known are the excellent reds of the **SALICE SALENTINO** and **COPERTINO** subzones, made chiefly from the dark-skinned Negroamaro grape.

BASILICATA Its spicy, Aglianico-based reds make Basilicata's best case for greatness, especially those from **AGLIANICO DEL VULTURE,** where vineyards planted on the slopes and foothills of the extinct Monte Vulture volcano yield potent wines. The newer DOCs of **TERRE DELL'ALTA VAL D'AGRI** and **MATERA** offer red, white and rosé blends based on grapes other than Aglianico.

CALABRIA Cirò, a delicate, floral-scented red based on the Gaglioppo grape, is Calabria's best wine.

CAMPANIA This region is a leader in southern Italy's native grape revival. Campania's *terroir*-driven wines include powerful Aglianico reds (top, ageworthy examples come from the **TAURASI** DOCG) and three distinctive whites: the expressive Falanghina; lush, nutty Fiano di Avellino; and floral, zesty Greco di Tufo.

SARDINIA The twin stars of this Mediterranean isle are its fresh Vermentino whites and spicy, supple Cannonau (Grenache) reds, the best of which come from old, low-yielding "bush" vines.

SICILY Sicily's most interesting wines are made from native varieties. Fruity Nero d'Avola is its signature red grape; when blended with Frappato it yields **CERASUOLO DI VITTORIA,** the island's only DOCG wine. From Mount Etna's slopes, reds designated **ETNA ROSSO** offer bold tannins and savory red fruit. White grapes grown in Etna's black soils can yield fresh, minerally wines. Elsewhere, standouts include citrusy whites made from Catarratto, Grillo and Inzolia, and reds based on Frappato.

❧ KEY GRAPES: WHITE

FALANGHINA, FIANO DI AVELLINO & GRECO DI TUFO Wines made from these varieties share crisp floral and mineral notes.

VERMENTINO Grown up and down Italy's coasts, Vermentino produces whites whose racy, lime- and herb-scented zesty flavors make them a terrific match for seafood.

❧ KEY GRAPES: RED

AGLIANICO Responsible for the top reds of Basilicata and Campania, this inky, earthy variety possesses high tannins and acidity that give its wines the ability to age.

CANNONAU, CARIGNANO & MONICA Sardinia's Spanish- and French-influenced history shows in its plantings of these foreign grapes. Cannonau (a.k.a. Grenache) bursts with supple red fruit; the island's top Carignano (Carignane) wines stand among the best examples of this rustic variety. Monica yields simple reds.

FRAPPATO Sicily's Frappato produces alluring, light-bodied reds with fragrant, silky red-fruit tones.

GAGLIOPPO Bottlings of this Calabrian grape are perfumy and supple, with sweet red cherry and floral notes.

NEGROAMARO Depending on how it's used, this Apulian grape can yield simple, light reds or concentrated, muscular wines.

NERELLO MASCALESE & NERELLO CAPPUCCIO Indigenous to the slopes of Sicily's Mount Etna, these varieties offer rich, firm reds.

NERO D'AVOLA Sicilian winemakers prize this native grape for its lush, earthy flavors redolent of sweet blackberries and spice.

PRIMITIVO Plush tannins and rich, brambly red-berry notes are the hallmarks of this Zinfandel relative.

Producers/ Southern Italy

ARGIOLAS

Argiolas kick-started Sardinia's wine revolution in the early 1990s and remains its leading producer. Brothers Franco and Giuseppe Argiolas hired enologist Mariano Murru and famed consultant Giacomo Tachis to transform the family's bulk-wine business. Their efforts yield some of the planet's best Vermentinos, as well as ripe, supple reds from Carignano, Monica and Cannonau. The red Turriga blend competes with Italy's best.

BOTTLES TO TRY

○ **Costamolino Vermentino di Sardegna** / $
● **Turriga Isola dei Nuraghi** / $$$$

AZIENDA AGRICOLA CEUSO

The Melia brothers earned their original *garagistes* moniker literally: They started Ceuso in their family garage in northwest Sicily in 1990. Now housed in a refurbished, purpose-built wine cellar, Ceuso still veers on the small side. The Melias crush just four estate-grown wines each year, showing an equal facility with local and international grapes. That's clear in the flagship Ceuso cuvée, a ripe, polished blend of Nero d'Avola, Cabernet and Merlot. The vibrant, accessible Scurati red showcases pure, juicy Nero d'Avola fruit.

BOTTLES TO TRY
- ● **Scurati Rosso** / **$**
- ● **Ceuso** / **$$$**

AZIENDA AGRICOLA COS

Few wineries succeed as brilliantly as COS at fashioning benchmark renditions of Sicilian grapes. This biodynamic estate (its name is an acronym of the last names of its founders—Cilia, Occhipinti and Strano) is on the cutting edge of retro/naturalist winemaking. A stroll into its cellar reveals, for example, giant clay wine amphorae, similar to those used by ancient Greeks. While COS is best known for its peppery, meaty Cerasuolo, it's hard to go wrong with any of its offerings—even the silky, berry-rich Frappato is complex.

BOTTLES TO TRY
- ● **Frappato** / **$$**
- ● **Cerasuolo di Vittoria** / **$$$**

DONNAFUGATA

The Rallo family named their estate Donnafugata (Italian for "woman in flight") after Maria Carolina, the queen of Naples who left the city in the early 1800s to escape Napoleon's troops and took refuge near the family's estate vineyards in Sicily. For more than a century, the Rallos used their grapes for fortified Marsala wines. Today it's Donnafugata's Nero d'Avola–based reds that have made it one of Sicily's leading estates. The juicy, dark-fruited Sedàra blend makes a terrific introduction to the reds, but the stealth choice is the floral, citrusy Anthìlia white.

BOTTLES TO TRY
- ○ **Anthìlia** / **$**
- ● **Sedàra** / **$**

MASTROBERARDINO

Dapper and charismatic, Piero Mastroberardino is the latest in 10 generations of vintners to guide this preeminent Campania winery. Decades ago, Mastroberardino's father and grandfather led the region's revival of indigenous grapes. Those years of research and expertise show in the wines, which include Radici, a tannic, complex red that's arguably Campania's greatest Aglianico. Less-expensive offerings—like the stony, citrusy Lacryma Christi white, made from the Coda di Volpe grape—make excellent introductions to Campania's varieties.

BOTTLES TO TRY

○ **Lacryma Christi del Vesuvio** ∕ **$$**
● **Radici Taurasi** ∕ **$$$**

MORGANTE

Sicilian star Morgante produces two of Italy's standard-setting Nero d'Avolas: a juicy, inexpensive basic bottling, and Don Antonio, a muscular, spicy reserve cuvée made from old vines. The Morgante family—including Antonio and sons Carmelo and Giovanni—transitioned from grape growers into vintners only in the mid-1990s. But they found speedy success by hiring one of Italy's biggest winemaking talents, Riccardo Cotarella, as a consultant. His deft touch makes Morgante's Nero d'Avolas reliably terrific.

BOTTLES TO TRY

● **Nero d'Avola** ∕ **$$**
● **Don Antonio Nero d'Avola** ∕ **$$$**

OCONE

Domenico Ocone has taken this century-old Campania estate from good to great in recent decades. His father, Luigi, began the transition from bulk-juice producer to estate-bottled wines in the 1960s; today, thanks to Domenico's shift to biodynamic farming and other labor-intensive, neo-traditional steps, Ocone has become one of Campania's leading naturalist labels. Made from indigenous grape varieties without any additives, its wines include the zesty, intense Flora Falanghina and the graceful Apollo Aglianico.

BOTTLES TO TRY

○ **Flora Falanghina** ∕ **$**
● **Apollo Aglianico** ∕ **$$**

TASCA D'ALMERITA

In the late 1950s, when nearly all Sicilian wine grapes went into jug or bulk wine, Count Giuseppe Tasca aimed higher. He transformed his family's wine estate, founded in 1830, into a quality-driven producer and began creating expressive reds and whites to rival Italy's best. Sicily's largest winery, Tasca d'Almerita sources grapes from its 1,500 acres of vineyards spread across the island. Its top wine is the legendary Rosso del Conte. Easier to find is Lamùri, a floral, polished red that's also based on Nero d'Avola but costs about a third of the price of the flagship.

BOTTLES TO TRY
- ○ **Regaleali Bianco** / **$**
- ● **Lamùri** / **$$**

TENUTA DELLE TERRE NERE

Marco de Grazia, an Italian American living in Florence, exports Italian wine for a living. But he and his wife became so enamored of wines from the lava-covered slopes of Sicily's Mount Etna that they started a winery there, naming it after the area's black earth (*terre nere*). Their minerally whites, made from Carricante, and, especially, their muscular reds have become stars of Etna's emerging wine industry. Based on the Nerello Mascalese grape, the reds are firm and tight on release; try decanting them if you open them right away.

BOTTLES TO TRY
- ● **Etna Rosso** / **$$**
- ● **Calderara Sottana** / **$$$**

TERREDORA

When a dispute divided Campania's famous Mastroberardino winemaking clan (see p. 101), Walter Mastroberardino gave up the right to make wine under the family name but kept most of the historic vineyards. His Terredora wines come from an impressive collection of nearly 500 acres of estate vines, planted entirely with the region's native grapes. Its definitive wines include go-to renditions of Campania's key grapes, including Fiano di Avellino, crisp-but-creamy Falanghina and ageworthy Aglianico-based reds.

BOTTLES TO TRY
- ○ **DiPaolo Falanghina** / **$**
- ● **Aglianico** / **$**

RARITIES & COLLECTIBLES

COTTANERA Made from grapes grown on the slopes of an active volcano, Cottanera's extraordinary reds—especially the rare cuvées the Cambria family crafts from local varieties—have redefined Sicilian wine and put Mount Etna on the wine map.

FRANK CORNELISSEN Belgian wine trader–turned–vintner Frank Cornelissen practices ultra-minimalist winemaking on Mount Etna's mineral-rich slopes, turning out tiny quantities of wine, some from ancient vines. Bottled without sulfur, his wines can be inconsistent, but when they're good, they're brilliant.

QUINTODECIMO Campania's Taurasi Aglianicos can age for decades; arguably, none are greater than Quintodecimo's. Their fame can sometimes overshadow vintner Luigi Moio's other benchmark bottlings.

TORMARESCA

Tuscany's famed Antinori family (see p. 84) created this sprawling Apulia estate in 1998 and has applied its winemaking expertise to the region's emerging wine zones with dazzling effect: Tormaresca's value-driven portfolio includes Neprica, a dense blend of three grapes that makes a terrific house red, and a bright, oak-free Chardonnay. Slightly pricier reds based on Negroamaro, Primitivo and Aglianico are worth the step up.

BOTTLES TO TRY

○ Chardonnay / $
● Neprica / $
● Masseria Maìme Negroamaro Salento / $$

VITICOLTORI DE CONCILIIS

Former architect and jazz fan Bruno De Conciliis left Milan to turn a family property in Campania into a wine estate in 1996. The farm is located in Cilento, a coastal area famous for Greek ruins and olive groves, not wines. Nonetheless, De Conciliis has become a star, crafting brilliant renditions of local grapes. The basic Fiano, Donnaluna, whose name was inspired by the jazz standard "Donna Lee," emphasizes the variety's lush side; De Conciliis's Aglianico-based reds are smooth, plummy and dense.

BOTTLES TO TRY

○ Donnaluna Fiano / $$
● Donnaluna Aglianico / $$

Spain
Wine Region

Sir Alexander Fleming once wrote, "If penicillin can cure those that are ill, Spanish sherry can bring the dead back to life." Fleming discovered penicillin, so he knew whereof he spoke. And when it comes to fans of Spanish wine, his assessment is actually rather modest. Most of them would say that not just sherry but all Spanish wine has magical properties. That may be hard to prove, but Spain is producing remarkable wines at all levels: from the flavorful, affordable reds of its Mediterranean coastal regions, to the crisp, saline whites of Rías Baixas, to world-class, ageworthy wines from renowned regions like Rioja and Priorat. And those are only a few of Spain's more than 65 official wine regions (it's the third-largest wine-producing country, after France and Italy). And, of course, there's sherry. It may not raise the dead, but it wouldn't be a bad idea to buy a bottle or two, just in case.

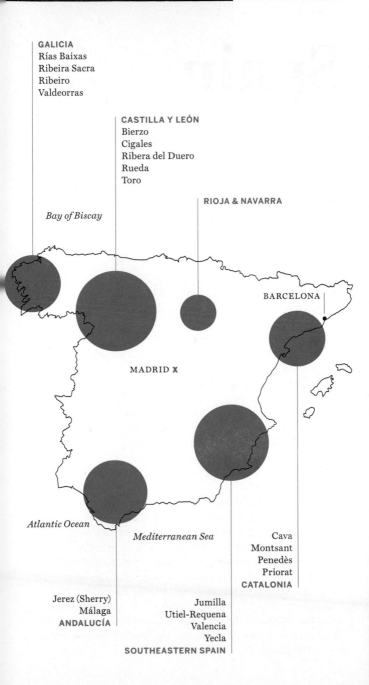

GALICIA
Rías Baixas
Ribeira Sacra
Ribeiro
Valdeorras

CASTILLA Y LEÓN
Bierzo
Cigales
Ribera del Duero
Rueda
Toro

RIOJA & NAVARRA

Bay of Biscay

BARCELONA

MADRID **X**

Atlantic Ocean

Mediterranean Sea

Cava
Montsant
Penedès
Priorat
CATALONIA

Jerez (Sherry)
Málaga
ANDALUCÍA

Jumilla
Utiel-Requena
Valencia
Yecla
SOUTHEASTERN SPAIN

Spain

WINE TERMINOLOGY

VINO DE LA TIERRA (VDT) Like French *vins de pays* (see p. 18), Spain's basic regional VdT wines are often dull and unremarkable, but they can offer great value, too.

VINO DE CALIDAD CON INDICACIÓN GEOGRAFICA A step up from VdT, this category recognizes improving regions. On labels, it's indicated by *Vino de Calidad* followed by a place name.

DENOMINACIÓN DE ORIGEN (DO) Spain's regional DOs set out legal standards for permitted grapes, harvest limits and vinification techniques, in addition to geographic sourcing requirements. Most quality wine belongs to this category.

DENOMINACIÓN DE ORIGEN CALIFICADA (DOCA) Just two areas, Rioja and Priorat, lay claim to the prestigious status of DOCa, the most rigorous regional wine designation.

DENOMINACIÓN DE ORIGEN DE PAGO/VINO DE PAGO Roughly equivalent to a French *grand cru* (see p. 35), the prestigious *vino de pago* classification is given to single, renowned estates; 13 *vinos de pago* have been approved since the category was introduced in 2003. Confusingly, many wines with *pago* on the label are not in this elite category (it's also a generic term for "estate" and/or "vineyard"), and some *vinos de pago* don't say *pago* at all, but list the name of the *pago* after *Denominación de Origen,* as in *Denominación de Origen Finca Élez.*

BODEGA & CELLER Both of these words mean "winery." The Catalan *celler* is used in Catalonia; the Spanish *bodega* is common throughout the rest of the country.

ROSADO Several regions in Spain produce superb *rosado* (rosé) wines, which are typically dry, with citrus and berry flavors.

VIÑA & VIÑEDO These terms for "vineyard" are often part of a winery's name. When not part of the winery name on a label, the words usually refer to a site from which the wine is sourced.

RIOJA & NAVARRA

CLAIM TO FAME
Though regions like Ribera del Duero and Priorat are now competing with Rioja for the title of Spain's greatest wine zone, this large region in the northeast still turns out an impressive percentage of the country's best reds. Many producers today strike a balance between earthy, old-school reds and superfruity modern versions. Meanwhile, up-and-coming neighbor Navarra has become a go-to source of value-priced reds and *rosados.*

REGIONS TO KNOW
RIOJA ALAVESA Distinctive chalky soils, an Atlantic-influenced climate and a high elevation define this region. As a result, its wines are lighter and more rustic than those of Rioja Alta. Quality is not as consistent as in Rioja Alta, but good values abound.

RIOJA ALTA The source of most of Rioja's greatest wines, the Alta ("high") subzone is located in the foothills of the Cantabrian mountains at the region's western end, where Atlantic-driven temperatures and limestone soils yield refined, ageworthy reds.

RIOJA BAJA Winemakers in Rioja Baja benefit from the warm, dry Mediterranean climate and rely more on Garnacha than on Tempranillo, which is dominant elsewhere. Their wines are softer, riper and less-structured reds made for early drinking.

🍇 KEY GRAPES: WHITE
VIURA Rioja's reputation rests on its reds, but both Rioja and Navarra produce lovely, vibrant whites based mostly on Viura, known elsewhere in Spain as Macabeo. By the 1990s, most white Riojas were made exclusively with Viura. Styles range from barrel-aged and often intentionally oxidized to fresh and bright.

♟ KEY GRAPES: RED

GARNACHA Supple, sultry and loaded with fragrant red-berry notes, this variety is a key component of many Rioja reds and was, until recently, Navarra's dominant grape. Winemakers use its velvety tannins and plump body to soften Tempranillo's firm, earthy structure in blends. Internationally, it's better known by its French name, Grenache.

GRACIANO & MAZUELO Grown in small amounts, these minor grapes are native to northeast Spain. Graciano is increasingly prized by winemakers for its ability to add acidity and fragrance to a blend, whereas Mazuelo—called Carignane in France and Cariñena elsewhere in Spain—is a tough and tannic grape.

TEMPRANILLO Tempranillo's fragrant cherry flavors, tart acidity and firm tannins have long made it the top grape for Rioja's long-lived blends. Today it's also popular in Navarra, where it recently supplanted Garnacha as the most planted variety.

WINE TERMINOLOGY
While used widely throughout Spain, these terms are most closely associated with Rioja wines.

ALTA EXPRESIÓN An unofficial term for high-end reds typically aged in French (rather than American) oak for shorter periods than usual. These wines are darker, with bolder fruit.

JOVEN Made to be drunk within a year or two of release, *joven* (young) wines—also called *cosecha*—spend little time in oak, which keeps them fresh (and reasonably priced).

CRIANZA Matured at least two years, one in oak, *crianzas* are more complex than *jovens*. Rioja's top *crianzas* offer great value.

RESERVA Aged in barrel for at least 12 months and not released until at least three years after harvest, *reservas* showcase soft tannins, mellower fruit and oak-driven spicy vanilla.

GRAN RESERVA Only wine vinified from the best, most intense grapes can survive the required five years of aging—at least two of them in oak—and emerge more balanced and delicious.

Producers/ Rioja & Navarra

ARTADI

This cult producer began in the mid-1980s as a bootstrapping co-op in the harsh, high-altitude hinterlands of Rioja Alavesa. Grape grower–turned–vintner Juan Carlos López de Lacalle convinced his fellow farmers to band together and crush their own grapes, rather than selling them. Superb fruit—most from ancient vines—and a flair for rich, robust reds have made Artadi a fine-wine powerhouse. Its top cuvées compete with Rioja's best.

BOTTLES TO TRY
- **Viñas de Gain** / **$$**
- **Pagos Viejos** / **$$$$**

BODEGA ABEL MENDOZA MONGE

The small scale of this northwest Rioja estate—just 45 acres—means that owners Abel and Maite Mendoza are able to do much of the labor by hand. They painstakingly destem their red grapes, bunch by bunch, and in the case of their youngest Tempranillo, they even crush the fruit by foot. That they lavish such effort on even their least expensive red helps explain how the Mendozas achieve the rare purity and finesse in their wines.

BOTTLES TO TRY
- **Abel Mendoza Limoso** / **$$**
- **Abel Mendoza Pedregoso** / **$$**

BODEGAS CHIVITE

Navarra's leading estate, Bodegas Chivite has been passed down from father to son since 1647. Its wines epitomize Navarra's greatest strengths: refreshing, fruity *rosado;* lush, old-vine Garnacha; and modern wines made from nontraditional grapes. In addition to the flagship Chivite label, the family owns Rioja's Viña Salceda and Arínzano, Navarra's first estate to gain the elite *vino de pago* designation (see p. 106).

BOTTLES TO TRY
- **Gran Feudo Rosado** / **$**
- **Gran Feudo Crianza** / **$**

BODEGAS FERNANDO REMÍREZ DE GANUZA

Fernando Remírez de Ganuza's notorious fastidiousness helps him make some of Rioja Alavesa's most coveted wines. Remírez de Ganuza is so picky about the fruit that goes into his best wines that he uses only the ripest, darkest grapes at the top of each bunch. No surprise, then, that even his less-exalted bottlings, like the Fincas de Ganuza, show impressive depth. Made in a modern style, Remírez's output reflects his taste for muscular, polished wines with intense fruit flavors.

BOTTLES TO TRY

- Fincas de Ganuza Reserva / $$$
- Remírez de Ganuza Reserva / $$$$

BODEGAS LAN

When a group of Basque families created this ambitious winery in the early 1970s, the name they chose for it was an acronym taken from the three provinces of the Rioja wine region: Logroño (now La Rioja), Álava and Navarra. Today LAN also produces wines from Ribera del Duero, Rías Baixas and Rueda and is owned by Portugal's Sogrape group (see p. 133), but its center of gravity is still in Rioja and quality remains high. The vibrant Crianza is a steal, as is the classically styled, single-vineyard Viña Lanciano Reserva.

BOTTLES TO TRY

- Rioja Crianza / $
- Viña Lanciano Reserva / $$

BODEGAS LUIS CAÑAS

When Juan Luis Cañas took over his family's bodega in 1989, it was drawing from superb old vineyards but turning out fairly unremarkable wine. Cañas transformed it into one of Rioja Alavesa's top estates by upgrading farming methods and constructing a modern, elegant winery. Today Cañas's offerings compel at every level, from juicy young reds made by fermenting whole grapes in a carbon dioxide–rich environment (a technique known as carbonic maceration) to ageworthy reserve wines. The latter include, only in great vintages, the dense, formidable Hiru 3 Racimos.

BOTTLES TO TRY

- Rioja Reserva / $$
- Hiru 3 Racimos / $$$$

COMPAÑÍA DE VINOS TELMO RODRÍGUEZ

The dashing, Bordeaux-educated Telmo Rodríguez has left an indelible mark on contemporary Spanish wine, producing brilliant bottlings from established and emerging Spanish regions. His success in making compelling, affordable reds and whites using native varieties grown on ancient "bush" vines helped spur a national revival of indigenous grapes. One terrific example is Rodríguez's trio of reds from Rioja Alavesa's Lanzaga district. They showcase old vines, minimal winemaking (native yeasts, subtle oak), and pure, elegant flavors. The fresh, silky LZ is unbeatable at the price.

BOTTLES TO TRY

- ● LZ / $
- ● Lanzaga / $$

CVNE

It's hard to keep this important Rioja producer's labels straight, but the effort is worth it. CVNE (the Spanish acronym for Wine Company of Northern Spain) is responsible for two venerable Rioja Alta labels, Cune and Imperial, and the Viña Real label, whose five wines come from Rioja Alavesa (and are made in a cedar-lined cellar that evokes the interior of a gigantic wine barrel). The affiliated Contino brand offers pricey, prestigious single-vineyard reds crafted by Jesús Madrazo.

BOTTLES TO TRY

- ○ Cune Monopole Blanco / $
- ◐ Cune Rosado / $
- ● Viña Real Reserva / $$

FINCA ALLENDE

Finca Allende's Miguel Ángel de Gregorio fashions flashy, concentrated reds that put this young Rioja Alta winery firmly in the region's modernist camp. Based out of a magnificent 1675 mansion built by a Mexican millionaire, Ángel is best known for bottlings that zero in on small plots of outstanding *terroir*, like the famous Calvario cuvée. Other wines focus on varietal character, like the 100 percent Tempranillo Finca Allende. But the stealth choice is the fresh, mouth-filling Allende Blanco.

BOTTLES TO TRY

- ○ Allende Blanco / $$
- ● Calvario / $$$$

LA RIOJA ALTA

This benchmark producer's reputation for high-quality wines goes back more than a century. Founded in 1890 as a partnership among five of the finest estates in the area, La Rioja Alta now deftly straddles tradition and modernity. Its lineup includes both classically mellowed, old-school bottlings such as the Gran Reserva 904 and powerful cuvées like the Viña Ardanza. The silky, cherry-inflected Alberdi Reserva, made entirely from Tempranillo, is a perennial overachiever.

BOTTLES TO TRY
- **Viña Alberdi Reserva** ∕ **$$**
- **Gran Reserva 904** ∕ **$$$**
- **Viña Ardanza Reserva** ∕ **$$$**

MARQUÉS DE MURRIETA

Murrieta, one of the greatest producers in Rioja, sources grapes for its famous wines solely from its vast 741-acre Ygay estate at Rioja Alta's southern tip. That's a remarkable resource in Rioja, where most large wineries buy grapes from dozens of growers. Such control gives Murrieta and its supertalented winemaker María Vargas an edge. The advantage is clear in more traditionally styled wines like the graceful, spicy Finca Ygay Reserva, as well as in the winery's modern offering, Dalmau, a smoky, splurge-worthy blend of Tempranillo, Cabernet and Graciano.

BOTTLES TO TRY
- **Finca Ygay Reserva** ∕ **$$**
- **Dalmau Reserva** ∕ **$$$$**

MARQUÉS DE RISCAL

The grand scale of Marqués de Riscal's glittering City of Wine complex—which includes a Frank Gehry–designed hotel and a Michelin-starred restaurant—fits right into this Rioja producer's celebrated history. Founded by a Francophile marquis, Marqués de Riscal produces traditionally styled wines that have helped define Rioja for more than 150 years. They include a light, popular Crianza and a savory, long-aging Gran Reserva. The collectible Barón de Chirel, a complex and elegant Tempranillo blend, is worth seeking out.

BOTTLES TO TRY
- **Rioja Reserva** ∕ **$$**
- **Rioja Gran Reserva** ∕ **$$$**

MARQUÉS DE VARGAS

A relatively new label from an old Rioja family, Marqués de Vargas fulfills a long-held ambition of Hilario de la Mata and his son, Pelayo de la Mata, the current marquis (*marqués*) of Vargas. Established in 1989 in a section of Rioja Alta nicknamed Los Tres Marqueses for its three influential landholders, the winery produces a trio of sustainably farmed, estate-grown reds—all *reservas*. The smooth, licorice-edged Reserva has lovely depth, while the smoky, intense Reserva Privada, from low-yielding older vines, is built for aging.

BOTTLES TO TRY
- **Rioja Reserva** / **$$**
- **Rioja Reserva Privada** / **$$$**

MUGA

Although Muga is part of Rioja's old guard (it was founded in 1932), the winery's reputation for traditionalism is only partially true. In addition to earthy, long-aged *reservas* and *gran reservas*, Muga's lineup includes newer, more voluptuously styled bottlings. And while scions Jorge and Manuel Muga continue to ferment and age their wines exclusively in oak, their experimental streak shows in their huge diversity of barrels, which hail from France, the U.S., Hungary, Russia, Spain and beyond.

BOTTLES TO TRY
- **Rosado** / **$**
- **Rioja Reserva** / **$$**
- **Prado Enea Gran Reserva** / **$$$**

RAMÓN BILBAO

Even in Rioja, where it's easy to find wines that outperform their price, Ramón Bilbao stands out. That's because this Haro-based producer has been completely revitalized by Diego Zamora, the Spanish beverage company that purchased it in 1999. With a renovated winery, a new winemaker and new equipment, the quality shot up, yet the wines themselves remain comparatively under the radar. The *crianza*, *reserva* and *gran reserva* wines are fashioned traditionally; the Limited Edition is bolder, more modern and pure Tempranillo.

BOTTLES TO TRY
- **Rioja Crianza** / **$**
- **Limited Edition** / **$$**

R. LÓPEZ DE HEREDIA VIÑA TONDONIA

This ultra-traditional estate releases its definitive Riojas only when it judges them ready to drink—generally years later than its peers. Extended aging for reds is the norm in Rioja, but López de Heredia is nearly unique in also aging its white and *rosado* (rosé) wines in oak for four or more years and then in bottles. The use of mostly old, neutral barrels and high-quality fruit results in wines that are gorgeously polished and mellow.

BOTTLES TO TRY

○ Viña Tondonia Reserva ∕ $$$

● Viña Tondonia Reserva ∕ $$$

GALICIA

CLAIM TO FAME

The green river valleys of Galicia, on the Atlantic coast of northwestern Spain, look more like Ireland than Iberia, with drizzly wet weather to match. But those valleys produce some of Spain's most outstanding white wines, especially the vibrant, mineral-laden offerings of Rías Baixas (*REE-ahs BYE-shus*), Galicia's top subzone. Based on the Albariño grape, Rías Baixas whites are fantastically fresh, with pronounced citrus.

✌ KEY GRAPES: WHITE

ALBARIÑO Most white grapes rot in weather as rainy as Galicia's, but this variety thrives in it. Crisp, citrusy and marked by a hint of sea-salt minerality, Albariño is typically made into refreshing, unoaked wines that are best drunk young (preferably with any kind of seafood). That said, the handful of ambitious, high-end bottlings (some of which are aged partially in oak) deliver flavors that actually improve with a few years of bottle age.

GODELLO Rescued from oblivion in the 1970s by a few dedicated vintners, this once-rare grape is gaining popularity as a single-variety wine, especially in the Valdeorras and Ribeira Sacra sub-regions, where it yields tangy, quince- and citrus-inflected whites.

TREIXADURA The chief grape of the Ribeiro DO (located along the Miño River and its tributaries), Treixadura creates wines with perky acidity and vibrant citrus and apple layers.

❦ KEY GRAPES: RED

MENCÍA It's rare to find a Galician red wine in the U.S., but if you do, chances are it's made from this grape. Most of it grows in the warmer, inland subregions of Valdeorras and Ribeira Sacra, where it yields light-bodied, high-acid reds with floral and licorice notes. In the hands of the right winemaker, it can display the earthy complexity of Pinot Noir.

Producers/ Galicia

DO FERREIRO

Vintner Gerardo Méndez fashions his wines from ancient family vines—some more than 200 years old—in the Salnés Valley, Galicia's coolest and wettest part. *Ferreiro* means "ironworker" (the profession of Méndez's grandfather), an appropriate name for an estate whose rocky, granite-based soils give its vibrant wines a steely strength. Méndez employs low-tech, traditional techniques—farming organically and handpicking grapes, for example—to create extraordinary whites. His old-vines cuvée, Cepas Vellas, offers a complexity few Albariños achieve.

BOTTLES TO TRY
○ **Albariño / $$**
○ **Albariño Cepas Vellas / $$$**

DOMINIO DO BIBEI

When they're not fashioning sought-after wines from Priorat and Montsant, star winemakers Sara Pérez and René Barbier, Jr., are working with a pocket of ancient, perilously steep vineyards deep in Ribeira Sacra's Bibei Valley. Using traditional blends of native grapes, plus small amounts of experimental varieties, the spouses mastermind thrilling wines for visionary Dominio do Bibei owner Javier Dominguez. Of the two Mencía-based reds, Lalama is lighter, offering minerally, red-berry flavors. The Lapola white blend is reliably zesty and intense.

BOTTLES TO TRY
○ **Lapola / $$$**
● **Lalama / $$$**

PAZO DE GALEGOS

Pazos are a unique Galician class of country mansions. Some of these grand estates along the Camino de Santiago have offered lodging to travelers since religious pilgrims started trekking by on their way to Santiago de Compostela in medieval times. The family-owned Pazo de Galegos, located in the prime subzone Ribera del Ulla, still rents out rooms, though guests these days are as likely to be seeking good wine and a taste of history as they are a religious experience. From a modern facility housed in a 400-year-old building, the winery turns out fantastically fresh, citrus-inflected Albariño.

BOTTLE TO TRY
○ **Premium Selection Albariño / $$**

PAZO DE SEÑORÁNS

Rías Baixas was nowhere on the world's fine-wine radar when Marisol Bueno and her husband acquired Pazo de Señoráns in the Salnés Valley in 1979. She painstakingly restored the historic 16th-century property and was instrumental in the campaign to gain DO status (granted in 1988) for the region. Her riveting Albariños have long been a Rías Baixas standard-bearer. A rare second wine, Selección de Añada, is made only in great vintages; it is one of the few Albariños that can improve with extended aging in bottle, developing complex honeyed flavors.

BOTTLES TO TRY
○ **Albariño / $$**
○ **Selección de Añada Albariño / $$$$**

VIÑA MEÍN

Galicia's Ribeiro region has arguably its greatest champion in Javier Alén, the creator and owner of Viña Meín. In 1988 Alén recruited friends and relatives to help him on a quest to create 40 acres of vineyards in a hilly corner of rural Ribeiro, an area he'd gotten to know on vacations as a child. Alén focused on traditional, indigenous varieties, chiefly the white grape Treixadura, and built a small winery on-site. The resulting offerings have become Ribeiro benchmarks, especially the fragrant, melony whites, which have brought new appreciation for Treixadura, their primary grape.

BOTTLE TO TRY
○ **Viña Meín / $$**

RARITIES & COLLECTIBLES

BODEGA CONTADOR After 15 years as the winemaker at the great Rioja estate Artadi, Benjamín Romeo left to focus on his own boutique label. His powerful, opulently styled flagship wine, Contador, has quickly become a Rioja benchmark.

BODEGAS EL NIDO Australian virtuoso Chris Ringland fashions a scarce and superexpensive namesake Barossa Shiraz. Easier to find are the two voluptuous Mourvèdre-Cabernet El Nido reds he makes in Jumilla with the Gil family.

CLOS MOGADOR Although René Barbier makes other wines from Priorat, including one that is even more expensive than Clos Mogador, this cuvée remains the region's iconic red. First made in 1989, it redefined Priorat wine with its dense black fruit and formidable structure.

SOUTHEASTERN SPAIN

CLAIM TO FAME

Ambitious winemakers have rediscovered Spain's Mediterranean coast and are turning out terrific offerings from vines both new and very old that thrive in the hot, dry region. Jumilla's and Yecla's Monastrells and Valencia's Bobal-based wines are the region's top emerging stars, often delivering amazing value.

♣ KEY GRAPES: RED

BOBAL This distinctive native grape creates dark, brooding reds (plus attractive *rosados*) and accounts for most of the production of the southeast's up-and-coming Utiel-Requena DO.

MONASTRELL The signature grape of Jumilla and of the adjacent Murcia region's only DO, Yecla, Monastrell makes spicy, inky, high-alcohol reds. It's the same grape as France's Mourvèdre.

SYRAH, MERLOT & CABERNET SAUVIGNON Jumilla has led the adoption of these international grapes in the southeast. Now they are steadily gaining ground throughout the region.

TEMPRANILLO The southeast's best examples of this cherry-inflected grape come from the Utiel-Requena DO.

Producers/ Southeastern Spain

BODEGAS OLIVARES

Olivares' Monastrell-based reds reliably outclass their Jumilla peers, thanks to a rare cache of old, ungrafted vines and the coolness of a prime, higher-altitude location. Owner Paco Selva shifted the winery's focus from bulk to estate-bottled wines in 1998. Its output today showcases the spicy, plush Monastrell grape at its best, from the ridiculously affordable Altos dc la Hoya to a juicy *rosado* and even a luscious dessert red, Dulce.

BOTTLES TO TRY
- Olivares Rosado / $
- Altos de la Hoya / $

CASA DE LA ERMITA

Jumilla native Marcial Martínez Cruz made wine all over Spain before returning home in the late '90s to help create this stellar estate. Zeroing in on some of Jumilla's highest mountains, Martínez planted French grapes in addition to the region's signature Monastrell. The Crianza blends both to create a supple, early-drinking red; the powerful Petit Verdot proves that Jumilla can make dry, luscious reds with the structure to age.

BOTTLES TO TRY
- Crianza / $
- Petit Verdot / $$

SEÑORÍO DE BARAHONDA

Señorío de Barahonda turns out some of the best value wines not just in Yecla—a tiny, up-and-coming DO—but in all of Spain. The Candela family have been making wine commercially in Yecla longer than anyone else, and their expertise shows in the full-bodied reds. Based mostly on the Monastrell grape, these include round, richly fruity bottlings such as the oak-free, all-Monastrell Sin-Madera and a spicy Monastrell-Syrah blend, Nabuko.

BOTTLES TO TRY
- Barahonda Sin-Madera / $
- Nabuko / $

CATALONIA

CLAIM TO FAME
In addition to sparkling cava (see p. 283), northeastern Spain's Catalonia region produces the reds of Priorat, which are ranked among the world's most prized wines. Top bottles, like Álvaro Palacios' L'Ermita (see below), command a small fortune; nearby DOs such as Montsant offer similar, if usually less ambitious, blends at a fraction of the price.

KEY GRAPES: RED
CARIÑENA (CARIGNANE) A good companion to Garnacha, Cariñena delivers structure that boosts Garnacha's soft tannins, giving more power and increased longevity to the blend.

GARNACHA (GRENACHE) Catalonia's star variety, Garnacha grows best on old vines, preferably on hillsides, where lean soils concentrate its plush berry and cherry flavors. Garnacha is usually blended with such grapes as Cabernet, Cariñena, Syrah and Tempranillo.

Producers/ Catalonia

ÁLVARO PALACIOS

Some wines are so great that they change the perception of an entire region, which is what happened in 1993, when Álvaro Palacios created L'Ermita, a red made from ancient Garnacha vines in Priorat. L'Ermita and Palacios' earlier effort, Finca Dofí, established the Priorat area as Spain's most exciting wine frontier and Palacios as one of the country's greatest stars. Today Palacios also crafts more-affordable wines, such as the plush, black-fruited Camins del Priorat and Les Terrasses, a polished, old-vines blend.

BOTTLES TO TRY
● **Camins del Priorat** ⁄ $$
● **Les Terrasses** ⁄ $$$

CELLER DE CAPÇANES

Until the late 1990s, Celler de Capçanes was just another sleepy Montsant cooperative. But a request from Barcelona's Jewish community to create custom-made kosher wine sparked a transformation. After mastering modern winemaking equipment, Capçanes' member families were soon getting inquiries about their remarkable kosher reds. The winery still makes superb kosher wines, such as Peraj Petita and Peraj Ha'abib, as well as reds that range from some of Montsant's priciest to some of its best bargains, like the supple, licorice-tinged Mas Donís blend.

BOTTLES TO TRY
- Mas Donís Barrica ⁄ $
- Peraj Petita ⁄ $$

CELLER EL MASROIG

Not long ago, Montsant's cooperative wineries were best known for churning out generic wines high in alcohol and low in enjoyment (many still do). Celler el Masroig is a happy example of an elite new echelon of co-ops focused on quality. In fact, Celler el Masroig winemaker Carles Escolar sells off low-quality fruit rather than bottle it under the Masroig label. The careful selection shows in wines such as the refreshing, full-bodied Les Sorts Rosat (rosé) and the co-op's fruity, affordable reds.

BOTTLES TO TRY
- Les Sorts Rosat ⁄ $
- Castell de Les Pinyeres ⁄ $$

TORRES

When Miguel A. Torres joined his family's wine business in 1962, its success was built on the Sangre de Toro red blend (known for its kitschy plastic-bull bottle ornament) and the value-priced Coronas label, both from Catalonia. Today Torres is a global pioneer, with properties in Jumilla, Toro, Rioja, Ribera del Duero and beyond. Its wines are emblematic of modern Spain—from the world-class Mas La Plana Cabernet to terrific everyday reds and whites.

WINE INTEL
Miguel Torres recently retired to devote himself to fighting climate change. He has reduced his company's carbon footprint and is a key recruiter for the Wineries for Climate Change coalition.

BOTTLES TO TRY
- Sangre de Toro ⁄ $
- Mas La Plana ⁄ $$$

CASTILLA Y LEÓN

CLAIM TO FAME

The Castilla y León region located in northwestern Spain is home to Vega Sicilia (see p. 125), a legendary winery that put the Ribera del Duero subregion on the fine-wine map nearly a century ago. Vega Sicilia's Único—a Tempranillo-Cabernet blend renowned for its longevity—is among the world's most collectible (and most expensive) reds. But not until the debut in the 1980s of Alejandro Fernández's Pesquera did interest in Ribera del Duero really take off. Today the nearby Toro region competes with Ribera reds in quality, while the Cigales DO is moving beyond its reputation for *rosados* and producing more bold reds. The long-underrated Rueda zone shines as a source of crisp whites—an anomaly in a region dominated by red wine—and in Bierzo, an influx of winemaking talent is turning out impressive reds from the local Mencía grape.

♥ KEY GRAPES: WHITE

VERDEJO Once nearly consigned to oblivion, the signature grape of the Rueda region makes fragrant, citrus-laden white wines that recall Sauvignon Blanc (a grape that Verdejo is frequently blended with).

♥ KEY GRAPES: RED

MENCÍA This red grape variety has become increasingly popular with winemakers in recent years. Indigenous to Spain, it is best known for giving the fragrant reds of Bierzo in northwestern León their alluring floral aromas, licorice tinge and bright, often-rustic cherry notes.

TEMPRANILLO Known locally under a handful of different aliases, including Tinto Fino, Tinta del País and Tinta de Toro, this is Castilla y León's star grape variety. Many of Ribera del Duero's savory, spicy, medium- to full-bodied wines are pure Tempranillo (although regional regulations permit the addition of small amounts of other varieties). The Tempranillo-based wines of Toro are fuller-bodied and more concentrated than those of Ribera, and they're usually made to be consumed earlier. As in Rioja, many Ribera reds require many years to soften.

Producers/ Castilla y León

ABADÍA RETUERTA

Because this sprawling estate lies just outside the borders of the prestigious Ribera del Duero DO, its wines carry the humble *vino de la tierra* designation. But don't let that deter you: Abadía Retuerta turns out wines that rival Ribera's best, as well as some terrific bargains. Winemaker Ángel Anocíbar is known for his Tempranillo-based blends, including spicy, succulent and affordable bottlings like Rívola

> **WINE INTEL**
> In 2012 Abadía Retuerta opened a luxury hotel, LeDomaine, in a medieval abbey on the estate. The abbey's orchard provides produce for the Gothic-style dining hall.

and its stellar elder sibling, Selección Especial, the estate's best-known wine. Layering Cabernet Sauvignon and Syrah or Merlot on a Tempranillo base, Selección Especial is reliably polished and elegant (and easier to find than the luxury-priced Pago reds).

BOTTLES TO TRY
- Selección Especial / $$
- Pago Negralada / $$$$
- Pago Valdebellón / $$$$

BODEGAS AALTO

Former Vega Sicilia (see p. 125) winemaster Mariano García— one of the planet's most famous and respected winemakers—is the most prominent of the powerful names behind this culty Ribera del Duero label. Bodegas Aalto's two sumptuous wines are made entirely from Tinto Fino, a.k.a. Tempranillo, with nearly all of the grapes going into the namesake red. Powerful and polished, it showcases García's genius for blending diverse wines from dozens of small vineyards into a seamless whole. This bottling has quickly become a Ribera benchmark, with a substantial structure that gives it the ability to age. García reserves a tiny fraction of fruit for the collectible PS cuvée, which he crafts only in stellar vintages.

BOTTLES TO TRY
- Aalto / $$$
- Aalto PS / $$$$

BODEGAS ALEJANDRO FERNÁNDEZ/ TINTO PESQUERA

Until Alejandro Fernández's powerhouse Tempranillo, Pesquera, came along, the Ribera del Duero region had only one superstar winery—Vega Sicilia. Pesquera's instant acclaim helped galvanize the quality-wine revolution in Ribera, and Fernández went on to create a mini dynasty of four wineries in emerging areas throughout Spain: Pesquera and Condado de Haza in Ribera del Duero; Dehesa La Granja in Castilla y León; and El Vínculo in La Mancha.

BOTTLES TO TRY
- Dehesa La Granja / $$
- Tinto Pesquera Reserva / $$$

BODEGAS JOSÉ PARIENTE

Victoria Pariente created a stir when she and a colleague, Victoria Benavides, fashioned a revelatory 1998 Verdejo from her father José's Rueda vineyards. That white, called Dos Victorias, established the younger Pariente as a rising star. Today she's on her own and makes some of Rueda's best white wine. Her three Verdejos showcase the range of Rueda's signature white grape—a tangy, grapefruity, steel-aged bottling; a silky cuvée fermented in concrete-clay tanks; and a rare, old-vines selection that gets its seductive creaminess from fermentation in oak.

BOTTLES TO TRY
- ○ Varietal Verdejo / $$
- ○ Verdejo Fermentado en Barrica / $$

BODEGAS LOS ASTRALES

Son of the legendary Mariano García, former winemaster at iconic Vega Sicilia, Eduardo García has a winemaking resumé that name-checks some of the world's greatest estates, from Bordeaux's Cos d'Estournel to California's Ridge Vineyards. García puts that heritage and experience to use at Ribera del Duero's Los Astrales, where he works with the Romera de la Cruz family's 71 acres of vines. Planted to Tinto Fino (Tempranillo), they yield fruit for two deeply flavored reds: a flagship bottling and Christina, a spicy, single-vineyard sibling.

BOTTLES TO TRY
- Astrales / $$$
- Astrales Christina / $$$$

BODEGAS TORREMORÓN

Wine importers Patrick Mata and Alberto Orte, of Olé Imports, have a knack for sleuthing out phenomenal values from unknown and unlikely wineries all across Spain. A case in point: the flat-out delicious Tempranillos of Bodegas Torremorón, a cooperative located in the delightfully named hamlet of Quintanamanvirgo (population: 100 or so) in north-central Ribera del Duero. Torremorón's wines benefit from the age of its members' vines, which ranges from 30 to 60 years and older, with some vines hitting the century mark. That translates into juicy, intense, affordable reds of surprising depth.

BOTTLE TO TRY
- Torremorón Tempranillo / $

BODEGAS VIZCARRA

Ribera del Duero star Juan Carlos Vizcarra Ramos manages to turn out phenomenal Tempranillo-based wines at both ends of the price spectrum. His two tough-to-find luxury cuvées, Celia and Inés (named for his daughters), are among the region's most expensive and acclaimed. But Vizcarra takes as much care with his boldly styled, more affordable wines, which outclass many at twice the price. The JC Vizcarra, for example, spends 15 months aging in American and French oak, which gives its intense fruit flavors a toasty edge.

BOTTLES TO TRY
- JC Vizcarra / $$
- Vizcarra Senda del Oro / $$

CAMPO ELISEO

Campo Eliseo is a supergroup of sorts. Like the Traveling Wilburys, it's a high-profile collective project created by big-time stars: "flying winemaker" Michel Rolland and his wife, Dany, and brothers Jacques and François Lurton, scions of an influential Bordeaux-based wine dynasty. All are known for wines made in a modern style, meaning reds packed with deep, ripe fruit, plush tannins and generous oak. First crushed in 2001, their pricey Campo Eliseo wines come from Toro, where the Lurtons already owned a winery and where the local Tempranillo clone, Tinta de Toro, yields especially powerful, dense reds.

BOTTLE TO TRY
- Campo Eliseo / $$$$

DESCENDIENTES DE J. PALACIOS

Ricardo Pérez Palacios teamed up with his uncle, Priorat wine-making legend Álvaro Palacios (see p. 119), in 1998 to make red wines in the up-and-coming Bierzo region. Relying on grapes from old vines planted on steep hillsides, the pair have helped illuminate the region's tremendous potential, as well as the alluring qualities of its signature grape, Mencía. Their single-vineyard reds are Bierzo benchmarks but are hard to find. Look for the entry-level Pétalos, a fragrant, juicy red full of wild berry and mineral flavors, or its pricier Villa de Corullón sibling.

BOTTLES TO TRY
- Pétalos ∕ $$
- Villa de Corullón ∕ $$$

NUMANTHIA

This acclaimed Toro winery bears a name that recalls a grisly chapter in local history: The villagers of Numantia burned down their town, with themselves in it, rather than be taken as slaves by invading Romans. If that's depressing, never mind— Numanthia's three red wines are good enough to cheer up even a besieged Numantian. Made from Tinta de Toro (the local clone of Tempranillo), they're exactly what great Toro should be: rich and bold yet elegant, with a velvety texture and exotically spiced black fruit.

BOTTLES TO TRY
- Termes ∕ $$
- Numanthia ∕ $$$

VEGA SICILIA

Since 1915, this Ribera del Duero legend has been producing some of the greatest wines in the world. Vega Sicilia ages its wines in barrel longer than many wines last in bottle, and once bottled, its best vintages improve for decades more. Its current owners, the Álvarez family, have established sister wineries, including Alión in Ribera del Duero (1992) and Pintia in Toro (2001), but Vega Sicilia itself produces just three highly coveted wines: Valbuena 5°, Único and a near-mythical, nonvintage Reserva Especial.

BOTTLES TO TRY
- Único ∕ $$$$
- Valbuena 5° ∕ $$$$

Portugal

Wine Region

Portugal is home to one of the most picturesque wine regions in the world: the Douro Valley, where vineyards cling to sheer hillsides above more than a hundred miles of winding river. But the Douro is difficult to visit—there are almost no tasting rooms, and transportation is a challenge. Similarly, Portuguese wine is beautiful, but not many people experience it. After an extraordinary renaissance in quality, Portugal now produces spicy, intense reds and vibrant, incredibly refreshing whites, most of which are underpriced relative to their quality. And port, the Douro's famed sweet wine, continues to be one of the greatest wines in the world, with the best vintage bottlings able to age for decades. The Douro may be a difficult place to get to, but exploring the variety and depth of Portuguese wines is easy—all it takes is reaching for a different bottle or two in your local wine store.

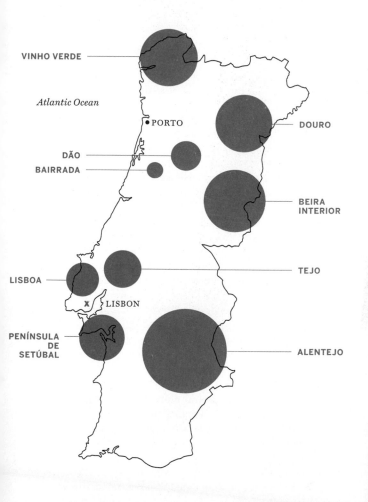

VINHO VERDE

Atlantic Ocean

● PORTO

DOURO

DÃO

BAIRRADA

BEIRA INTERIOR

TEJO

LISBOA

✕ LISBON

PENÍNSULA DE SETÚBAL

ALENTEJO

Portugal

REGIONS TO KNOW

DOURO The oldest officially demarcated wine region in the world, the Douro follows the path of the Douro River from Portugal's border with Spain in the far east toward the Atlantic coast. The region is famous for long-lived, deeply flavored port wines (see p. 294) and produces a growing number of rich, dry reds, nearly always with the same grapes used to make port.

ALENTEJO While most of Portugal's winemaking regions are dominated by the cool breezes of the Atlantic Ocean, Alentejo is located in the hot, sunny plains of the country's southeast corner. The weather there helps translate grapes into plump, full-bodied red wines with pronounced fruit flavors.

BAIRRADA Best known for inky, full-bodied reds made from the local Baga variety, as well as still and sparkling whites made from the fresh, aromatic Maria Gomes grape, Bairrada is now turning out red wines from smoother varieties such as Touriga Nacional and Cabernet Sauvignon.

DÃO This high north-central plateau is starting to fulfill its tremendous promise. Cool nights and granite soils yield crisp, juicy red blends that range from light and simple to complex and ageworthy.

LISBOA & TEJO Located not far from the capital city of Lisbon, these two regions are dominated by large cooperatives making dull wine. But increasingly, small independent producers in these areas are releasing quality red wines that deliver excellent value. Until recently, Lisboa was known as Estremadura, and Tejo was known as Ribatejo.

PENÍNSULA DE SETÚBAL The calling-card wine of this sandy southwest zone is Moscatel de Setúbal, a fragrant, fortified dessert wine, though dry reds from the peninsula's Palmela zone are gaining notice.

VINHO VERDE Portugal's biggest winegrowing district, this cool, rainy region on the country's northwest coast is best known for light, dry, slightly spritzy white wines with crisp citrus notes. Vinho Verde wines possess a comparatively low alcohol content, which makes them especially refreshing and a great choice for summertime drinking.

♥ KEY GRAPES: WHITE

ALVARINHO This aromatic variety—known as Albariño in Spain—helps give the wines of Vinho Verde their bright, citrus-driven flavors. Usually made into light-bodied, crisp whites that offer mineral-laden notes of white peach and orange rind uplifted by a slight prickle of effervescence, Alvarinho can create fuller-bodied, more complex wines, too.

LOUREIRO & TRAJADURA While both of these grapes are used as supporting players to Alvarinho in Vinho Verde, occasional single-variety bottles of Loureiro are making their way to the U.S. Similar to Alvarinho, Loureiro offers mouthwatering acidity and floral aromatics.

♥ KEY GRAPES: RED

BAGA The signature grape of the Bairrada region, thick-skinned Baga produces tannic, often-rustic red wines with high acidity.

TINTA RORIZ (ARAGONEZ) In Spain, where it's called Tempranillo and is frequently blended with Garnacha, this grape yields medium-bodied red wines marked with distinctive cherry flavors. In Portugal, vintners more commonly combine Tinta Roriz with native grapes such as Touriga Nacional and Touriga Franca to craft their hardy reds.

TOURIGA FRANCA The most widely planted grape in the Douro, Touriga Franca is rarely bottled on its own; instead, it's valued for the fragrant aromas and firm, fine-grained tannins it contributes to red blends.

TOURIGA NACIONAL The country's star grape has a very thick skin that gives wines made from it their firm tannins. This factor, along with the grape's high acidity, also helps give these wines their ability to age—which is why Touriga Nacional forms the backbone of so many port wines and dry red blends. It offers spicy depth and juicy black currant, floral and licorice notes and is increasingly gaining favor as a single-variety wine.

WINE TERMINOLOGY

DENOMINAÇÃO DI ORIGEM CONTROLADA (DOC) Portugal's "protected place of origin" labeling applies only to wines produced in designated growing regions that have been vinified according to a strict set of rules designed to ensure quality. Regulations cover factors such as maximum yields, winemaking techniques and required aging periods.

RESERVA Wines labeled *reserva* must be at least half a percent higher in alcohol than wines at the DOC or IGP (similar to the French IGP; see p. 18) level, meaning that they have more body.

QUINTA A common term on many wine labels, this can mean farm, vineyard or estate.

Producers/ Portugal

ÁLVARO CASTRO

There's no better way to grasp the enormous potential of the emerging Dão region than through the wines of Álvaro Castro. This visionary vintner and his daughter Maria make some of the Dão's best wines, as well as some of its top values. The reasonably priced Quinta de Saes bottlings make a terrific starting point, as does the mid-priced Dão tier; old-vine cuvées from the Pellada vineyard are a worthy splurge. Deep fruit and smooth finesse define the reds; whites are silky, crisp and minerally.

BOTTLES TO TRY
○ **Quinta de Saes / $**
● **Quinta da Pellada / $$$**

AVELEDA

The innovative Guedes family has helped set the standard for wines from Portugal's northwest coast as far back as the 1880s. Their rambling Aveleda estate—set amid formal French gardens dotted with fountains, a thatched cottage and a goat tower—is best known for white Vinhos Verdes. Made from local grapes, they're invariably crisp, light and dry, with reasonable prices and an easy-drinking charm that make them terrific house wines. The top white, a zesty, citrusy Alvarinho, is made from a single grape variety.

BOTTLES TO TRY

○ **Alvarinho** / **$**
○ **Quinta da Aveleda Vinho Verde** / **$**

DUORUM

Alentejo star João Portugal Ramos and ex-Barca-Velha wine-maker José Maria Soares Franco have teamed up to create this high-profile wine label in the Douro (*Duorum* is Latin for "of two"). They source grapes from two distinctly different climates: the Douro's midzone, Mediterranean-like Cima Corgo, and the hot, dry upper Douro. They've also established a spectacular, sustainably farmed estate called Quinta de Castelo Melhor. Blending grapes from both regions yields three spicy, elegant dry reds and a single citrusy white.

BOTTLES TO TRY

● **Colheita** / **$$**
● **Reserva Vinhas Velhas** / **$$$**

NIEPOORT

Although he's the descendant of a centuries-old Dutch port-producing family, Dirk Niepoort has the dynamism and drive of a Silicon Valley start-up guru. Niepoort masterminds two of Portugal's greatest modern reds (Batuta and Charme) and a stable of go-to Douro bottlings. Beyond the Douro, the energetic Niepoort makes a fresh, fragrant Vinho Verde and juggles joint ventures with an all-star cast of winemakers from Spain to South Africa and beyond.

BOTTLES TO TRY

○ **Dócil Louriero Vinho Verde** / **$$**
● **Twisted** / **$$**
● **Charme** / **$$$$**

PRATS & SYMINGTON

Bruno Prats seems to like life in the fast lane. While running his family's famous Bordeaux château, Cos d'Estournel, he raced sports cars on the side. After Prats sold Cos d'Estournel in 1998, he teamed up with famous vintners all over the world, including the Symingtons, of Graham's and Warre's ports. They created Chryseia, an ambitious Douro red based on native grapes, and the less costly Post Scriptum bottling. In 2009 P&S added the Prazo de Roriz red and a port to its lineup.

BOTTLES TO TRY

- **Prazo de Roriz ⁄ $$**
- **Chryseia ⁄ $$$**

QUINTA DO CRASTO

In 1997 the Roquette family had released just two vintages of their fledgling Quinta do Crasto wines when one of their reds bested thousands of wines to win a prestigious trophy at an international wine competition. That award helped catapult Quinta do Crasto—and Portugal's dry reds—into the spotlight. Today Crasto is a sought-after name in Douro wine, known for plummy, polished reds made from blends of indigenous grape varieties. The stealth choice in Crasto's lineup, though, is its luscious, minerally white.

BOTTLES TO TRY

- ○ **Crasto ⁄ $$**
- **Crasto ⁄ $$**
- **Quinta do Crasto Reserva Old Vines ⁄ $$$**

QUINTA DO NOVAL

Two decades ago, AXA Millésimes—owner of several Bordeaux châteaus, including Château Pichon-Longueville—purchased Noval, marking an important turnaround for the then-ailing port house. The new owners invested heavily and, in addition to reviving Noval's glorious port heritage, kick-started its foray into nonfortified wines. Newer vineyards rely heavily on Touriga Nacional, arguably Portugal's greatest red grape, which lends complexity to the powerful, savory Quinta do Noval, the flagship red. Cedro do Noval is the lighter, spicier little sibling.

BOTTLES TO TRY

- **Cedro do Noval ⁄ $$**
- **Quinta do Noval ⁄ $$$$**

QUINTA DO VALLADO

A trio of cousins, all sixth-generation descendants of Quinta do Vallado's founding Ferreira family, owns this important Douro estate. One of the cousins, the phenomenally talented Francisco "Xito" Olazabal, directs his own much-admired winery (Quinta do Vale Meão) but consults for Vallado and created, most famously, its red *reserva* and an ambitious Touriga Nacional. Both wines are pricey, but, happily, Vallado's entry-level red offers a taste of the quinta's rich, herb-inflected style at a price that's easier to swallow.

> **WINE INTEL**
> The Ferreira family has created the Douro's most stylish new boutique hotel, a slate-and-concrete structure featuring modern furnishings and views over the Corgo River.

BOTTLES TO TRY
- Vallado ⁄ $$
- Quinta do Vallado Touriga Nacional ⁄ $$$

RAMOS PINTO

Founded in 1880 and owned for the past 24 years by the French Champagne house Roederer, Ramos Pinto was a pioneer of single-variety viticulture—a huge shift for a country in which different grapes traditionally had been planted and picked together. The winery's four estates—two in the upper Douro Valley and two in the middle Douro (Cima Corgo)—provide grapes for an array of affordable wines, including the Duas Quintas and Collection labels.

BOTTLES TO TRY
- Duas Quintas ⁄ $
- Duas Quintas Reserva ⁄ $$$

SOGRAPE

Sogrape owns wineries across Portugal that together offer a dizzying tour of Portuguese wine. From ports to pink wines (think Mateus rosé) and from everyday plonk to world-class reds (like the iconic Barca-Velha), this megaproducer covers all of the country's major bases. The jewel of its portfolio is Casa Ferreirinha, a Douro estate that's been producing benchmark wines since 1751.

BOTTLES TO TRY
- ○ Azeveda Vinho Verde ⁄ $
- ● Callabriga Dão ⁄ $$
- ● Casa Ferreirinha Vinha Grande ⁄ $$

Germany

Wine Region

The problem with German wine is simple: It's that one word like *Trockenbeerenauslese* (a type of sweet dessert wine) can scare off a hundred potential German-wine fans. The good things about German wine, though, are myriad, and at the top of the list is Riesling, one of the world's greatest white grapes. When grown in Germany's ancient hillsides of crumbling slate, Riesling achieves an unmatched mix of stony purity and perfumed elegance. Even entry-level bottlings have tongue-tingling citrus and mineral notes, and top German Rieslings can stand up to the best white wines in the world. Not many other German wines come to U.S. stores, but fans of lean, crisp Pinot Noir should look out for Germany's Spätburgunders. And though most German wine labels have, thanks to the *Trockenbeerenauslesen* of the world, all the easy decipherability of a particle physics textbook, they're incredibly helpful once you've cracked the code.

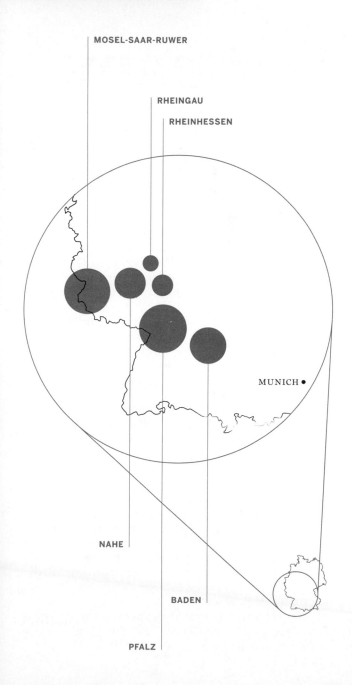

MOSEL-SAAR-RUWER

RHEINGAU

RHEINHESSEN

MUNICH ●

NAHE

BADEN

PFALZ

Germany

REGIONS TO KNOW

RHEINGAU Home to storied estates with vineyards dating back to Roman times, the Rheingau traces the course of the Rhine River and produces many of Germany's greatest wines. Its Rieslings, which are generally drier and fuller-bodied than those of Mosel, display a mineral purity rarely equaled elsewhere; the best examples are monumental whites that age well for decades.

MOSEL-SAAR-RUWER South-facing slopes along the Mosel River and its tributaries, the Saar and the Ruwer, make the most of Germany's available sunshine. Vines rooted in rocky slate terraces produce delicate, minerally Rieslings with racy acidity.

RHEINHESSEN The hilly terrain of the Rheinhessen region produces many low-quality sweet wines, but excellent bargains exist among the bulk offerings. Some of the best Scheurebes and Silvaners—two other German white varietals—are made here.

PFALZ, NAHE & BADEN The relatively warmer Pfalz, Nahe and Baden regions have been the source of some of Germany's best values recently, thanks to an influx of ambitious new winemakers. Look for lusher Rieslings and interesting wines from lesser-known grapes, including Grauburgunder (Pinot Gris) and Gewürztraminer. Some of Germany's best Pinot Blanc—a.k.a. Weissburgunder—comes from Baden and Pfalz. Baden also produces most of the country's Pinot Noir (Spätburgunder).

KEY GRAPES: WHITE

GEWÜRZTRAMINER & MUSCAT (MUSKATELLER) Marked by floral, intensely fragrant aromas, these white grapes thrive in Germany's cool climate.

MÜLLER-THURGAU (RIVANER) & SILVANER Wines made with these grapes are rare in the U.S., mainly because there's not much worth importing. Typically used for refreshing, simple table wines, these popular varieties can sometimes yield sleek, exciting whites when grown for quality rather than quantity.

PINOT GRIS & PINOT BLANC Members of the Pinot family, these whites come in both sweet and dry versions, with Pinot Blanc generally dry. Pinot Gris is called Grauburgunder when made in a crisp style; sweeter versions are often named Ruländer.

RIESLING Germany's most widely planted and prestigious grape is made into a vast range of wine styles, from bracingly dry to unctuously sweet, from fruity and floral to searingly mineral.

SCHEUREBE Often used for dessert wines, this unusual white variety displays black currant aromas and citrusy flavors.

KEY GRAPES: RED

DORNFELDER First cultivated in 1979, this new grape yields juicy, deeply colored reds that are catching on in Germany.

PINOT NOIR Spätburgunder, as Pinot Noir is called in Germany, is still far from a household name in the U.S., but if you can find them, these wines offer delicate, fresh cherry notes.

WINE TERMINOLOGY

German labels provide more information than most, and their wealth of detail can overwhelm at first glance, but cracking the code is easy with a few hints. Labels identify the producer, the place of origin and, sometimes, a ripeness level. If grapes come from a single village, that town is identified and given the suffix *er;* the vineyard name follows if it's also a single-vineyard wine. Sometimes a cuvée name is given. The two primary quality categories are QbA and QmP; QmP wines include a ripeness designation at the end of the wine name (see p. 138). So, Dr. Loosen Wehlener Sonnenuhr Riesling Spätlese is made by Dr. Loosen near the town of Wehlen in the Sonnenuhr vineyard from Riesling grapes that were picked at a Spätlese level of ripeness. Grape varieties are usually listed, though in regions like the Rheingau, Riesling is assumed.

**QUALITÄTSWEIN OR QUALITÄTSWEIN BESTIMMTER ANBAUGE-
BIETE (QBA)** This basic category includes most German wine,
meaning it's the designation used on everything from bulk wines
to solidly made value bottlings.

QUALITÄTSWEIN MIT PRÄDIKAT (QMP) A big step up from QbAs,
wines labeled QmP are held to higher quality standards; they
are ranked by the grapes' sugar levels, or ripeness, at the time
of harvest (see below).

RIPENESS LEVELS & SWEETNESS In theory, grapes with higher
sugar levels have the potential to make sweeter wines. Yet in
practice, perceived sweetness depends more on the balance
between acidity and sugar or the amount of natural grape sugar
allowed to ferment into alcohol. So, wines in less-ripe categories
are usually drier than those made from riper grapes, but not
always. The least-ripe category is Kabinett, which can taste dry
or slightly sweet. Spätlese wines, the next designation up, range
from dry to sweet with more-concentrated flavors than Kabinett.
Richer and typically sweeter than Spätleses, Auslese wines come
from handpicked grapes that ripen on the vine long after most
fruit is picked. The sweetest designations are Beerenauslese (BA)
and Trockenbeerenauslese (TBA). Made with superripe grapes,
these opulent dessert wines can age beautifully for decades.

TROCKEN & HALBTROCKEN *Trocken* wines taste dry, while *halbtrocken* (half-dry) bottlings have a very subtle sweetness. *Spätlese trocken* means the wine is dry in style yet made from grapes
picked at Spätlese levels of ripeness.

CLASSIC & SELECTION These terms denote wines that are high
quality and dry. Classic wines are usually made with a single
variety and bear the name of the producer but not the vineyard.
Selection wines are higher in quality; they must be made from
hand-harvested grapes and list the producer and vineyard.

**ERSTES GEWÄCHS, GROSSES GEWÄCHS, ERSTE LAGE & GROSSE
LAGE** These relatively new, elite designations are reserved for
top-quality wines sourced from specific vineyards recognized
as superior. Erstes Gewächs and Grosses Gewächs denote (relatively) dry wines, with the former used exclusively in the

Rheingau and the latter abbreviated "GG" on labels. Erste Lage (comparable to the French *premier cru;* see p. 35) wines are identified by an icon—the number 1 next to a bunch of grapes—placed after the vineyard name. Grosse Lage, a term approved in 2012, is comparable to the French *grand cru* designation.

Producers/ Germany

DR. LOOSEN

Ernst Loosen had intended to become an archaeologist but ended up taking over his family's Mosel estate, in 1988. Lucky for wine lovers that he did: Loosen's then-radical insistence on low crop yields and his focus on old, ungrafted vines (as well as his unbridled enthusiasm) inspired winemakers across the country. In collaboration with winemaker Bernard Schug, Loosen crafts expressive single-vineyard Rieslings that put the estate in the ranks of Mosel's elite. The Dr. L label, meanwhile, offers fantastically reliable wines for everyday drinking.

BOTTLES TO TRY

○ Dr. L Riesling / $
○ Blue Slate Riesling Kabinett / $$

GEORG BREUER

Rheingau vintner Bernhard Breuer left an out-size legacy when he died in 2004. His racy, dry Rieslings and sleek Spätburgunders were so good that they inspired a movement toward drier wines in the region, and his zeal for quality was legendary. After Breuer's death, his daughter Theresa stepped into her father's boots, working in collaboration with winemaker Hermann Schmoranz. Together they have kept the caliber of the wines extraordinarily high.

WINE INTEL
Surprisingly, Germany is now the world's third-largest source of Pinot Noir, or Spätburgunder. Georg Breuer produces some of the country's best renditions of the popular grape.

BOTTLES TO TRY

○ GB Charm Riesling / $$
○ Terra Montosa Riesling / $$$
● Spätburgunder-Pinot Noir / $$$

MAXIMIN GRÜNHAUS/
SCHLOSSKELLEREI C. VON SCHUBERT

The double-barreled name of this Ruwer Valley estate reflects its history: Lands from the ancient Abbey of St. Maximin eventually ended up in the hands of the von Schubert family. One of Germany's greatest estates, it produces filigreed Rieslings that epitomize the Ruwer Valley's delicate, flinty style. Grapes come from a trio of exalted vineyards: Abtsberg, Herrenberg and Bruderberg. Single-site cuvées can be hard to find; alternatively, look for the estate's two intro-level, multivineyard Rieslings.

BOTTLES TO TRY

○ Abtsberg Riesling Kabinett∕$$
○ Riesling Trocken∕$$

REICHSGRAF VON KESSELSTATT

Director Annegret Reh-Gartner, daughter of Reichsgraf von Kesselstatt's owner Günter Reh, and winemaker Wolfgang Mertes can afford to be choosy about which vineyards they showcase in the winery's famous site-specific cuvées: With 90 acres of vines in enviable spots along the Mosel, Saar and Ruwer rivers, this is one of the larger of Germany's top wine estates. Von Kesselstatt's single-vineyard wines, whether delicate, steely, fruity or lush, reflect the range of places they're from. Its multi-vineyard blends deliver affordable quality.

BOTTLES TO TRY

○ RK Riesling∕$
○ Piesporter Goldtröpfchen Riesling Kabinett∕$$

S.A. PRÜM

A handful of wineries in the Mosel Valley bear the name of the Prüm family, which has been making wine for close to nine centuries. Raimund Prüm—known as "the red Prüm" for his carrot-colored hair—took the tiny, prestigious winery he inherited and made it into one of the valley's most prominent estates. Its reputation rests on electrifying single-vineyard Rieslings from ancient vines in legendary sites such as Wehlener Sonnenuhr. Easier to find are Prüm's multivineyard blends, including the lightly sweet Essence and two Kabinetts.

BOTTLES TO TRY

○ Essence Riesling∕$
○ Blue Riesling Kabinett∕$$

WEINGUT BARON KNYPHAUSEN

For more than six centuries, the vineyards of this Rheingau estate belonged to Eberbach Abbey, one of the most powerful Cistercian monasteries in Germany and a major medieval wine producer. In 1818, an ancestor of the current baron, Gerko Freiherr zu Knyphausen, purchased a chunk of prime church vineyards and created the family's namesake estate. The winery's small-lot bottlings are scarce, but its Baron K' Riesling is relatively findable. Reliably zesty and fruity, it usually delivers a kiss of sweetness that makes it a perfect match for spicy foods.

BOTTLE TO TRY

○ **Baron K' Riesling Kabinett ∕ $$**

WEINGUT DÖNNHOFF

Arguably the greatest producer in the small, less-heralded Nahe region, and among the greatest in Germany, Dönnhoff makes masterfully balanced wines that command cultlike devotion from fans. Its coveted sweet Rieslings and dry Grosses Gewächs bottlings get their stunning intensity partly from Nahe's slightly warmer climate, where grapes ripen more easily than in the Mosel. Even Dönnhoff's duo of delicate, entry-level Rieslings— one dry (Trocken) and the other lightly sweet—offer rare precision and purity.

BOTTLES TO TRY

○ **Riesling ∕ $$**
○ **Riesling Trocken ∕ $$**

WEINGUT DR. H. THANISCH ERBEN MÜLLER-BURGGRAEF

The Thanisch name is closely associated with one of the Mosel's most famous sites, the Doctor vineyard in the village of Bernkastel. Two branches of the family still hold important stakes in Bernkasteler Doctor; both, confusingly, make wine under the Dr. H. Thanisch name. The Müller-Burggraef branch has gained new dynamism under Barbara Rundquist-Müller, who took over in 2007 and upgraded the winery and vineyards. Minerally Rieslings from Bernkasteler Doctor are its calling card, but excellent, affordable alternatives abound.

BOTTLES TO TRY

○ **Classic Riesling ∕ $$**
○ **Berncasteler Doctor Riesling Kabinett ∕ $$$**

WEINGUT KARTHÄUSERHOF

While some wine labels shout out from store shelves, Karthäuserhof's labels whisper. The small neck labels on mostly bare bottles give few clues about Karthäuserhof's renown, although just the winery name is enough for most Riesling lovers. That's because all of Karthäuserhof's wines come from estate-owned vines along the Ruwer River, whose quality has been recognized for centuries. Owner Albert Behler, who took over the estate in 2012, and winemaker Christian Vogt fashion Rieslings that are famous for their juicy, vibrant freshness.

BOTTLES TO TRY

○ **Riesling Kabinett Grosse Lage** ∕ **$$$**
○ **Riesling Spätlese Grosse Lage** ∕ **$$$**

WEINGUT LEITZ

Johannes Leitz (pronounced *lites*) is no longer a rising star in the world of German wine—he's too widely admired and established now. The son of Rheingau winegrowers whose family winemaking history goes all the way back to 1744, Leitz took over the family cellar in 1985, at the age of 21. Learning by trial and error, he has enlarged the estate from tiny (7 acres) to substantial (nearly 100). The estate's Rieslings range from affordable bottlings with cheeky names (e.g., Leitz Out and Eins Zwei Dry) to serious, gorgeously fragrant single-vineyard wines that can age for decades.

BOTTLES TO TRY

○ **Leitz Out Riesling** ∕ **$**
○ **Leitz Eins Zwei Dry** ∕ **$$**

WEINGUT REICHSRAT VON BUHL

The Reichsrat von Buhl estate landed in good hands when businessman Achim Niederberger bought it in 2005, a lucky break for one of the most historic wineries in Pfalz. Niederberger—a businessman and passionate wine collector—hired a skilled team that is making the most of von Buhl's 128 acres under vine, which include some of the best sites in Pfalz. Now biodynamically farmed, the vineyards yield superb Riesling and a smattering of wines made from other varieties.

BOTTLES TO TRY

○ **Armand Riesling Kabinett** ∕ **$$**
○ **Kirchenstück Riesling Grosses Gewächs** ∕ **$$$$**

WEINGUT ROBERT WEIL

Robert Weil dessert wines are so famous (and famously expensive) that they can overshadow the winery's phenomenal dry Rieslings. Although this 139-year-old Rheingau estate was already well regarded, Wilhelm Weil made radical changes when he took over nearly three decades ago. His meticulousness—insisting, for example, on picking a vineyard 17 or more separate times in order to harvest only choice grapes—has paid off in the form of Rieslings with rare elegance and intensity.

BOTTLES TO TRY

○ **Estate Dry Riesling** ⁄ **$$**
○ **Kiedrich Turmberg Riesling Trocken** ⁄ **$$$**

WEINGUT ST. URBANS-HOF

Named for the patron saint of wine producers, St. Urban of Langres, this family-owned Mosel estate produces two fabulous, value-driven Rieslings: the stony, crisp estate bottling and a light, barely sweet cuvée named for proprietor Nik Weis. Even Urbans-Hof's more expensive single-site wines, the best of which come from Goldtröpfchen (in Mosel) and the Bockstein vineyard (in Saar), deliver terrific quality for their comparatively reasonable prices.

BOTTLES TO TRY

○ **Nik. Weis Selection Urban Riesling** ⁄ **$**
○ **Estate Riesling** ⁄ **$$**
○ **Piesport Goldtröpfchen Riesling Spätlese** ⁄ **$$$**

Austria

Wine Region

Austria has an unusual distinction: It's the only major European wine country that is entirely landlocked. But it does have one of Europe's most gorgeous rivers, the Danube, and the vineyards by its banks yield many of Austria's wines. This white wine country's greatest bottlings are its peppery Grüner Veltliners and regal, minerally Rieslings; gracefully proportioned wines of invigorating freshness, both are fantastic complements to food. Those qualities alone are probably why U.S. sommeliers have been so obsessed with convincing their customers of the virtues of Austrian wine. But Austria's reds— particularly its spicy Zweigelts and subtle Blaufränkisches (otherwise known as Pinot Noir)—are also well worth exploring. So hum a waltz, have some schnitzel and get started.

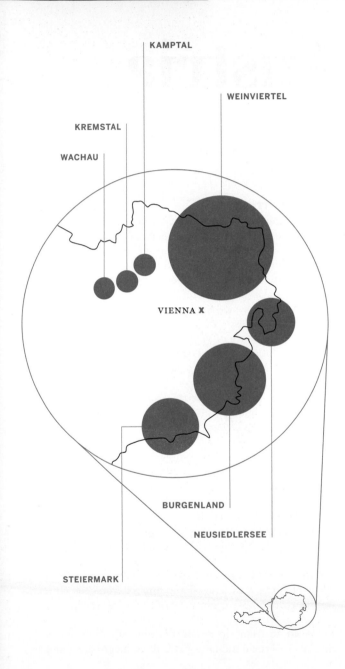

KAMPTAL

WEINVIERTEL

KREMSTAL

WACHAU

VIENNA **X**

BURGENLAND

NEUSIEDLERSEE

STEIERMARK

Austria

REGIONS TO KNOW

NIEDERÖSTERREICH (LOWER AUSTRIA) Austria's great white wines come mainly from this sprawling province in the northeast, where vineyards line the Danube River. Its small **WACHAU** subregion produces many of the country's richest Grüner Veltliners and Rieslings; the neighboring **KREMSTAL** and **KAMPTAL** areas also make stellar examples. The region's largest subzone, **WEINVIERTEL**, is a good source of affordable Grüner Veltliner.

BURGENLAND South of Vienna and bordering Hungary, this warm zone produces most of the country's reds, along with stunning dessert wines.

STEIERMARK (STYRIA) Austria's southernmost wine region makes vivid, aromatic whites from grapes such as Sauvignon Blanc, Chardonnay, Welschriesling and Gelber Muskateller.

WIEN (VIENNA) Wine from the hills just outside Vienna is made from blends of different varieties harvested and crushed together (called *gemischter satz*). A little is now available in the U.S.

♥ KEY GRAPES: WHITE

GELBER MUSKATELLER U.S. sommeliers have championed this rare grape, which yields delicate, floral-scented whites.

GRÜNER VELTLINER Austria's signature grape is a crisp, peppery white bursting with mineral and apple flavors. Top Grüners improve over time, gaining notes of honey and smoke.

RIESLING Austrian versions of this minerally white tend to be drier than German Rieslings and fruitier than Alsace examples.

SAUVIGNON BLANC (MUSKAT-SYLVANER) & CHARDONNAY (MORILLON) These international whites are gaining ground in Austria; Sauvignon Blanc from Steiermark is the finest.

WEISSBURGUNDER The most famous examples of this grape variety (a.k.a. Pinot Blanc) come from Burgenland, where it is the basis of superb dessert wines and many dry whites; southern regions, such as Südsteiermark, are also good sources of dry Weissburgunder wines.

WELSCHRIESLING & MÜLLER-THURGAU (RIVANER) These high-yielding varieties are responsible for much of Austria's simple, everyday whites, though a handful of excellent sweet Welschrieslings can be found.

❧ KEY GRAPES: RED

BLAUFRÄNKISCH This spicy red grape yields medium-bodied wines that are exceptionally food-friendly.

ST. LAURENT Though rarely imported, this local variety may be Austria's most seductive red, with lush, smoky flavors and exuberant aromas reminiscent of Pinot Noir.

ZWEIGELT Fresh cherry and licorice tinges and juicy acidity define Zweigelt, Austria's most popular red.

WINE TERMINOLOGY

Austrian wine labels list grape and region, and, except for table wines, use rankings similar to Germany's Qualitätswein designations, which define the ripeness of grapes for quality wines and hence the finished wine's potential alcohol and sweetness (see p. 137). In 2002 Austria introduced the Districtus Austriae Controllatus (DAC) regional wine-classification system.

DISTRICTUS AUSTRIAE CONTROLLATUS (DAC) Similar to the French AOC and Italian DOC systems, DAC categories have rules that cover yields, permitted grapes, winemaking requirements and geographic limits for sourcing. The wines must also adhere to a certain taste profile. DAC terms are intended to ensure that wines represent quality examples of the country's most important styles; today there are eight appellations.

FEDERSPIEL A Wachau term for wines made from riper grapes that are then fermented into medium-bodied dry wines similar to those made in a Kabinett style (see p. 138).

GEMISCHTER SATZ A wine made from a traditional "field blend" of different grape varieties. For these bottlings, winemakers grow and ferment the grape varieties together, rather than blending them after fermentation.

SMARAGD Used only in the Wachau, this term applies to wines made from grapes that were picked later than those for Federspiel wines (see above). The extra hang time on the vine gives Smaragd wines exceptional richness and body, and occasionally a touch of sweetness.

STEINFEDER A term used in the Wachau to define light, low-alcohol wines that are made for drinking young (and perfect for picnics and parties).

Producers/ Austria

F.X. PICHLER

F.X. Pichler's Rieslings and Grüner Veltliners inspire cultlike devotion, thanks to their phenomenal depth, concentration and penetrating minerality. Franz Xaver and son Lucas together fashion their richly styled whites from some of the Wachau's most famous vineyards. Whether a result of vintage conditions or a stylistic tweak, the wines have dialed back some of their baroque lushness, and are better than ever for the shift. Top wines get snapped up by collectors; look for the fresh, enticing Federspiel cuvées, which are more readily available.

WINE INTEL In 2006 F.X. Pichler's daughter Elisabeth and her husband, Erich Krutzler, started their own label. The talented duo's Pichler-Krutzler wines gained instant acclaim and have made their estate one to watch.

BOTTLES TO TRY
○ **Burgstall Riesling Federspiel / $$$**
○ **Urgestein Terrassen Grüner Veltliner Smaragd / $$$**

HÖGL

Tucked away in the Spitzer Graben, a steep, green glen opening out to the Danube, Högl is one of the Wachau's finest producers, with one of its most unassuming proprietors. Josef Högl apprenticed with two living legends, winemakers F.X. Pichler (see opposite) and Franz Prager, for 15 years before shifting his attention to his parents' tiny mountainside estate. Högl (with the assistance of his son Georg) farms 17 acres of stacked-stone terraces, turning his grape crop into precise, stony white wines of remarkable depth.

BOTTLES TO TRY

○ Schön Grüner Veltliner Federspiel / $$
○ Steinterrassen Riesling Federspiel / $$

MORIC

Moric's Roland Velich spent decades studying winemaking techniques used by Burgundy's greatest domaines and adapting them to his vineyards in Burgenland. Instead of treating the local Blaufränkisch grape like the bold, heat-loving varieties Syrah and Cabernet Sauvignon (e.g., aging it in new oak and extracting maximum concentration), Velich employs a delicate touch suited to cool-climate grapes such as Pinot Noir. The result of Velich's approach is revelatory: spicy, silky Blaufränkisch with captivating finesse.

BOTTLES TO TRY

● Blaufränkisch / $$
● Reserve Blaufränkisch / $$$

NIKOLAIHOF WACHAU

The Nikolaihof estate oozes history: Records of winegrowing here go back a mind-boggling two millennia, to the year AD 90; the wine cellar was originally a Roman-era crypt. In that context, Nikolaihof's newly refurbished 17th-century wooden wine press seems practically modern. The Saahs family, who purchased the former monastery in 1894, have vinified small amounts of white grapes in much the same way for 200 years. Aged in massive, ancient oak casks, the wines display rare harmony and grace.

BOTTLES TO TRY

○ Im Weingebirge Grüner Veltliner Federspiel / $$$
○ Vom Stein Riesling Federspiel / $$$

SCHLOSS GOBELSBURG

Until 1996 Michael Moosbrugger was an obsessive young wine collector with a burning desire to make his own wine. Then Willi Bründlmayer (see below) gave him the opportunity of a lifetime: to lease the vineyards at Schloss Gobelsburg, a 12th-century monastery with grapevines growing in some of Kamptal's finest *terroir*. Since then, the quality of the wines has soared, and Moosbrugger has made the leap from winemaking novice to established star.

BOTTLES TO TRY
- ○ Gobelsburger Riesling / $$
- ○ Grüner Veltliner Reserve Steinsetz / $$
- ○ Tradition Reserve Riesling / $$$

UMATHUM/ZANTHO

Josef "Pepi" Umathum is one of Austria's red wine masters, though when he took over his family's Burgenland farm, it was growing mostly white grapes. His biodynamically farmed Zweigelt, Blaufränkisch and St. Laurent set standards for these varieties, with spicy, lithe Zweigelt the winery's signature pour. One of Umathum's gifts is his ability to turn out good wines even in difficult vintages—a skill evident in his affordable Zantho wines, which he makes with Wolfgang Peck.

BOTTLES TO TRY
- ● Zantho Zweigelt / $
- ● Umathum Zweigelt / $$

WEINGUT BRÜNDLMAYER

If you want to memorize just one name in Austrian wine, Bründlmayer is a good one to choose. That's because Willi Bründlmayer fashions wines that are consistently ranked among Austria's best, and because, in a country where most family-owned estates are pocket-size, he owns nearly 200 acres of vineyards, making Bründlmayer bottlings easier to find. The estate is best known for Rieslings from the magnificent Heiligenstein vineyard, but the quality is terrific across the entire portfolio, including its Grüner Veltliners, acacia-aged red wines and zesty sparkling wines.

BOTTLES TO TRY
- ○ Kamptaler Terrassen Grüner Veltliner / $$
- ○ Kamptaler Terrassen Riesling / $$

WEINGUT EMMERICH KNOLL

It's debatable whether Emmerich Knoll makes better Riesling or Grüner—this Wachau winemaker excels at both. A leading figure in Austria's wine renaissance of the 1980s, Knoll owns, along with his son Emmerich III, 37 acres of steep vineyards along the warmer, eastern stretch of the Wachau Valley. Knoll's wines combine freshness, power and stony minerality to create some of the Wachau's most ageworthy whites; his top cuvées can improve for many years. Knoll's Pfaffenberg wines come from a vineyard just across the Wachau border, in Kremstal.

BOTTLES TO TRY

○ **Ried Loibenberg Grüner Veltliner Smaragd** / **$$$**
○ **Ried Pfaffenberg Riesling Kabinett** / **$$$**

WEINGUT FRANZ HIRTZBERGER

At harvest, Franz Hirtzberger and son Franzi make several passes through their Wachau vineyards, plucking only the ripest grapes from a vine at each foray. It's a monstrously difficult, thigh-burning task: Their fruit grows on some of the region's steepest terraces, towering stadium-high over the Danube. Their obsession with perfect ripeness means that even the Federspiel (lighter) wines are among the weightiest of their kind, while the seductive, coveted Smaragds offer silky richness and seamless balance.

BOTTLES TO TRY

○ **Rotes Tor Grüner Veltliner Federspiel** / **$$$**
○ **Hochrain Riesling Smaragd** / **$$$$**

WEINGUT HIRSCH

While still in his 20s, Johannes Hirsch convinced his family to let him rip out every red variety growing in their Kamptal vine-yards—never mind that Hirsch's reds were among the region's best. As it turned out, Hirsch's progressive streak was just getting started: He converted the estate to biodynamic farming and became the first Austrian to use screw-caps for all of his wines. His six stellar Grüners and Rieslings include the juicy, compulsively drinkable Veltliner #1 and stony whites from the famous Heiligenstein vineyard.

BOTTLES TO TRY

○ **Veltliner #1** / **$$**
○ **Heiligenstein Riesling** / **$$$**

WEINGUT KURT ANGERER

Though Kurt Angerer fashions wines from 11 grape varieties, this up-and-coming Kamptal vintner is obsessed mostly with Grüner Veltliner. Angerer showcases the grape in a series of cuvées that get their distinctiveness from different soils (gravel, granite, loess and loam) and aging techniques (oak barrels and steel tanks). Taken together, the collection reflects Grüner Veltliner's amazing range, from zippy to lush to fruity to austere. The peppery, refreshing entry-level cuvée, Kies, comes from a vineyard of pure red gravel (*kies* in German).

BOTTLE TO TRY

○ **Kies Grüner Veltliner** ∕ **$$**

WEINGUT LOIMER

Fred Loimer's Kamptal winery, a modernist black glass box, wouldn't seem at all out of place in a fashionable Los Angeles neighborhood; yet it sits on top of vaulted brick wine tunnels that date to the 19th century, and some of the surrounding vineyards are plowed by horse, not tractor. That contradiction neatly embodies Loimer's cutting-edge-yet-traditionalist approach, which has helped put him at the forefront of Kamptal's new guard. His wines aim for balance over sheer power, with succulent freshness prized as much as richness.

BOTTLES TO TRY

○ **Lois Grüner Veltliner** ∕ **$**
○ **Terrassen Reserve Riesling** ∕ **$$$**

WEINGUT NIGL

First-generation winemaker and rising star Martin Nigl makes Rieslings and Grüner Veltliners on his Kremstal estate that are impressive enough to compete with those of the more prestigious, and more expensive, Wachau region. Nigl's grapes are all picked by hand, and those from the estate's oldest vineyards are reserved for the more expensive Privat line. Though they are layered with complex flavors, even Nigl's top wines retain a sense of delicacy, partly a result of his reliance chiefly on steel tanks (rather than barrels) to mature them.

BOTTLES TO TRY

○ **Dornleiten Riesling** ∕ **$$**
○ **Freiheit Grüner Veltliner** ∕ **$$**
○ **Privat Riesling Pellingen** ∕ **$$$$**

WEINGUT PAUL ACHS

Blaufränkisch specialist Paul Achs apprenticed in California in the late 1980s, then returned to his family's Burgenland estate to create some of Austria's most seductive red wines. Located not far from the shores of Neusiedler Lake, Achs's biodynamically farmed vineyards bask in the region's relatively warm climate. Ripe grapes and a focus on intense fruit flavors give Achs's wines rare concentration. Other varieties to look for include his polished renditions of Zweigelt and St. Laurent.

BOTTLES TO TRY
- Heideboden Blaufränkisch / $$
- Zweigelt / $$

WEINGUT STADT KREMS

Urban winemaking has become a legitimate trend in the U.S., but the Austrian city of Krems (Stadt Krems) had a six-century head start. Krems created its own municipal winery in the 15th century, after a nobleman donated his vineyards. A long history and ancient vines partly explain why these wines are so good today; the presence of über-talented winemaker Fritz Miesbauer explains the rest. Miesbauer's minerally and refreshing entry-level wines outclass many at their price; his top cuvées are among Kremstal's best.

BOTTLES TO TRY
- ○ Grüner Veltliner / $$
- ○ Steinterrassen Riesling / $$

Greece

Wine Region

Greece's Santorini—that tiny Cycladic island of whitewashed cliff villages and azure waters—is home to one of the world's greatest white wines for seafood. Made primarily with the local Assyrtiko grapes, Santorini whites fully capture the clear, sparkling sunlight and seaside freshness (and they're fantastic with fish, whether it's grilled, baked or fried). That's Greek wine in a nutshell: Despite the world's obsession with Cabernet and Chardonnay, Greek winemakers have concentrated on the country's evocative local grapes, and they use them to express the character of a place where wine has been made for thousands of years. In Macedonia, tannic, fragrant Xinomavros suggest the rugged mountain slopes; in the Peloponnese, ripe, rich Agiorgitikos reflect the Mediterranean sun and soft hillsides. If you haven't tried Greek wines recently, you're missing out on some of the great wines in the world today.

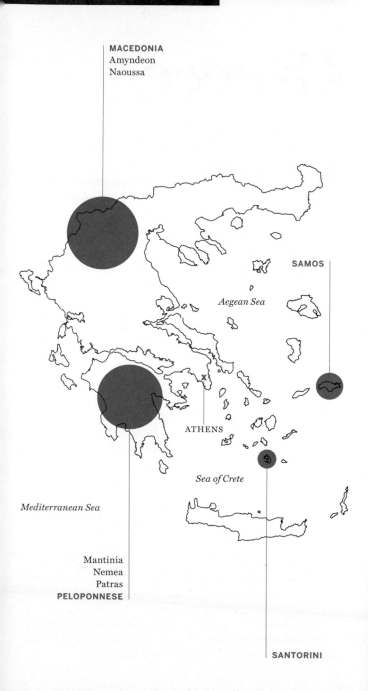

MACEDONIA
Amyndeon
Naoussa

SAMOS

Aegean Sea

X

ATHENS

Sea of Crete

Mediterranean Sea

Mantinia
Nemea
Patras
PELOPONNESE

SANTORINI

Greece

REGIONS TO KNOW

PELOPONNESE This large peninsula in southwestern Greece is a go-to zone for aromatic reds based on the Agiorgitiko grape, as well as for floral whites. Top subzones include **NEMEA,** for reds, and **MANTINIA,** for whites.

SANTORINI Greece's finest whites come from this small, arid island, where rainless summers, volcanic soils and native grapes give its wines a minerally intensity.

MACEDONIA This mountainous, northern zone produces young, fruity reds as well as tannic, ageworthy ones; the best come from **NAOUSSA** and neighboring **AMYNDEON**.

♣ KEY GRAPES: WHITE

ASSYRTIKO Of the hundreds of grapes cultivated in Greece, this is perhaps the best. A Santorini specialty, it yields bone-dry, mineral-rich wines that, at their best, can improve for decades.

ATHIRI This ancient white grape, often blended with Assyrtiko, is the source of succulent, citrusy whites.

MALAGOUSIA A satiny texture and lush, full-bodied stone-fruit flavors define wines made from this grape, which was brought back from the brink of extinction by Evangelos Gerovassiliou (see p. 158).

MOSCHOFILERO This pink-skinned Peloponnesian native stands out for crisp, low-alcohol white and rosé wines with floral, lightly spicy qualities reminiscent of Gewürztraminer.

ROBOLA The same grape as Friuli's Ribolla Gialla, Robola grows mostly on the mountainous island of Cephalonia, where it's responsible for minerally, citrus-inflected whites.

RODITIS This bulk-wine staple also produces charming, floral whites in the Peloponnese's Patras appellation.

SAVATIANO The common Savatiano grape is the usual basis for retsina, a simple, ubiquitous white wine flavored with pine resin.

♣ KEY GRAPES: RED

AGIORGITIKO Pronounced *ah-yor-YEE-tee-ko*, this grape also goes under the moniker St. George and is responsible for some of the country's best reds. A lush texture and juicy cherry notes are its hallmarks, whether it's made into fresh rosés or rich reds.

XINOMAVRO Macedonia's signature grape yields bold, ageworthy reds marked by savory black olive and herb notes.

WINE TERMINOLOGY

Greek wine labels typically feature regions rather than grapes, as a wine's region tends to determine the main grape from which it is made. Naoussa reds are required to be made from the Xinomavro grape; Nemea reds, from Agiorgitiko. Mantinia wines are mostly Moschofilero; on Santorini, Assyrtiko dominates.

Producers/ Greece

BOUTARI

Boutari's six wineries occupy strategic spots in Greece's top wine zones, making this dynamic producer one of the country's largest. It's also one of its best, thanks to Constantine and Yannis Boutari. The brothers transformed their family's successful *négociant* company into a premium winegrower after taking over in the early 1980s. Today Boutari produces Greece's most famous example of the Xinomavro grape, with its firm, savory Grande Reserve Naoussa bottling, as well as terrific examples of every major native grape and innovative blends.

BOTTLES TO TRY

○ **Santorini Boutari** ⁄ $$
● **Grande Reserve Naoussa** ⁄ $$

DOMAINE GEROVASSILIOU

Evangelos Gerovassiliou trained in France under the late, great enologist Émile Peynaud, then returned to his homeland to revolutionize Greek wine. By planting French grapes such as Syrah on his Macedonian estate in the 1980s, Gerovassiliou helped establish the country's potential for foreign varieties. And by creating stunning wines from obscure native varieties—especially the lush, peach-scented Malagousia grape—he helped save them from possible extinction. His benchmark single-vineyard cuvée features Malagousia straight; the crisp Epanomi bottling blends Malagousia with Assyrtiko.

BOTTLES TO TRY
○ **Domaine Gerovassiliou Epanomi** / **$$**
○ **Malagousia** / **$$**

DOMAINE SIGALAS

Paris Sigalas is a Sorbonne-trained mathematician who spent much of his childhood on the island of Santorini and became fascinated by its wines, especially those made from very old varieties. Inspired in part by the stellar wines he drank while studying in France, Sigalas started winemaking as a hobby, applying French techniques (such as fermenting grapes in oak barrels) to Santorini grapes. In 1992 he went commercial, and today he's one of the country's most respected winemakers, thanks to chiseled, minerally Assyrtiko-based whites and elegant red wines made from local grapes.

BOTTLES TO TRY
○ **Asirtiko Athiri** / **$$**
○ **Assyrtiko Santorini** / **$$**

ESTATE HATZIMICHALIS

Onetime turkey farmer Dimitris Hatzimichalis has almost single-handedly created the Atalanti Valley's modern reputation for fine wine, although this green basin northwest of Athens was celebrated for its vintages in ancient times. Protected by mountains and open to the Euboean Gulf, the valley benefits from an exchange of cool mountain air and sea breezes—a temperate microclimate that Hatzimichalis exploits to grow more than 20 native and international grape varieties.

BOTTLE TO TRY
○ **Lefkos** / **$**

GAIA WINES

While Yiannis Paraskevopoulos was working for Boutari (see p. 157), the company sent him to Santorini to research vineyards. Paraskevopoulos—a Bordeaux-trained wine wonk with a PhD in enology—got so excited by the island's potential that he founded a winery there with vineyard expert Leon Karatsalos. Their pure, razor-sharp Santorini Assyrtikos made their Gaia winery an instant success—though today they're even better known for turning out polished, velvety Agiorgitikos from a mountaintop vineyard in remote Nemea.

BOTTLES TO TRY

○ **Thalassitis ∕ $$**
● **Agiorgitiko by Gaia ∕ $$**

MERCOURI ESTATE

One of Mercouri's least expensive wines is also one of its reliably best: Folói is a fragrant, crisp white blend that demonstrates just how good wines based on the pink-skinned Roditis grape can be. The secret to its quality is elevation: The oldest vineyards of this 150-year-old Peloponnese estate occupy a flat coastal peninsula (complete with private bay), but its Roditis comes from mountain-grown vines. Its reds, meanwhile, benefit from temperate seaside breezes, and include Cava, a juicy, peppery red based on the Friulian variety Refosco.

BOTTLES TO TRY

○ **Folói ∕ $**
● **Cava ∕ $$$**

NEW
WOR

United
States/
Australia/
New
Zealand/
Argentina/
Chile/
South
Africa/

162
UNITED
STATES

248
ARGENTINA

LD

222 AUSTRALIA

238 NEW ZEALAND

256 CHILE

266 SOUTH AFRICA

United States

Thirty years ago most U.S. wine grapes
went into green jugs with handles, which
sold for $2. These days you can walk into
a wine shop and find bottles of California
wine selling for $200—in fact, just the
cork in that bottle of superstar Cabernet
may have cost $2. What happened
between then and now was a U.S. wine
revolution. Today there are more than
450 wineries in Oregon, over 750
in Washington and more than 3,500 in
California—plus additional wineries
in every other state. All that growth has
been driven by an incredibly vibrant wine
culture that produces everything from
those fantastically pricey cult Cabernets
to some of the world's greatest wine
values. Now, a wave of young, ambitious
U.S. producers is pushing the boundaries
of both winemaking and viticulture.
It is, without question, a sensational time
to be drinking American wine.

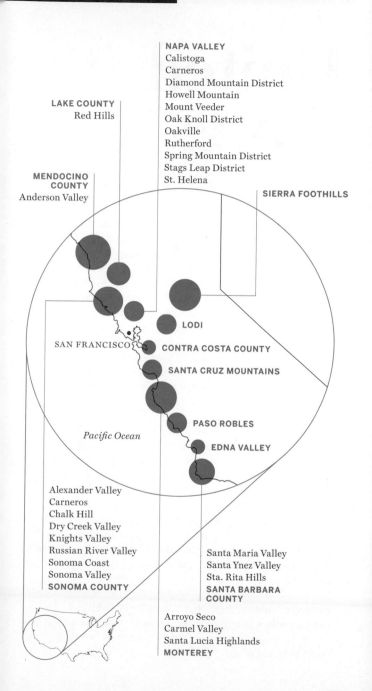

NAPA VALLEY
Calistoga
Carneros
Diamond Mountain District
Howell Mountain
Mount Veeder
Oak Knoll District
Oakville
Rutherford
Spring Mountain District
Stags Leap District
St. Helena

SIERRA FOOTHILLS

LAKE COUNTY
Red Hills

MENDOCINO COUNTY
Anderson Valley

LODI

SAN FRANCISCO

CONTRA COSTA COUNTY

SANTA CRUZ MOUNTAINS

PASO ROBLES

EDNA VALLEY

Pacific Ocean

Alexander Valley
Carneros
Chalk Hill
Dry Creek Valley
Knights Valley
Russian River Valley
Sonoma Coast
Sonoma Valley
SONOMA COUNTY

Santa Maria Valley
Santa Ynez Valley
Sta. Rita Hills
SANTA BARBARA COUNTY

Arroyo Seco
Carmel Valley
Santa Lucia Highlands
MONTEREY

United States

WINE TERMINOLOGY

AMERICAN VITICULTURAL AREA (AVA) Most U.S. labels carry an AVA, showing the legally defined region from which the wine comes. Unlike many European designations, AVAs don't stipulate how a wine must be produced, which grapes may be used or the maximum yields allowed per vineyard. Rather, U.S. law dictates that at least 85 percent of the grapes in a wine labeled with an AVA must come from that region. If an AVA wine lists a vintage date, 95 percent of the fruit is required to be from that year's harvest. Wines with the name of one grape, often called varietal wines, must contain 75 percent of that grape variety. Some states go beyond these requirements. Oregon, for example, mandates a higher minimum percentage for most varietal wines and for geographic designations.

MERITAGE Pronounced like "heritage," this category recognizes multivariety blends made from traditional Bordeaux grapes—chiefly Cabernet Sauvignon and Merlot in reds and Sauvignon Blanc and Sémillon in whites. Many producers use proprietary names for these wines, e.g., Mondavi's Opus One.

OLD VINES The U.S. government does not regulate the phrase *old vines* on labels, meaning that vintners can define it however they like. Many vintners agree that vines older than 35 years qualify as old, though some believe only those a half century or older make the cut.

RESERVE Another term that has no legal definition, *reserve* can be applied to any wine regardless of its age or how it was made; how much the designation is actually worth depends entirely on the brand.

VITIS LABRUSCA Native to North America, this hardy grape species has largely been supplanted in the U.S. by European *Vitis vinifera* grapes. The *Vitis labrusca* species includes such varieties as Concord and Catawba.

VITIS VINIFERA All of Europe's so-called "noble" grape varieties, such as Chardonnay, Cabernet Sauvignon, Sauvignon Blanc and Pinot Noir, belong to this grape species.

CALIFORNIA

CLAIM TO FAME
When it comes to U.S. wine, there's California, and then there's everywhere else. California is the country's viticultural powerhouse, producing about 90 percent of the nation's wine. Although it boasts a winemaking history that dates to the late 1700s, the state became one of the world's top wine zones in just the past few decades. Many of California's best regions hug the coast: Vines depend on ocean-driven wind and fog to chill the grapes nightly and help create thick-skinned, complexly flavored fruit. Still, vineyards grow across much of the state. And while plantings are dominated by international varieties such as Cabernet Sauvignon and Chardonnay, California's experimental winemakers work with a vast array of other grapes, producing wines of every type and style.

REGIONS TO KNOW
CARNEROS Straddling the southern ends of Napa and Sonoma counties, Carneros has a blustery climate that's perfect for Chardonnay and Pinot Noir; sparkling versions are a specialty.

CENTRAL COAST Not to be confused with the scorching-hot Central Valley (which is bulk-wine country), this stretch of the Pacific Coast is a premium growing region that extends between San Francisco and Santa Barbara. Of its 32 subregions, a few stand out. **MONTEREY** occupies a peninsula south of San Francisco and specializes in Chardonnay and Pinot Noir (though it successfully grows aromatic whites like Sauvignon Blanc and Riesling, too). Halfway to Los Angeles, **PASO ROBLES** offers terrific bold, fruity reds, especially Zinfandel, Rhône varietals

(Syrah, Grenache, Mourvèdre) and Cabernet Sauvignon. Southern California's **SANTA BARBARA COUNTY** owes its success with cool-climate wines (notably Chardonnay, Syrah and Pinot Noir) to a geological oddity: coastal valleys that run east–west and serve as superhighways for chilly ocean air. Subregions include the **SANTA MARIA** and **SANTA YNEZ** valleys and **STA. RITA HILLS.**

LAKE COUNTY This district has long been a top source of delicious Sauvignon Blanc; now its **RED HILLS** subzone is gaining fame for Napa-like Cabernets at refreshingly gentle prices.

LODI & THE SIERRA FOOTHILLS Located inland and east of San Francisco Bay, Lodi, in the Central Valley, and the Sierra Foothills region are famous for old-vine Zinfandels.

MENDOCINO COUNTY Home to an unlikely mix of loggers, liberals and vintners, this rugged North Coast region grows an equally unlikely mix of grapes ranging from Charbono to Carignane. Easier to find are its fantastic old-vine Zinfandels and cherry-driven Pinot Noirs. The cool, rainy subregion of **ANDERSON VALLEY** has emerged as an excellent source of silky Pinot Noirs, crisp Chardonnays and refined sparkling wines.

NAPA VALLEY California's most prestigious wine region produces benchmark Cabernet Sauvignons that are among the world's finest reds. (It produces great Merlot and Cabernet Franc, too, but they're less fashionable at the moment.) Northeast of San Francisco, Napa, which includes 16 subregions, is blocked from the Pacific by the Mayacamas Mountains, making it warmer than its western neighbor Sonoma County. The most tannic, powerful Cabernets come from hillside vineyards on famous slopes such as **HOWELL, SPRING** and **DIAMOND** mountains; more-restrained versions, like those from **OAK KNOLL DISTRICT, STAGS LEAP DISTRICT** and **ST. HELENA,** are made from grapes grown on the valley floor or on benchlands.

NORTH COAST This large umbrella region encompasses all of Northern California's best-known AVAs, including those in Napa, Sonoma, Mendocino and Lake counties. The designation is typically used for larger-production blends sourced from multiple vineyards.

SANTA CRUZ MOUNTAINS Though it's home to Ridge Vineyards, one of the best U.S. producers, this forested district south of San Francisco remains under the radar. But that's slowly changing as boutique vintners discover its superb terrain.

SONOMA COUNTY Thanks to its patchwork of varied soils and microclimates, Sonoma's million-plus acres grow heat-seeking Cabernet and Merlot as easily as they do such heat-shy grapes as Sauvignon Blanc and Pinot Noir. Located an hour north of San Francisco, the county is hemmed in between the Pacific and the Mayacamas Mountains, which funnel ocean-driven fog. The prestigious **RUSSIAN RIVER VALLEY** turns out world-class Pinot Noir and Chardonnay, as does the newer **SONOMA COAST,** which offers elegant wines from Sonoma's western extreme. Warmer regions such as parts of the **ALEXANDER VALLEY** and **KNIGHTS VALLEY** produce polished Cabernet and Merlot, along with some lush Chardonnays. **DRY CREEK VALLEY** is one of Sonoma's warmer subregions and an ideal spot for Zinfandel, as well as Cabernet and Syrah. **SONOMA VALLEY** yields perhaps the most diverse wines, with firm reds coming from hillside vines and cool-climate grapes thriving in the valley's southern end.

❦ KEY GRAPES: WHITE

CHARDONNAY The state's most planted variety makes wines that range from rich and heavily oaked to minerally and crisp.

PINOT GRIGIO Most California Pinot Grigio used to be pretty bad, but today winemakers are crafting some delicious, citrusy wines with the grape, particularly from cooler regions.

RIESLING The popularity of this crisp, aromatic white has risen in recent years, along with the skill level of its producers. Though a handful of wineries have been making ambitious, small-lot Rieslings for decades, today they are joined by many larger wineries that are producing fresh, fruity and often lightly sweet bottlings, many of which come from Monterey.

SAUVIGNON BLANC California versions of this zippy white variety display succulent tropical fruit and citrus flavors; these distinguish it from grassier New Zealand versions and minerally white Bordeaux.

VIOGNIER, MARSANNE & ROUSSANNE Often blended to create lush, stone fruit– and apple-inflected white wines, these Rhône Valley grape varieties are most associated with the Paso Robles and Santa Barbara regions.

❦ KEY GRAPES: RED

CABERNET SAUVIGNON This is the grape that put California on the international map in the 1970s, and Cabernet remains the state's iconic wine. Though world-class Cabernets are made in many top West Coast regions, Napa Valley's complex, ageworthy examples still set the standard, at least for prestige and price.

MERLOT Although its reputation took a hit as a result of over-production in the 1990s, Merlot has bounced back in quality and, somewhat less quickly, in prestige—which means shrewd shoppers can now find great Merlots that are much less expensive than Cabernets.

PETITE SIRAH A traditional grape often misidentified in field blends, most California Petite Sirah is actually Durif, a French-originated cross of Syrah with the humble Peloursin. The spicy grape is used primarily to add color and tannin to blends. On its own, Petite Sirah has a small but passionate following.

PINOT NOIR A cool climate is essential for good Pinot, and the state's best bottles come from coastal regions, including western Sonoma, the Anderson Valley and Santa Barbara County.

SYRAH Syrah is the most important Rhône red in California. Often blended with Grenache and/or Mourvèdre, it thrives in the California sun, particularly in the so-called Rhône Zone around Paso Robles. Syrahs made in warm regions like Paso Robles, are lush and fruity; taut, elegant bottlings are made in cooler areas such as Santa Barbara.

ZINFANDEL Although Zinfandel is not a native variety (it's actually an obscure Croatian grape related to Italy's Primitivo), California winemakers have been cultivating it for some time, giving it a distinctive American identity. Paso Robles, Sonoma County's Dry Creek Valley, Mendocino County and Contra Costa County are top spots for the grape.

Producers/ California

ACACIA VINEYARD

Part of the Chalone Wine Group (now owned by beverage titan Diageo), Acacia was a pioneer of Pinot Noir and Chardonnay in the San Francisco Bay–cooled Carneros region. The winery continues on its Burgundian mission, and at their best the wines can be very good indeed, with Pinots and Chardonnays that tend to be leaner-framed and more European in profile. In a good vintage, the Carneros Chardonnay can be a steal for the quality.

BOTTLES TO TRY

○ **Carneros Chardonnay** / **$$**
● **St. Clair Vineyard Pinot Noir** / **$$$$**

ALBAN VINEYARDS

Far from the Napa-Sonoma limelight, in San Luis Obispo, contrarian John Alban is one of the most influential California winemakers of the past 25 years. On the cutting edge of planting Rhône varieties, including finicky Viognier and a bevy of others—Roussanne, Grenache, Mourvèdre—when Rhône wasn't cool, Alban is a Rhône Ranger who walks the walk as a highly talented winemaker and interpreter of the grapes.

BOTTLES TO TRY

○ **Roussanne** / **$$$$**
● **Seymour's Vineyard Syrah** / **$$$$**

ALTAMURA VINEYARDS AND WINERY

Frank and Karen Altamura cleared land for their grapes in 1985 from a cattle ranch Karen's family had worked since 1855. The vineyards are located in Wooden Valley, a hidden pocket of the Napa appellation, and yield distinctive grapes that make exuberant, complex wines. Best known for estate-grown mountain Cabernet Sauvignon, Altamura is also among California's top producers of Sangiovese.

BOTTLES TO TRY

○ **Sauvignon Blanc** / **$$$**
● **Sangiovese** / **$$$**

ARNOT-ROBERTS

Childhood pals Nathan Lee Roberts and Duncan Arnot Meyers grew up around wine in Napa Valley, but moved over to Sonoma to start their own venture in 2001. They produce a highly allocated 2,000 cases of a dozen or more high-personality, single-vineyard bottlings: obscure old-vine field blends and overlooked varieties like Ribolla Gialla, in addition to Cabernet Sauvignon, Chardonnay and Syrah. Wines are fermented with native yeasts, and bottled unfined and unfiltered. Bonus: Roberts is a second-generation cooper who builds and toasts the label's Cabernet barrels himself.

BOTTLES TO TRY

○ **Ribolla Gialla** ⁄ **$$$**
● **Bugay Vineyard Cabernet Sauvignon** ⁄ **$$$$**

AU BON CLIMAT

Both Jim Clendenen and his wines are instantly recognizable: Wild haired, voluble and partial to loud shirts, Clendenen is as idiosyncratic as he is famous. His wines, meanwhile, are sleek and coolly elegant, with a structure that bears the stamp of a formative stint Clendenen spent working in Burgundy in 1981, the year before he founded Au Bon Climat in Santa Barbara County. Today his trailblazing work yields some of California's most flavorful but refined Chardonnay and Pinot Noir. The Santa Barbara County entry-level bottlings are striking bargains.

BOTTLES TO TRY

○ **Santa Barbara County Chardonnay** ⁄ **$$**
● **Sanford & Benedict Vineyard Pinot Noir** ⁄ **$$$**

BABCOCK WINERY & VINEYARDS

The Babcock family came to wine from food—father Walt and mother Mona founded the well-known restaurant Walt's Wharf in Seal Beach—and in 1978 were among the early believers in Santa Barbara County. Winemaker son Bryan is a vineyard theorist ("saturasion irrigation," anyone?) whose most profound discovery is that Babcock's own dirt in the heart of the Sta. Rita Hills produces exceptionally vibrant, full-character Pinot Noir. The signature micro-lot Pinot Noirs of the Terroir Extraordinaire series are available only through the winery.

BOTTLE TO TRY

● **Psi Clone Pinot Noir** ⁄ **$$$**

BEAULIEU VINEYARD

Founded in 1900, this landmark Napa Valley winery survived Prohibition through a legal loophole, producing altar wine. Its Georges de Latour Private Reserve, a Bordeaux-inspired red, helped define world-class California Cabernet Sauvignon. That wine today tops a sprawling portfolio sourced from vineyards in Napa Valley and other areas of the state. The Napa-sourced wines constitute a very solid line, including the entry-level Napa Valley Cabernet and the pricier Tapestry blend; the Georges de Latour can be exceptional.

BOTTLE TO TRY
- Reserve Tapestry / $$$

BECKMEN VINEYARDS

Well known to aficionados, Beckmen deserves a much wider audience for some of the south Central Coast's most intriguing Rhône-style wines (at still-reasonable prices). The Beckmen family's core offerings come from its biodynamically farmed and magically scenic Purisima Mountain Vineyard, above the Santa Ynez Valley. The winery produces some of California's most nuanced Syrahs, and certainly among the very finest Grenaches— luscious, tongue-purpling wines with great energy and lift. But don't overlook its popular Cuvée Le Bec red and Le Bec Blanc— serious upgrades to your house wine.

BOTTLES TO TRY
- ○ Le Bec Blanc / $$
- ● Purisima Mountain Vineyard Grenache / $$$

BEDROCK WINE CO.

Morgan Twain-Peterson crushed his first wine at the tender age of five, with some help from his famous winemaker dad, Ravenswood founder Joel Peterson. His early training definitely paid off: Today 33-year-old Twain-Peterson has an expert hand with grapes that include Zinfandel, Syrah, Cabernet Sauvignon and Pinot Noir. Look for both of his fine labels: the value-driven Sherman & Hooker's and the boutique Bedrock Wine Co., a hyperartisan Sonoma winery located in a converted chicken coop, where Twain-Peterson hand crushes every grape in a traditional basket press.

BOTTLE TO TRY
- ● Monte Rosso Zinfandel / $$$

BERINGER VINEYARDS

Brothers Jacob and Frederick Beringer established this Napa winery 138 years ago. Today, at the much-visited tasting bar in in what was Frederick's gabled and turreted stone mansion, visitors can sample Beringer's higher-end offerings. The huge portfolio ranges from mass-market White Zinfandel to Cabernets that compete with Napa Valley's best—like the Private Reserve Cabernet. The portfolio's sweet spot, value-wise, lies in its mid-priced wines, including those sourced from Beringer's own vineyards in Knights Valley, just over the Sonoma line.

BOTTLES TO TRY

○ **Private Reserve Chardonnay** / **$$$**

● **Knights Valley Cabernet Sauvignon** / **$$**

BLACK KITE CELLARS

This winery is a family affair for Donald and Maureen Green, who acquired their acreage in the remote redwoods above Mendocino's Anderson Valley in 1995. Three generations of the Green family are involved in Black Kite today. They craft three elegant vineyard-designated Pinot Noirs from their 40 acres, including the acclaimed Redwoods' Edge, an intense Pinot from the highest plantings on the land; a combo offering, Kite's Rest, blended from the three vineyards; and in top years the reserve Angel Hawk. The winery stepped outside its estate in 2010 to produce a dark, full-bodied wine from the Santa Lucia Highlands.

BOTTLE TO TRY

● **Redwoods' Edge Pinot Noir** / **$$$**

BONNY DOON VINEYARD

Talented Central Coast vintner Randall Grahm is the winemaking equivalent of the pop star who hit it big with Top 40 tunes, then gave it up to record idiosyncratic alt rock. Grahm sold his wildly successful Cardinal Zin and Big House brands in 2006 to focus on an eclectic range of biodynamically farmed, *terroir*-driven wines—made mostly from Rhône varieties and lesser-known Italian and Spanish grapes. Grahm is capable of hitting the heights and of disappointing, but this has been one of the most dynamic, cutting-edge wineries in California for many years.

BOTTLES TO TRY

● **Vin Gris de Cigare** / **$$**

● **Le Cigare Volant** / **$$$**

BREWER-CLIFTON

Steve Clifton and Greg Brewer are two very talented winemakers whose skills are on display at Palmina (Clifton), and Diatom and Melville (Brewer). They convene here to celebrate the Cal-Burgundian possibilities of Pinot Noir and Chardonnay in the extended growing seasons of the cool-climate Sta. Rita Hills of Santa Barbara County. Their sure-handed track record in producing sophisticated, full-bodied wines has placed them in the forefront of this intriguing appellation.

BOTTLES TO TRY

○ **Mount Carmel Chardonnay** / **$$$**
● **Ampelos Pinot Noir** / **$$$**

CADE ESTATE WINERY

The in-crowd behind PlumpJack—Gordon Getty, Gavin Newsom and John Conover—built this small stunner of a winery 1,800 feet up on Napa Valley's Howell Mountain to showcase organic grapes and a more supple style of mountain Cabernet. The first few vintages have proved that the estate itself can produce wines that keep company with Napa's finest, but two Cabernets made partly from purchased grapes—the Napa Valley and Howell Mountain bottlings—are also well worth pursuing. A sometimes overlooked gem: the estate's layered, linger-on-the-tongue Sauvignon Blanc.

BOTTLES TO TRY

○ **Estate Sauvignon Blanc** / **$$$**
● **Howell Mountain Cabernet Sauvignon** / **$$$$**

CAIN VINEYARD & WINERY

Part of the Napa Valley wave of the early 1980s, Cain consists of 550 spectacularly scenic acres at the top of Spring Mountain, carved from a historic sheep ranch. The winery today concentrates its efforts on three Bordeaux-style reds: Cuvée, a multi-grape blend based on Merlot, Cabernet Franc and Cabernet Sauvignon; Five, an estate wine composed of the five major Bordeaux blending grapes; and Concept, a blend of richer, lower-elevation grapes. As a general rule, Cain's wines eschew the prevalent blockbuster style in favor of classical weight—so they're not always a big hit with the wine raters.

BOTTLE TO TRY

● **Cain Five** / **$$$$**

CAMERON HUGHES WINE

A man with a plan since he began selling wine out of his station wagon in 2002, Cameron Hughes is a *négociant* who buys wine from others, bottles it and sells it, often at a fraction of the wine's price under its original name. Consumers have responded to his eye—and palate—for a bargain, evident in his globe-spanning five labels, from the anonymous Lot Series (each of whose wines is assigned a unique lot number) to the "grapes-to-glass" Hughes Wellman Napa Valley Cabernet Sauvignon. Hughes's success at selecting terrific wines is impressive.

BOTTLE TO TRY
- Zin Your Face Zinfandel / $

CAYMUS VINEYARDS

Caymus's Special Selection Cabernet Sauvignon defined classic Napa Valley Cab in the 1970s, when it helped create the California cult wine phenomenon. The torch was passed from father to son—the winery is now in its third generation under the Wagner family—and Special Selection is still going strong. The Wagners also offer two less-costly wines that have a taste of Caymus's big, bold style: the Napa Valley Cabernet and a small-lot Zinfandel.

BOTTLES TO TRY
- Napa Valley Zinfandel / $$$
- Napa Valley Cabernet Sauvignon / $$$$

CHIMNEY ROCK

This familiar Napa Valley winery, with its whitewashed Cape Dutch architecture, was acquired in 2004 by the Terlato family of Chicagoland-based wine import and distribution powerhouse Terlato International. They have poured resources into upgrading the winery's facilities while wisely retaining its root philosophy: producing Cabernet Sauvignons that express the privileged Stags Leap District growing site. The result is a sometimes confusing array of estate-grown Cab bottlings, which are generally full-bodied but typically fleshy, supple and palate flattering. There is also an estimable white, Elevage Blanc, a blend of Sauvignon Blanc and Sauvignon Gris.

BOTTLES TO TRY
- ○ Elevage Blanc / $$$
- Stags Leap District Cabernet Sauvignon / $$$$

RARITIES & COLLECTIBLES

AUBERT WINES Mark Aubert's fanaticism for tiny yields of explosively intense fruit is abetted by his star vineyard manager, Ulises Valdez. The Chardonnays that Aubert crafts are large scale and hedonistic, with years-long waiting lists.

KONGSGAARD John Kongsgaard takes his layered Chardonnays to the edge, leaving them to an extended fermentation in barrel that would make other vintners lose sleep. The secret: his unique fruit, including grapes from his grandfather's vineyard for his stunning The Judge Chardonnay.

MARCASSIN Cult-wine icon Helen Turley owns this label with her viticulturist husband, John Wetlaufer. Despite the fog and chill of the extreme Sonoma Coast, Turley's small yields and late harvests result in mouth-filling, rich and ripe Chardonnays.

CLIFF LEDE VINEYARDS

The scion of a Canadian construction company fortune, Cliff Lede has put his passion—and his considerable capital—to work in this showplace Napa Valley floor winery, in his art-filled home situated on a knoll above it and in the luxurious Poetry Inn perched on a hillside across the way. The winery's Bordeaux-style wines more than hold their own in their super-premium-priced competitive set; the flagship Poetry bottling is a benchmark in the dense, ripe-fruit Napa style, but it's wrapped up with a sure-handed Stags Leap–area elegance.

BOTTLES TO TRY
- ○ Sauvignon Blanc / $$
- ● Claret / $$$

CLOS LACHANCE

Bill and Brenda Murphy began as hobby winemakers, but they have built Clos LaChance into one of the Central Coast's most respected wineries. Next door to the Santa Cruz Mountains appellation, Clos LaChance crafts well-priced wines, including vanilla- and toast-inflected Chardonnays and, among the reds, an estate Zinfandel, single-vineyard Pinots and Rhône-inspired blends from younger vineyards in warmer San Martin.

BOTTLES TO TRY
- ○ Santa Cruz Mountains Chardonnay / $
- ● Estate Zinfandel / $$

COPAIN WINES

Francophile Wells Guthrie turns out some exceptionally graceful and subtle Pinot Noirs, Chardonnays and Syrahs—yes, subtle California Syrahs. Though his winery is located in Sonoma County, most of his grape sources are up north in cool, coastal-influenced Mendocino, from which he manages to coax flavorful wines with moderate—you might even say traditionally French—alcohol levels and richness profiles. Copain's Tous Ensemble wines are notable bargains, the food-friendly Pinot Noir in particular.

BOTTLES TO TRY

○ **Tous Ensemble Chardonnay** ∕ **$$**
● **Tous Ensemble Pinot Noir** ∕ **$$**

CORISON WINERY

Highly respected winemaker Cathy Corison lent her talents to such star producers as Staglin Family Vineyard and Long Meadow Ranch before devoting herself to her own boutique Napa Valley label. She produces small amounts of four cuvées, including a Gewürztraminer and a Cabernet Franc, but her best wines are the Cabernet Sauvignons: the single-vineyard, sustainably grown Kronos and the Napa Valley, which is sourced from the Rutherford Bench. In both, Corison crafts expertly balanced, assured wines that aim for finesse and harmony over sheer strength.

BOTTLES TO TRY

○ **Gewürztraminer** ∕ **$$$**
● **Kronos Vineyard Cabernet Sauvignon** ∕ **$$$$**

DASHE CELLARS

From their base in downtown Oakland, co-owners and husband-and-wife team Michael and (French-trained) Anne Dashe seek out old vines, rocky hillsides and special locales for their *terroir*-based, small-production wines. Though Dashe produces wines from a number of grapes, it is best known by far as a Zinfandel specialist, with styles ranging from the chewy, dark, deeply concentrated Todd Brothers Ranch bottling to a sweet, dessert-style late-harvest Zin. Les Enfants Terribles is a special line of limited-production wines made from cool-climate vineyards.

BOTTLE TO TRY

● **Todd Brothers Ranch Zinfandel** ∕ **$$$**

DAVID ARTHUR VINEYARDS

Pritchard Hill, on the eastern slope of Napa Valley, is now hallowed Cabernet Sauvignon ground, but when Donald Long and his son David came along in 1978, they had to wrestle their first vines out of the rocky ground at 1,200 feet. That 21-acre vineyard now yields four reds, including the Cabernet-Sangiovese blend Meritaggio and the top-end Elevation 1147, as well as a Chardonnay that is grown downvalley and closer to sea level.

BOTTLES TO TRY

○ **Chardonnay** / **$$$**
● **Elevation 1147 Cabernet Sauvignon** / **$$$$**

DELOACH VINEYARDS

The 2003 purchase of DeLoach by French wine entrepreneur Jean-Charles Boisset gradually shifted the venerable brand's emphasis from Zinfandel and Chardonnay to Pinot Noir, while retaining strong footholds in both of those varietals. Boisset's passion for biodynamic viticulture and Burgundian winemaking (low intervention, limited new oak, traditional methods) has brought a new attention to detail to the top bottlings, which include the Vineyard Designate, Estate and OFS lines. DeLoach is a generally high-percentage bet, though you need to be sure of what you're buying: The label encompasses a bewildering variety of price tiers.

BOTTLES TO TRY

○ **OFS Chardonnay** / **$$**
● **Estate Collection Pinot Noir** / **$$$**

DONKEY & GOAT

An in-town Berkeley-based winery, Donkey & Goat is owned and run with evangelical fervor by Jared Brandt and his wife, Tracey. The bread and butter here is Rhône-style wines, particularly the Syrahs sourced from several cool-climate North Coast vineyards, but the winery also turns out some well-regarded Pinot Noir and versions of Chardonnay. All of the wines are made naturally (no adding lab yeast or enzymes, fining or filtering, or overoaking), which allows the fruit and *terroir* to come to the fore.

BOTTLES TO TRY

○ **Grenache Blanc 100% Skin Fermented** / **$$**
● **The Recluse Syrah** / **$$$**

DREW

Jason Drew's evolving artisan operation will eventually feature Pinot Noir from the farthest west—that is, closest to the ocean—vineyard in Mendocino County (planted in 2011). Meanwhile, mailing-list members have the best chance of tasting his impressive translations of grapes from some of Mendocino's finest small-grower vineyards. These aren't the easiest places in California to ripen grapes—that's the point—but the best wines that emerge have a taut, lively distinctiveness.

BOTTLES TO TRY

○ **Albariño / $$**

● **Fog-Eater Pinot Noir / $$$**

EDMUNDS ST. JOHN

Steve Edmunds is a true California maverick, making Rhône-style wine—in Berkeley—long before Rhône was fashionable. He's the kind of talented, charming anomaly the North Coast wine business could use more of. Edmunds's wines are personal, *terroir*-driven (he's a committed vineyard scout) and defiantly out of the high-alcohol, heavy-extraction mainstream. They are often built for the long haul—particularly the Syrahs—and are less immediately palate-flattering when young, but the best offer up astonishments as they mature.

BOTTLES TO TRY

○ **Heart of Gold / $$**

● **Bassetti Vineyard Syrah / $$$**

EHLERS ESTATE

In the mid-1980s, French entrepreneur Jean Leducq began buying parcels of Napa Valley land centered on Bernard Ehlers's historic 1886 winery. By the time of Leducq's death in 2002, the property had expanded to include 43 contiguous acres of prime vineyard land plus the winery, and was left in trust as part of his and his wife Sylviane's substantial philanthropic endeavors. Farmed biodynamically and organically by winemaker Kevin Morrisey, the property specializes in rich, expressive Bordeaux-grape reds, including Cabernet Franc and Merlot, and produces an estimable Sauvignon Blanc as well.

BOTTLES TO TRY

○ **Sauvignon Blanc / $$**

● **1886 Cabernet Sauvignon / $$$$**

FAILLA

One of California's quieter winemaking superstars, Ehren Jordan (whose résumé includes a stint in the Rhône Valley with Jean-Luc Colombo) last year left his longtime job at Turley Wine Cellars to concentrate on multiappellation winemaking at Failla, which is named for his wife and partner, Anne-Marie Failla. Though the winery is in Napa, nearly all of its often-superb Pinot Noirs (plus some Chardonnay, Viognier and Syrah) are sourced from the cool, foggy Pacific Coast, mostly in Sonoma County's rugged coastal range. The flagship Pinots are grown in marginal climates and made with low-tech, traditional winemaking techniques.

BOTTLES TO TRY

○ **Estate Vineyard Chardonnay** / **$$$**
● **Keefer Ranch Pinot Noir** / **$$$**

FLORA SPRINGS

A familiar presence to Napa Valley visitors thanks to its multi-venue tasting room near St. Helena on Highway 29, Flora Springs was an abandoned 19th-century winery revived in the 1970s by Flora Komes and her husband, Jerry. Along with their children, the Komeses turned into dedicated producers and growers, farming what would eventually grow to 650 acres of vines. The third generation of the family—grandchildren Nat Komes and Sean Garvey—now run this Cabernet-focused winery, which also makes some terrific whites, including the stylish Sauvignon Blanc Soliloquy.

BOTTLES TO TRY

○ **Soliloquy Vineyard Sauvignon Blanc** / **$$**
● **Trilogy** / **$$$**

FROG'S LEAP

Former Stag's Leap Wine Cellars winemaker John Williams crafts Frog's Leap wines in a restrained, food-friendly style that was ahead of its time when he started in the 1980s but is now in fashion. Also forward-looking: Since the 1980s, Frog's Leap has been committed to eco-friendly farming, and forgoes chemicals, pesticides and even irrigation in its vineyards.

BOTTLES TO TRY

○ **Sauvignon Blanc** / **$$**
● **Zinfandel** / **$$**

GALLO SIGNATURE SERIES/ESTATE WINES

This is the upscale, local-*terroir* face of the global megabrand (the mother ship, E. & J. Gallo Winery, is behind a multitude of labels from Alamos to Wycliff). Winemaker Gina Gallo and her brother Matt teamed up on this higher-end label anchored by bottlings from Gallo vineyards in Sonoma, Napa and Monterey counties. At the top of the pyramid are two acclaimed estate cuvées created from the best of Gallo's deep vineyard holdings in Sonoma County.

BOTTLES TO TRY

○ **Signature Series Chardonnay** / **$$**

○ **Estate Chardonnay** / **$$$**

● **Estate Cabernet Sauvignon** / **$$$$**

HALL WINES

Hall was founded in 2001 by the charismatic Kathryn Hall, a former U.S. ambassador to Austria, and her husband, Dallas financier Craig Hall. The winery's full-bodied California takes on Bordeaux-style blends are sourced from the Rutherford estate's 400 or so acres, most of which are sustainably farmed. The Napa Valley Collection, four wines blended from estate vineyards, including the flagship Kathryn Hall Cabernet, are the winery's main offerings. But there are a slew of smaller-production, single-vineyard Artisan Collection wines as well.

BOTTLES TO TRY

○ **T Bar T Ranch Sauvignon Blanc** / **$$**

● **Kathryn Hall Cabernet Sauvignon** / **$$$$**

HANZELL VINEYARDS

Burgundy-loving James Zellerbach, who served as the U.S. ambassador to Italy in the late 1950s, planted some of California's first post-Prohibition Chardonnay and Pinot Noir in Sonoma County in 1953, and Hanzell continues its founder's vision today. The winery's bottlings are somewhat closer to the European ideal than the California mainstream of instant gratification (i.e., loaded with sweet fruit and oak). Tightly wound when released, Hanzell's long-lived wines typically benefit from extended cellaring.

BOTTLES TO TRY

○ **Chardonnay** / **$$$$**

● **Pinot Noir** / **$$$$**

HARTFORD FAMILY WINERY

Attorney Don Hartford and his wife, Jennifer, had a potent calling card when they decided to found a winery: Her father was the late Jess Jackson of megabrand Kendall-Jackson. The Hartfords carved out their own niche in Sonoma County's Russian River Valley, making a range of generously bodied, expressive Pinot Noirs from coastal-influenced, cool-climate vineyards, including the well-known Velvet Sisters and Sevens Bench bottlings. The winery's other great claim to fame is its inky, old-vine Zinfandels, also typically vineyard designated.

BOTTLES TO TRY

○ **Far Coast Vineyard Chardonnay** ∕ **$$$**
● **Hartford Court Velvet Sisters Pinot Noir** ∕ **$$$**

HENDRY WINERY

In a land of Johnny-come-latelies, the Hendrys have been farming their Napa acreage since 1939. They show their confidence in their land—and in their skills—by working 10 different grapes, from Albariño to Zinfandel, right in the Cabernet heartland. But for fans of Hendry's wines (all of which are estate bottled), Cabernet rules—especially the well-priced, richly aromatic 100 percent–varietal bottling. Most of that wine's grapes are pulled from the ranch's top Block 8, which has received a separate bottling in some years.

BOTTLES TO TRY

○ **Hendry Vineyard Pinot Gris** ∕ **$$**
● **Hendry Vineyard Cabernet Sauvignon** ∕ **$$$**

HIRSCH VINEYARDS

David Hirsch was the pioneering visionary of far-western Sonoma. His wind-scoured mountaintop vineyards lie at the edge of the continent, less than a mile from the San Andreas Fault, and are subject to every peril from frost to flood to earthquake. His very low yielding vines set enough fruit for six extraordinary Pinot Noirs and a tiny amount of Chardonnay, all wines whose flavors reflect not only the marginal climate but also the jumble of soils thrown up along the fault zone in the Fort Ross–Seaview AVA.

BOTTLES TO TRY

○ **Chardonnay** ∕ **$$$**
● **San Andreas Fault Pinot Noir** ∕ **$$$**

HONIG VINEYARD & WINERY

A rare American winery that made its reputation on Sauvignon Blanc, Napa Valley's Honig produces three versions: the crisp, lively Napa bottling, aged in stainless steel tanks to retain its freshness; the Rutherford appellation estate bottling, which gets barrel aging; and a late-harvest dessert wine. The family's solar-powered winery and sustainably farmed vineyard acreage rest in the heart of Cabernet country, though, and Honig also produces well-regarded reds.

BOTTLES TO TRY

○ **Napa Valley Sauvignon Blanc** ⁄ **$$**

● **Campbell Vineyard Cabernet Sauvignon** ⁄ **$$$$**

HUNDRED ACRE/LAYER CAKE WINES

Hundred Acre wines are rarified, cult reds that sell for hundreds of dollars—if you can get your hands on them (join the waiting list). Layer Cake bottlings, often representing excellent values, can be found on supermarket shelves at very gentle prices. Their common denominator is Jayson Woodbridge, a flamboyant, obsessive, Harley-riding Canadian and former investment banker who, despite zero experience, plunged into winemaking in 2000—proving that you don't need decades of practice to fashion compelling wines.

BOTTLES TO TRY

○ **Layer Cake Chardonnay** ⁄ **$**

● **Layer Cake Malbec** ⁄ **$**

INGLENOOK

Only a storyteller like owner Francis Ford Coppola could do justice to this saga: One of Napa Valley's seminal 19th-century vineyards was split up over the years and its name slapped on countless bottles of jug wine. Starting with his Niebaum-Coppola tract four decades ago, Coppola managed to reunite the property and purchase the Inglenook name in 2011. The winery today produces a bewildering variety of wines; if none of them now hit the heights of Coppola's old Rubicon bottlings—including the current Rubicons—they are generally solid. The tasting room and museum are must-visits.

BOTTLES TO TRY

○ **Blancaneaux** ⁄ **$$$**

● **Edizione Pennino Zinfandel** ⁄ **$$$**

RARITIES & COLLECTIBLES

ARAUJO ESTATE WINES Bart and Daphne Araujo's Cabernets combine palate-flattering California ripeness with Margaux-like finesse—a magic act that relies on superb fruit. Its source is the Araujos' 125-year-old Eisele vineyard, one of Napa's top sites.

GRACE FAMILY VINEYARDS Committed to producing Cabernets as "a catalyst for healing our planet," this tiny estate is farmed organically and biodynamically. Said to be the creator of Napa's original cult Cabernet, Grace Family Vineyards makes wines that display balance and harmony as opposed to pure power.

SCREAMING EAGLE This celebrated Napa estate's Cabernet is arguably the New World's most sought-after collectors' wine. Its scarcity and soaring prices all but obscure the exceptional quality of the wine, with its lively, perfumed aromatics and suppleness.

JAFFURS WINE CELLARS

Although he owns no vineyards, Rhône-wine specialist Craig Jaffurs has propelled his label to the forefront of California Syrah in particular, thanks to his skill in prospecting vineyards and making the most of their fruit. His winery, located in downtown Santa Barbara (conveniently close to the surfing he loves), remains for all its accolades a small operation (4,500 cases); many of its very limited production wines are either available only to club members or sold out all too quickly.

BOTTLES TO TRY

○ **Viognier** / **$$**
● **Bien Nacido Vineyard Syrah** / **$$$**

J. DAVIES ESTATE/DAVIES VINEYARDS

Hugh Davies, proprietor of the premier sparkling wine producer Schramsberg (see p. 289), manages this twin-pronged effort. The graceful, well-knit J. Davies Cabernet Sauvignons come from the estate's own vineyards surrounding the house and winery on Napa's Diamond Mountain—land far better suited to Cab and Malbec than to sparkling wine grapes. New with the 2009 vintage are a series of Davies Vineyards Pinot Noirs from top vineyards like Ferrington and Londer.

BOTTLES TO TRY

● **Londer Vineyard Pinot Noir** / **$$$**
● **J. Davies Cabernet Sauvignon** / **$$$$**

JOSEPH SWAN VINEYARDS

Joe Swan, a former airline pilot who became an early 1970s pioneer in the cool-climate Russian River Valley—and a much admired figure in his generation—passed away in 1989. The winery today is headed by his son-in-law, Rod Berglund, who follows in Swan's footsteps with very reasonably priced Pinot Noirs and Zinfandels, plus small bottlings of seemingly whatever interests him from a particular vintage. These are the kind of hands-on, personal-scale and occasionally idiosyncratic wines that make California vineyards worth exploring.

BOTTLES TO TRY
- The Vineyard Next Door Rosé / $$
- Cuvée de Trois Pinot Noir / $$$

JUSTIN VINEYARDS & WINERY

With its boutique inn and restaurant and handsome tasting room, Paso Robles's Justin is a center of wine tourism on the Central Coast. Former investment banker Justin Baldwin's winery operation offers a fine Bordeaux-style flagship, the Cabernet-based Isosceles; its sister wine, the Merlot–Cabernet Franc blend Justification; and varietal bottlings of Cabernet Sauvignon. This high-energy enterprise also produces numerous other varietals, notably the allocated Focus Syrah, available through Justin's wine club.

BOTTLES TO TRY
- ○ Viognier / $$
- ● Isosceles / $$$$

KENDALL-JACKSON

This Sonoma-based megabrand has a straightforward formula for maintaining quality despite its huge size: source grapes from estate-owned vineyards instead of buying them from growers; use high-end techniques (like barrel aging) even on inexpensive wines; and rely on one of the industry's best palates, winemaster Randy Ullom, to mastermind the cellar. Best known for its ubiquitous Vintner's Reserve Chardonnay, the deep KJ portfolio also includes terrific single-vineyard offerings. Its top wine is the limited-production Bordeaux-style blend Stature.

BOTTLES TO TRY
- ○ Highland Estates Alisos Hills Viognier / $$$
- ● Highland Estates Hawkeye Mountain Cabernet Sauvignon / $$$

LA CREMA

In recent years, La Crema has rebuilt its reputation for high-quality Chardonnay and Pinot Noir, an impressive feat given the winery's significant output and very reasonable prices (this is a go-to label at restaurants). A key to its success is sourcing: With vineyards in some of Northern California's most Burgundy-variety-loving, cool-climate zones, such as the Russian River Valley and Sonoma Coast, La Crema builds from a foundation of fine grapes. The 2010 handover to former assistant wine-maker Elizabeth Grant-Douglas appears to be seamless.

BOTTLES TO TRY

○ **Sonoma Coast Chardonnay** / $$
● **Sonoma Coast Pinot Noir** / $$

LADERA VINEYARDS

When a film production company wanted to use Anne and Pat Stotesbery's vast Montana ranch for shooting one summer, the couple decamped to Napa Valley and fell in love with the wine business. The vineyard they purchased, on the site of a famous 19th-century winery, is perched high up (at 1,800 feet) on Howell Mountain, where well-drained, nutrient-poor soils produce the small, intensely flavored berries that give Ladera wines their concentrated, mountain-grown character.

BOTTLE TO TRY

● **Stile Blocks Cabernet Sauvignon** / $$$

LA FOLLETTE WINES

You'd never know from winemaker Greg La Follette's habitual uniform—worn overalls and a kind smile—that he's one of America's great masters of Pinot Noir and Chardonnay. A protégé of the late, great André Tchelistcheff, La Follette is as humble as he is accomplished, with a résumé filled with top brands such as Flowers, Hartford Court and Londer. At his namesake label, La Follette crafts several expressive, elegant wines from elite vineyards in Sonoma and one site in coastal Mendocino.

WINE INTEL
The Barlow, a new retail complex in a former apple cannery in the Sonoma town of Sebastopol, hosts La Follette's first tasting room, plus other artisan wine, food, beer and spirits producers.

BOTTLES TO TRY

○ **Sangiacomo Vineyard Chardonnay** / $$$
● **Manchester Ridge Vineyard Pinot Noir** / $$$

LAIL VINEYARDS

Founder Robin Lail is Napa Valley aristocracy. She is the great-grandniece of the legendary Gustave Niebaum, who founded Inglenook—and some would say Napa's reputation—in 1879, and the daughter of John Daniel, Jr., who continued Niebaum's legacy into the 1960s. Lail's daughter Erin Dixon, the winery's general manager, is the family's fifth generation in the Napa wine business. The winery produces five bottlings—three Cabernets and two Sauvignon Blancs—all with the renowned winemaker Philippe Melka's silky touch.

BOTTLES TO TRY

○ **Blueprint Sauvignon Blanc** / $$$
● **J. Daniel Cuvée** / $$$$
● **Mole Hill Cabernet Sauvignon** / $$$$

LANG & REED WINE COMPANY

Napa Valley veteran (and former Niebaum-Coppola general manager) John Skupny became obsessed with the potential of Cabernet Franc, Bordeaux's aromatic underdog grape, which gets blended into many California reds but rarely takes center stage. Since 1996 Skupny, in partnership with his wife, Tracey, has combed vineyards and nurseries to determine the finest Cabernet Franc clones—his latest discovery, from the Loire, is 214, now an eponymous wine—and the best sites in Napa Valley to grow them. The resulting reds show off the variety's seductive side, brimming with blueberry and spice notes.

BOTTLE TO TRY

● **North Coast Cabernet Franc** / $$

LARKIN WINES

Scotsman Sean Larkin, a self-described "bon vivant and bona fide Napa Valley Cabernet Franc producer," is the talented winemaker behind Larkin Wines. The label produces an extremely limited amount of wine that sells out quickly, with a defining character of bold flavor and concentration. Larkin's other labels include Jack Larkin—named for his son—and Grand Wines, touted as "genuine Napa quality at recessionary prices," which means $20 to $35 in Napa Valley.

BOTTLES TO TRY

○ **Grand Sauvignon Blanc** / $$
● **Cabernet Franc** / $$$

LARKMEAD VINEYARDS

One of a handful of Napa Valley heritage properties to operate continuously since the 19th century (through Prohibition), Larkmead today is a top-notch producer of Bordeaux-style reds but doesn't always receive the popular recognition it has earned. The 7,000 all-estate-grown cases produced by this family-owned property are overseen by the well-regarded Scottish-born winemaker Andy Smith and include a series of distinctive, luxury-priced reds: the LMV Salon, Solari and the Lark. But the more wallet-friendly Napa Valley Cabernet is extraordinary, too, though heading skyward in price itself.

BOTTLE TO TRY

● Cabernet Sauvignon / $$$$

LAUREL GLEN VINEYARD

Beginning with the first vintage in 1981, Patrick Campbell's elegant, firmly structured Sonoma Mountain wines helped prove that Napa's neighbor could produce top-tier Cabernet Sauvignon, too. In 2011, Campbell sold the winery to industry veteran Bettina Sichel, who enlisted star consultant David Ramey and organic-viticulture guru Phil Coturri to put their stamp on the wines, which are made from grapes grown on a single 16-acre estate. In keeping with tradition, the winery focuses on two bottlings—Laurel Glen Vineyard and the more affordable Counterpoint—both 100 percent Cabernet Sauvignon.

BOTTLE TO TRY

● Laurel Glen Vineyard Cabernet Sauvignon / $$$$

LEWIS CELLARS

Founded by former Indy car driver Randy Lewis ("driven ... to create world-class wines") and his wife, Debbie, this well-regarded small producer—Lewis Cellars turns out about 9,000 cases annually—made its mark with spicy, full-throttle reds. The connoisseur's choice is the pricey Cabernet Sauvignon–based Cuvée L, produced only in top vintages. But Lewis followers also appreciate the far more affordable Alec's Blend, a juicy combo of Syrah and Merlot with a touch of Cabernet that showcases the winery's deep-fruit style.

BOTTLES TO TRY

○ Barcaglia Lane Chardonnay / $$$$
● Alec's Blend / $$$$

LIOCO

Former Spago Beverly Hills sommelier Kevin O'Connor and his buddy Matt Licklider, a onetime wine importer, share a passion for Chardonnay and Pinot Noir with lithe, vibrant flavors—the kind grown in Burgundy and in California's coolest wine regions. In 2005 they teamed up to create their own versions with LIOCO, a label focusing on naturally made Pinot Noir and Chardonnay—and a few lesser-appreciated, underdog varieties—sourced from a handful of top vineyards. The often-outstanding wines are all natural-yeast fermented, low- to non-oak impacted, and bottled with minimal intervention.

BOTTLES TO TRY

○ **Sonoma County Chardonnay** ╱ **$$**

● **Sonoma Coast Pinot Noir** ╱ **$$$**

LORING WINE COMPANY

Brian Loring, a self-confessed "Pinot freak," has a nose for great California and Oregon vineyards and seemingly wants to bottle a wine from each of them. His punk rockish, purple spray-paint-stenciled logo adorns the bottles, which list an all-star team of growers: Shea, Garys' Vineyard, Keefer Ranch. There is also a less costly line of AVA blends. The wines are purposely varied—Loring wants them to reflect the vineyards and growers—but they are typically at the rich, fruity, boisterous end of both the Pinot Noir and Chardonnay spectrums.

BOTTLES TO TRY

○ **Durell Vineyard Chardonnay** ╱ **$$$**

● **Rosella's Vineyard Pinot Noir** ╱ **$$$**

LOUIS M. MARTINI WINERY

A focus on big, bold Cabernet Sauvignons has reinvented this old-time Napa Valley producer, which started out making jug wines after the repeal of Prohibition. Mike Martini, grandson of Louis M., and the winemaker for nearly 40 years, fashions five exemplary Cabernets, among them the amazingly value-priced Sonoma County bottling, all the way up to the famous flagship Monte Rosso. Martini carries a well-deserved name for Zinfandel, too, including the exemplary Gnarly Vine version—also sourced from the Monte Rosso Vineyard.

BOTTLE TO TRY

● **Monte Rosso Cabernet Sauvignon** ╱ **$$$$**

MARSTON FAMILY VINEYARD

Michael and Alexandra Marston began farming a portion of their 500-acre ranch on the southern slopes of Napa Valley's Spring Mountain in 1969. However, it wasn't until 1998 that they went back to the drawing board (under the tutelage of star wine consultant Philippe Melka) and concentrated on the estate-bottled Cabernet Sauvignons they're known for today. Their vineyard is well situated above the fog line for plenty of sunshine, but at an elevation of up to 1,100 feet, which gives it a cooler, more extended growing season than the valley floor. Beginning with the 2010 vintage, Melka handed over the reins to Sierra Leone–born consultant winemaker Marbue Marke.

BOTTLE TO TRY
- Cabernet Sauvignon / $$$$

MATTHIASSON

Many winemakers talk about how "wine is made in the vineyard," but Steve Matthiasson, a FOOD & WINE Winemaker of the Year in 2012, has lived it: In his day job, he is a much-sought-after vineyard consultant. At the heart of his efforts as a winemaker are the Red, a Merlot-based Bordeaux blend with an emphasis on finesse as much as on power, and the White, a kitchen-sink blend based on Sauvignon Blanc but with portions of Ribolla Gialla, Sémillon and Tocai Friulano that somehow merge into a flavorful harmony.

BOTTLES TO TRY
- ○ Napa Valley White / $$$
- ● Napa Valley Red / $$$$

MERRY EDWARDS WINERY

You could call Merry Edwards a grande dame of California winemaking, except that she's too down-to-earth. Besides, she prefers "Reine de Pinot" (Queen of Pinot)—the title that appears on her business cards. A pioneer of clone-specific winegrowing, Edwards has been perfecting her sure-handed style of lush, nuanced Pinot Noir for more than 40 years. One secret: a creamy, grower-style (estate grown and vinified) sparkling wine that fans wish she would make more often.

BOTTLES TO TRY
- ○ Sauvignon Blanc / $$$
- ● Olivet Lane Pinot Noir / $$$$

MINER FAMILY WINERY

Miner is familiar to Napa Valley visitors for its Silverado Trail tasting room, featuring a nearly bewildering array of generally high-quality, reasonably priced (for Napa) wines. Owner Dave Miner left the software business back in 1993 to follow his vinous dreams and founded the winery in 1996. He owns some prime land but also pursues contracts with numerous vineyards around the state, with the proviso that he specifies the farming practices. The most famous result of these collaborations is The Oracle, a complex, concentrated red Bordeaux blend sourced from the Stagecoach Vineyard high up on Atlas Peak.

BOTTLES TO TRY

○ **Wild Yeast Chardonnay** / **$$$**
● **The Oracle** / **$$$$**

MORLET FAMILY VINEYARDS

Luc Morlet was slated to take over his family's Champagne domaine. Instead– *cherchez la femme*—he fell in love with an American woman, settled in California and worked his way up to become one of the state's most vaunted artisan winemakers. A veteran of cult producers Peter Michael Winery (where brother Nick now presides) and Staglin Family Vineyard, Morlet created his own instantly coveted label in 2006, with his wife, Jodie. Morlet is best known for tiny lots (join the mailing list) of meticulously produced Pinot and Chardonnay, but he also crafts notable Cabernets and Syrah.

BOTTLES TO TRY

○ **Ma Douce Chardonnay** / **$$$$**
● **Côteaux Nobles Pinot Noir** / **$$$$**

NALLE WINERY

Doug Nalle is a humorous man with a serious intent and a major stubborn streak. At his winery in the Zinfandel heartland of Sonoma's Dry Creek Valley, he steadfastly refuses to produce the jammy, high-alcohol Zins that have been an industry fashion for many years. Nalle has carved out a niche for graceful, claret-like Zins with plenty of stuffing but also a food-loving elegance. His son Andrew, now the winemaker, is a fifth-generation Dry Creek Valley farmer who also turns out a notable Pinot Noir.

BOTTLE TO TRY

● **Zinfandel** / **$$$**

RARITIES & COLLECTIBLES

PAUL LATO WINES By dint of his passion and talent—and vineyard choices—Polish-born sommelier-turned-winemaker Paul Lato has struck a chord with lovers of voluptuous, expressive Pinot Noirs like his Duende Gold Coast and Pisoni bottlings.

RHYS VINEYARDS Owner Kevin Harvey's elegant Burgundian Pinot Noirs have caught the attention of America's wine critics, who praise the ability of this Santa Cruz Mountains estate to imbue each of its complex wines with the distinct personality of its vineyard source.

SEA SMOKE In the foggy western reaches of Santa Barbara's Sta. Rita Hills AVA, Sea Smoke crafts vibrant, full-flavored, highly polished Pinot Noirs from a palette of 10 all-estate-grown clones—hence the name of the sought-after Ten bottling.

OPUS ONE

The late Robert Mondavi and the late Baron Philippe de Rothschild of Bordeaux's Château Mouton Rothschild modeled this Napa Valley joint venture winery after a *grand cru* Bordeaux, with their focus on a high-end Cabernet-based blend wine from vines so meticulously clipped they resemble topiary. The second wine, a junior version known as Overture, is crafted to be softer on the palate and more readily approachable in its youth. After a dip in quality in the 1990s, Opus One has reassumed its place among California's iconic reds.

BOTTLE TO TRY
- ● Opus One / $$$$

ORIN SWIFT CELLARS

The curious wine names here—The Prisoner, Mercury Head, Papillon—can be traced to the marketing mind of David Swift Phinney, who operates this modestly sized but growing Napa Valley–based endeavor, as well as other far-flung wine projects from Argentina to Corsica. The winery turns out a number of innovative, not to say idiosyncratic, blends (The Prisoner, for example, is Zin-based, but with Cabernet, Syrah and some Charbono for good measure), all with big, lively, exuberant flavors.

BOTTLES TO TRY
- ○ Veladora / $$
- ● The Prisoner / $$$

O'SHAUGHNESSY ESTATE WINERY

Inky, full-bodied, mountain-grown Cabernet Sauvignon–based reds from estate vineyards on Howell Mountain and Mount Veeder made the name of this boutique Napa Valley producer. Winemaker Sean Capiaux, famous among cognoscenti for his own Capiaux Cellars Pinots, makes these wines for Betty O'Shaughnessy Woolls and her family with a full appreciation for Cabernet's potential for depth and power. The Howell Mountain bottling is essentially a Meritage (see p. 164), with a slew of Bordeaux-derived blending grapes giving it nuance; the Mount Veeder is flat-out 100 percent Cabernet Sauvignon.

BOTTLE TO TRY

● **Mount Veeder Cabernet Sauvignon** ⁄ **$$$$**

PALI WINE COMPANY

Pali is a labor of love from two passionate Pinot Noir connoisseurs who roam from Oregon to Santa Barbara County—their facility is in Lompoc—searching out worthy vineyards, with notable success. Among other things, the winery's fans love its remarkable price-to-value ratio. The affordable line of Pinots offers regional blends named for neighborhoods in the proprietors' hometown of Pacific Palisades. The still gently priced vineyard-designated line includes bottlings from esteemed growers like Durell, Shea and Fiddlestix.

BOTTLES TO TRY

○ **Charm Acres Chardonnay** ⁄ **$$**

● **Durell Vineyard Pinot Noir** ⁄ **$$$**

PALMINA

Talented Steve Clifton of Brewer-Clifton fame (see p. 173) undertakes the Sisyphean task of producing and marketing Italian grape varieties—Nebbiolo, Sangiovese, Barbera, Malvasia—that have remained oddly obscure here, given the debt that California wine owes to Italian immigrants. No other great connoisseur's grape in the world has been as resistant to transplanted success as Piedmont's Nebbiolo, but Clifton at his best produces versions that are not just varietally correct but also juicy, dark, aromatically complex alternatives.

BOTTLES TO TRY

○ **Malvasia Bianca** ⁄ **$$**

● **Honea Vineyard Nebbiolo** ⁄ **$$$$**

PEAY VINEYARDS

The Peay vineyard is a 51-acre site spread over a dramatic ridge at Sonoma County's remote northwestern edge. Its cool, foggy, windy climate makes ripening grapes a nail-biting exercise for winemaker Vanessa Wong (formerly of Peter Michael) and the Peay brothers, Nick and Andy, who planted their vines in the late '90s. The payoff comes in riveting, world-class Pinot Noirs, Syrahs and Chardonnays—vibrant, expressive wines with an emphatic sense of place.

BOTTLES TO TRY

○ Estate Chardonnay / $$$
● Scallop Shelf Pinot Noir / $$$

PETER MICHAEL WINERY

One of California's most highly praised—and highly priced—producers, this winery was founded by a Briton, Sir Peter Michael, who bought close to a square mile of volcanic mountainside in Sonoma's Knights Valley in 1982. Limited production and a strong following make these French-named wines (Les Pavots, Point Rouge, Cuvée Indigène) hard to find, but persistence (or getting on the mailing list) will reward Chardonnay and red Bordeaux lovers with expressive, full-flavored, palate-saturating wines. Most of the acclaimed Pinot Noirs hail from the Seaview Vineyard, on the windy Sonoma Coast.

BOTTLES TO TRY

○ Mon Plaisir / $$$$
● Les Pavots / $$$$

PINE RIDGE VINEYARDS

Part of the Crimson Wine Group that owns Seghesio and Oregon's Archery Summit, Pine Ridge produces wine from its numerous vineyards across five Napa Valley appellations. The winery combines fruit from these varied locations into several Bordeaux-style proprietary blends, including the top-of-the-line Fortis, the Cave 7 and the new Tessitura. Even the generally excellent Stags Leap District Cabernet Sauvignon is blended from four estate vineyards within that single subregion. A secondary line of affordable wines is also available.

BOTTLES TO TRY

○ Chenin Blanc–Vicgnier / $
● Stags Leap District Cabernet Sauvignon / $$$$

QUPÉ

One of the Central Coast's original Rhône Rangers, Qupé founder Bob Lindquist fashions extraordinary Syrah, for starters, at his "modern stone age winery." And while most of his wines are small-lot, single-vineyard bottlings, his affordable Central Coast Syrah offers a fine sampling of his spicy, vibrant style. Lindquist's white wines, which are sometimes overshadowed by the reputation of his refined reds, offer incredible quality for the price.

BOTTLES TO TRY

○ **Sawyer Lindquist Vineyard Viognier** ∕ **$$$**
● **Bien Nacido Vineyard Syrah** ∕ **$$**

RAMEY WINE CELLARS

David Ramey is so affable and unpretentious that a stranger might not guess that he is one of California's most respected trendsetting winemakers. After running the show at prestigious producers like Chalk Hill, Dominus and Rudd, and gaining a reputation for groundbreaking Chardonnays and Cabernets—a relatively rare combination—Ramey and his wife, Carla, created their own label in 1996. Deep personal connections with growers allow Ramey to source grapes from a dazzling collection of top vineyards, including Chardonnay from Sonoma's sea-cooled reaches and Cabernet from the warmer Napa Valley.

BOTTLES TO TRY

○ **Hudson Vineyard Chardonnay** ∕ **$$$**
● **Claret** ∕ **$$$**

RAVENSWOOD

When Joel Peterson started making Zinfandel in the 1970s, he was an evangelist for bold, full-throttle, deeply purple Zins that were as far from the prevailing White Zinfandel blush wines as you could get. His "No Wimpy Wines" credo remains operative at Ravenswood to this day, even though the megabrand—encompassing affordable entry-level wines in the Vintners Blend series as well as the mid-priced County series and somewhat pricier single-vineyard offerings—has become part of the portfolio of the wine giant Constellation Brands.

BOTTLES TO TRY

○ **Sangiacomo Vineyard Chardonnay** ∕ **$$**
● **Dickerson Vineyard Zinfandel** ∕ **$$$**

RIDGE VINEYARDS

Ridge Vineyards' iconic reputation rests both on Monte Bello, the profound, world-class Cabernet-based blend that's sourced from the winery's home hilltop vineyard in the Santa Cruz Mountains, and on some of California's premier old-vine Zinfandels, notably Sonoma's Geyserville and Lytton Springs bottlings. But presiding guru Paul Draper turns out a plethora of exciting wines at a range of prices—this is one of California's most reliable fine-wine labels. Much underappreciated: Ridge's remarkable hand with silky Chardonnays.

BOTTLES TO TRY

○ **Estate Chardonnay** / **$$$**
● **Geyserville** / **$$$**

ROBERT KEENAN WINERY

Robert Keenan was a pioneer in the mid-1970s when he bushwhacked his way into the forests of Spring Mountain and bought a long-defunct 19th-century vineyard site. The winery, now run by his son Michael, with winemaking overseen by consultant Nils Venge (see Saddleback Cellars, p. 196), has largely stuck to its '70s roots, with plantings of Cabernet Sauvignon, Merlot and Chardonnay, but the quality level has risen since the mid-2000s on Michael's watch. In addition to the signature Cabs, a stellar lineup of Merlots includes the well-priced-for-Napa, non-estate Merlot and tops out with the curiously named Mernet estate blend of Cabernet and Merlot.

BOTTLE TO TRY

● **Keenan Reserve Cabernet Sauvignon** / **$$$$**

ROBERT MONDAVI WINERY

Robert Mondavi transformed the California wine industry with his namesake winery, founded in 1966. With the cellar in the hands of Geneviève Janssens for the past 15 vintages, Mondavi wines compete with Napa's best at the high end and offer some terrific values on less-pricey bottlings. Mondavi retains some of Napa's most prized sources for Cabernet, though the winery that invented the name Fumé Blanc (for Sauvignon Blanc) deserves its reputation for that wine as well.

BOTTLES TO TRY

○ **Fumé Blanc** / **$$**
● **Napa Valley Cabernet Sauvignon** / **$$**

SADDLEBACK CELLARS

Longtime Napa Valley stalwart Nils Venge is a winemaker's winemaker, not only because he consults for several prestigious outfits, but also because of his winemaking at Saddleback Cellars, his Oakville base, where he crafts numerous small lots of whatever strikes his fancy. But it was his way with luxuriously supple, palate-flattering Cabernet Sauvignon that put Venge on the map. The top offering is the pricey Cabernet Sauvignon Reserve, but the less expensive Napa Valley Cabernet can be luscious as well.

BOTTLES TO TRY

○ **Chardonnay** / **$$**
● **Napa Valley Cabernet Sauvignon** / **$$$**

SANDHI

A Pinot and Chardonnay specialist in the cool-climate Sta. Rita Hills, Sandhi is part of wine entrepreneur Charles Banks's international portfolio (Mulderbosch, Leviathan), founded in 2010 with two notable partners: sommelier Rajat Parr and winemaker Sashi Moorman. Its wines are defined both by what they are not (not over-rich, over-alcoholic or over-oaked) and by what they hope to be: naturally made, with finesse, structure and balance. Sourced from some of the area's top vineyards, Sandhi's first two releases were met with great acclaim.

WINE INTEL
Sandhi's success led Rajat Parr and Sashi Moorman to purchase a renowned 40-acre vineyard in the Sta. Rita Hills. They'll release Pinot Noir and Chardonnay wines from it under the new Domaine de la Côte label.

BOTTLE TO TRY

○ **Rita's Crown Chardonnay** / **$$$**

THE SCHOLIUM PROJECT

Former philosophy professor Abe Schoener defies the conventional wisdom of "Never let the public taste your experiments." Seemingly every one of the quirkily named wines he makes in small quantities has an envelope-pushing intent. Schoener runs basically a one-man operation, and he would be the last one to say that all of his wines are wonderful—but some certainly are. Ideal for those who are wine curious with a sophisticated palate, Scholium is the cutting edge in action.

BOTTLES TO TRY

○ **Lost Slough Vineyards Naucratis** / **$$**
● **Tenbrink Babylon Vineyards** / **$$$$**

SEGHESIO FAMILY VINEYARDS

Though their winery has recently become part of the Crimson Wine Group (Pine Ridge, Archery Summit), the Seghesios were one of the first names in Zinfandel: They were farming Zin in Sonoma County in 1895, and buying up prime vineyard land—300 acres of it—through the decades since. This affords certain luxuries: The vines that produce Seghesio's spicy, briary Old Vines Zinfandel, for example, are on average 90 years old. The winery also produces small lots of intriguing Italian specialties, like Arneis and Sangiovese.

BOTTLES TO TRY

○ **Arneis** ⁄ **$$**

● **Old Vine Zinfandel** ⁄ **$$$**

SHAFER VINEYARDS

Shafer's longtime winemaker, Elias Fernandez, has a definite talent for fashioning formidable wines that maintain balance despite their power. That quality is best seen in the estate's monumental flagship cuvée, Hillside Select, arguably the iconic Cabernet Sauvignon of Napa Valley's Stags Leap District, where one-time publishing executive John Shafer transplanted his family in 1972. Easier to find are Shafer's three other reds: the One Point Five Cabernet; an inky Merlot; and a full-throttle Syrah blend, Relentless; plus, the super-juicy, ever-popular Red Shoulder Ranch Chardonnay.

BOTTLES TO TRY

○ **Red Shoulder Ranch Chardonnay** ⁄ **$$$**

● **Relentless** ⁄ **$$$$**

SILVER OAK CELLARS

This venerable winery catapulted to fame in the 1980s and '90s, and has retained a hold on wine lovers' affections ever since. Despite the retirement of founding winemaker and guiding light Justin Meyer several years back, Silver Oak's two appellation Cabernet Sauvignons, one from its winery in Sonoma's Alexander Valley and the other from its winery in Napa Valley, retain the brand's trademark lusciousness—a character that derives partly from their traditional later release, after extended aging in the cellar.

BOTTLE TO TRY

● **Alexander Valley Cabernet Sauvignon** ⁄ **$$$$**

SOJOURN CELLARS

A partnership between two tennis partners, Erich Bradley and Craig Haserot, Sojourn is a boutique producer in the town of Sonoma with access to some stupendous Pinot Noir, Cabernet Sauvignon and Chardonnay grapes. Headliners include the Beckstoffer Georges III Vineyard Cabernet from Napa and Gap's Crown Vineyard Pinot Noir from out on the Sonoma Coast. The wines do justice to their sites of origin; this is a reliable source of fine wine at a reasonable price. Given Sojourn's small production, fans may want to get on the mailing list.

BOTTLES TO TRY

○ **Sangiacomo Vineyard Chardonnay** ⁄ **$$$**
● **Gap's Crown Vineyard Pinot Noir** ⁄ **$$$**

SONOMA COAST VINEYARDS

Owned by Sonoma-based Vintage Wine Estates (Cartlidge & Browne, Cosentino, Girard), SCV bottles Pinot Noirs, Syrahs, Chardonnays and a Sauvignon Blanc from what the winery calls "the extreme Sonoma Coast," meaning out near the ocean where fog, cold and rain result in an entirely different climate and growing season from those of inland vineyards. The aim is to create wines of nervosity, with a Burgundy-style tautness and liveliness—an admirable challenge in this highly changeable vineyard environment.

BOTTLES TO TRY

○ **Gold Ridge Hills Chardonnay** ⁄ **$$**
● **Balistreri Vineyard Pinot Noir** ⁄ **$$$$**

SPOTTSWOODE ESTATE VINEYARD & WINERY

Spottswoode has been producing classically structured Napa Valley Cabernet since 1982, which puts it among the old guard of Napa's modern wine scene, but its lovely Victorian house and grounds in St. Helena date to more than 100 years earlier. Its wines come chiefly from the estate, which the Novak family has farmed organically for more than a quarter century. Both the signature Cabernet Sauvignon and the much-acclaimed Sauvignon Blanc are notable for their balance and elegance, though neither is a shrinking violet by any means.

BOTTLES TO TRY

○ **Sauvignon Blanc** ⁄ **$$$**
● **Estate Cabernet Sauvignon** ⁄ **$$$$**

SPRING MOUNTAIN VINEYARD

A stunningly picturesque property high above Napa Valley, Spring Mountain has an elaborate history (it's made up of several 19th-century vineyard properties) and uses the impressive Miravalle mansion for sit-down tastings. It also has a reputation for experimental sustainable viticulture: Those flocks of bluebirds? They're combating sharpshooter vine pests. The winery farms 225 acres out of nearly 850 on an estate that rises to elevations of 1,650 feet and produces wines as diverse as Pinot Noir, Syrah and Sauvignon Blanc. The signature Cabernet Sauvignon–based Elivette is sourced from low-yielding mountain soils that infuse the wine with a notable intensity of flavor.

BOTTLE TO TRY
- **Elivette / $$$$**

STAGLIN FAMILY VINEYARD

Since its founding in 1985, this estate has become a cornerstone of Napa's Rutherford District—and Shari and Garen Staglin, pillars of its community. Managed by the talented Fredrik Johansson (winemaker), David Abreu (viticulturist) and Michel Rolland (consultant), Staglin produces some of Napa's most sought-after Cabernet Sauvignons. Offerings range from pricey (the entry-level Salus Chardonnay) to extremely pricey (the INEO Cabernet blend), and availability isn't always a sure thing.

BOTTLES TO TRY
- ○ **Estate Chardonnay / $$$$**
- ● **Estate Cabernet Sauvignon / $$$$**

STAG'S LEAP WINE CELLARS

In 2007 Warren Winiarski sold his landmark Napa winery to Chateau Ste. Michelle and Tuscan vintner Piero Antinori, who brought star consultant Renzo Cotarella on board. Quality, already good, has been notched up: It's easy to imagine current vintages competing with marquee Bordeaux, the way a Stag's Leap Cabernet famously did at the legendary Paris tasting in 1976. The winery's estate-vineyard Bordeaux-style reds (Cask 23, S.L.V. and Fay Estate) lead the way, but its relatively affordable Napa Valley bottlings can be wonderful as well.

BOTTLES TO TRY
- ○ **Karia Chardonnay / $$$**
- ● **Artemis Cabernet Sauvignon / $$$**

STOLPMAN VINEYARDS

Trial lawyer/wine nut Tom Stolpman went on a quest for a cool-climate, limestone-soil vineyard and bought this property in Santa Barbara's Ballard Canyon in 1990. After successfully selling its dry-farmed, organic grapes to prestigious labels, the Stolpman family plunged in and began bottling their own Rhône varietals in 1997. The results have generally been impressive, particularly for Syrah and Roussanne, and the prices remain reasonable for the quality. Some of the very limited production estate wines are available only through Stolpman's wine club.

BOTTLES TO TRY

○ L'Avion Roussanne / $$$

● Originals Syrah / $$$

TENSLEY WINES

Joey Tensley's small family operation—he and his wife, Jennifer, often staff the Los Olivos tasting room themselves—rings the chimes of critics and lovers of big-scaled but nuanced Rhône-style wines for very fair prices. The core of the 3,300-case offerings are the vineyard-designated Syrahs sourced from top sites around Santa Barbara County, arguably led by the meaty, intense Colson Canyon Vineyard bottling. A novelty: The winery's website also offers hands-across-the-water wines—Détente and Deux Terres—that combine Tensley and Lea (Jennifer's label) wines with French wines from Burgundy and the Rhône.

BOTTLES TO TRY

○ Lea Mormann Vineyard Chardonnay / $$$

● Colson Canyon Vineyard Syrah / $$$

TERRE ROUGE AND EASTON

Operating outside the Napa-Sonoma orbit in the Sierra Nevada slopes of Amador County, Bill Easton bottles under two labels: Terre Rouge for Rhône-style wines, and Easton for more traditional wines like Zinfandel. Between the two, he may produce 20 different wines a year, but it is fair to say that it is the Syrahs and old-vine Zins that most consistently put his operation on connoisseurs' radar. Though the winery's star, Terre Rouge Ascent Syrah, is expensive, the heart of the portfolio is very well priced, especially considering its quality.

BOTTLE TO TRY

● Easton Fiddletown Old Vines Zinfandel / $$

TRICYCLE WINE CO.

The Molnar brothers—who grew up on their father's Poseidon's Vineyard in Napa's Carneros region—and pal Michael Terrien joined forces in this three-label, small-batch wine company. The Molnar Family label produces cool-climate Chardonnay and Pinot Noir from Poseidon's; Kazmer & Blaise offers a gutsier style of Pinot; and Obsidian Ridge, from a vineyard over the mountains in Lake County's Red Hills zone, is for Cabernet and Syrah. The Molnars' Hungarian roots show up in the barrels, which brother Peter sources from the forests of Tokaj.

BOTTLES TO TRY

○ **Molnar Family Chardonnay** ╱ **$$**
● **Primo's Hill Kazmer & Blaise Pinot Noir** ╱ **$$$**

TRINCHERO NAPA VALLEY

Like other famous California wine families, the Trincheros made a fortune in popularly priced wine—specifically by inventing White Zinfandel at their Sutter Home Winery. Bob Trinchero plowed a chunk of those profits into the creation of an ambitious, high-end estate, spending the better part of two decades amassing an impressive collection of vineyards across Napa's subregions, then purchasing the old Folie à Deux winery in 2004. Winemaker Mario Monticelli (a protégé of star consultant Philippe Melka) uses the varied vineyards to create a number of concentrated reds (and one white) from Bordeaux grapes.

BOTTLE TO TRY

● **Meritage** ╱ **$$$**

TURLEY WINE CELLARS

Larry Turley's once-small Napa Zinfandel operation got a strong liftoff back in the 1990s from its first winemaker, superstar (and Larry's sister) Helen Turley. With the reins handed off to the estimable Ehren Jordan and now Tegan Passalacqua, Turley has never looked back. Alas, because of the long wait to get on the list to buy the wines, many will never taste these full-throttle, explosively flavorful—yet at their best, remarkably complex—Zinfandels and Petite Sirahs, many sourced from decades- or century-old vineyards. Your best bet: Look for them at wine-oriented restaurants.

BOTTLE TO TRY

● **Ueberroth Zinfandel** ╱ **$$$**

VARNER

Twins Jim and Bob Varner have raised the profile of their tiny Santa Cruz Mountains winery by becoming, of all things, Chardonnay specialists. They haven't turned their backs on the pure gratification that ripe California fruit brings to Chardonnay—and that often gets it dismissed by wine snobs. But the Varner brothers' deft hand with Chardonnay lends it a structured, delineated European finesse that puts their wines into a different league. Their fans also appreciate their touch with Pinot Noir and the often-remarkable value of their Foxglove second label.

BOTTLES TO TRY

○ **Bee Block Chardonnay** / **$$$**
● **Neely Hidden Block Pinot Noir** / **$$**

VIADER

Argentinean-born Delia Viader came to Napa Valley in the 1980s with an intimidating series of degrees (including a doctorate from the Sorbonne), four children she was raising on her own and a maverick sense of determination that led her to plant a then-unconventionally spaced and oriented vineyard on a steep slope of rocky Howell Mountain. Viader today produces her original proprietary blend of Cabernet Franc and Cabernet Sauvignon—the winery's signature—along with other outside-the-Napa-box offerings like Petit Verdot and Tempranillo.

BOTTLES TO TRY

● **Viader** / **$$$$**
● **Viader "Black Label" Estate Limited Edition** / **$$$$**

VINEYARD 7 & 8

This winery's history began in 1999, when New Jersey money manager Launny Steffens bought a 40-acre parcel 2,000 feet up on Spring Mountain in Napa Valley. But the real takeoff came in the mid-2000s, when former Peter Michael winemaker Luc Morlet came on board, joining Launny's son Wesley, who had apprenticed at Harlan Estate (and at the French Laundry). The winery makes small quantities of much-praised, premium-priced estate bottlings of Cabernet Sauvignon and Chardonnay, plus its 7 Cabernet and 8 Chardonnay from purchased grapes.

BOTTLES TO TRY

○ **Estate Chardonnay** / **$$$$**
● **Estate Cabernet Sauvignon** / **$$$$**

WILLIAMS SELYEM

One of California's top small wineries, Selyem has maintained its artisan cred despite immense consumer demand and an ownership transition from its founders. Winemaker Bob Cabral makes Pinot Noir, Zinfandel and Chardonnay with an attention to detail that allows the "minimal interference" mantra to actually work. The winery understood early on that cool, difficult-to-farm places could yield distinctive fruit, and its sources range from now-famous vineyards to off-the-grid grape patches.

BOTTLES TO TRY

○ **Drake Estate Chardonnay** / $$$
● **Estate Vineyard Pinot Noir** / $$$$

WIND GAP

Pax Mahle does things the hard way: sourcing tiny lots of grapes from ultra-cool, marginal growing sites; trodding grapes by foot; fermenting them on only natural yeasts; bottling them unfined and unfiltered. His wines are boldly original, sometimes visionary. They're also, considering the effort, reasonably priced, when you can find them. Mahle is best known for Pinot Noir, but check the winery's website for additional offerings.

BOTTLE TO TRY

● **Gap's Crown Vineyard Pinot Noir** / $$$

OREGON

CLAIM TO FAME

That Oregon, with its wet weather and short summers, could ever be famous for wine was in doubt until as recently as 30 years ago, when it began to receive international acclaim. Today the Willamette Valley is the epicenter of a world-class wine region famous for some of the country's best Pinot Noir.

REGIONS TO KNOW

COLUMBIA GORGE & WALLA WALLA VALLEY Northeast of the Willamette Valley, these regions run along the Washington State border. The Walla Walla Valley AVA lies mostly in Washington, but, like the Columbia Gorge, it straddles the border into Oregon. Warm, dry summers mean that reds reign: Cabernet is the flagship grape; Syrah and Merlot are made in lesser volumes.

ROGUE VALLEY Southern Oregon's Rogue Valley region includes the valleys of the Rogue River and three tributaries: the Illinois and Applegate rivers and Bear Creek. **APPLEGATE VALLEY,** with vineyards up to 1,500 feet in elevation, has its own AVA. Bordeaux and Rhône varieties are grown throughout the region.

UMPQUA Warmer than the Willamette Valley and cooler than Rogue, Umpqua produces small amounts of Pinot Noir and Pinot Gris, among others.

WILLAMETTE VALLEY Stretching virtually from the suburbs of Portland in the north to Eugene in the south, this broad valley is home to most of the state's population as well as most of its wine production. Protected against Pacific Ocean winds by the Coast Ranges, the region is divided into six subregions, each with its own AVA: **CHEHALEM MOUNTAINS, DUNDEE HILLS, EOLA-AMITY HILLS, MCMINNVILLE, RIBBON RIDGE** and the **YAMHILL-CARLTON DISTRICT.**

❦ KEY GRAPES: WHITE

CHARDONNAY Not much Chardonnay is crushed in Oregon compared with Pinot Noir and Pinot Gris, but as in Burgundy, the cool-climate conditions that work to create top Pinot Noirs also tend to favor graceful renditions of Chardonnay, with subtle fruit flavors and lively acidity.

PINOT GRIS Oregon's principal white grape is Pinot Gris, and though it ranges in style, its typical expression in the state leans toward the generous and full-bodied Alsace profile, with refreshing acidity, as opposed to the leaner Pinot Grigio style.

RIESLING & PINOT BLANC Aromatic whites such as these are making headway, with a handful of small vintners achieving notable success in the Willamette Valley.

❦ KEY GRAPES: RED

PINOT NOIR Representing more than half of the state's wine production, Oregon Pinot Noir is silky smooth, with delicate berry flavors and firm acidity. Somewhere between the earthy, astringent style of Burgundy and the robust offerings characteristic of California, Oregon Pinot Noir can be outstanding.

Producers/ Oregon

ANDREW RICH

Andrew Rich does indeed make very fine Oregon Pinot Noir—blending several cuvées from grapes sourced around the Willamette Valley—but he is too restless to be confined by one grape, or one state. Also under his label are a slew of generally delicious Rhône-style wines, from white Roussanne to Syrah and Grenache-Mourvèdre, typically produced in small lots.

BOTTLES TO TRY
- ○ **Roussanne** / **$$**
- ● **The Knife Edge Pinot Noir** / **$$$**

ANNE AMIE VINEYARDS

Ponzi veterans Thomas Houseman (winemaking) and Jason Tosch (viticulture) run the winery that business mogul Robert Pamplin, Jr., bought in 1999 (it was formerly Chateau Benoit). Anne Amie has made a name for itself not only in Pinot Noir, but also in the grape's white wine biological offshoots Pinot Gris and Pinot Blanc. This isn't a winery that typically scales the heights, but it does provide remarkable consistency across its line.

BOTTLES TO TRY
- ○ **Pinot Gris** / **$$**
- ● **Willamette Valley Pinot Noir** / **$$$**

ARGYLE WINERY

It remains to be seen what effect co-founder Rollin Soles's stepping aside in 2013 will have on this top-notch winery (Soles will continue to have input on the wines). Argyle has long been a producer of some of the state's finest Pinot Noir—under such beguiling names as Nuthouse and Spirithouse—plus top Riesling and Chardonnay, with a concentration on estate-grown fruit. But for many fans, Argyle is preeminently a maker of vibrant, world-class sparkling wines (see p. 286).

BOTTLES TO TRY
- ○ **Riesling** / **$$**
- ● **Nuthouse Pinot Noir** / **$$$**

A TO Z WINEWORKS

A to Z Wineworks owns neither vineyards nor a winery. Rather, the posse of talents behind this sizable label—including Michael Davies and Cheryl Francis (both ex-Chehalem) and Sam Tannahill (ex–Archery Summit)—buy finished wines, then use their masterful blending skills to create juicy, balanced blends. There's some luck of the draw in their offerings (compared with a single-vineyard wine made by the same winemaker vintage after vintage), but a fine track record has made A to Z a go-to label for often-superior wines at fantastic prices.

BOTTLES TO TRY

○ Chardonnay / $

● Pinot Noir / $$

BERGSTRÖM WINES

Bergström has put itself on wine lovers' maps of the Willamette Valley in relatively short order. Founded by Portland surgeon John Bergström and his wife, Karen, in 1999, Bergström is managed by their son Josh, who studied winemaking (and met his future wife) in Burgundy. The five estate vineyards—now encompassing 85 acres around the valley—are biodynamically farmed and yield much-sought-after Pinot Noirs of impressive poise and depth. Some of the winery's offerings are available only through its wine club.

BOTTLES TO TRY

○ Old Stones Chardonnay / $$$

● Bergström Vineyard Pinot Noir / $$$$

BROADLEY VINEYARDS

Craig and Claudia Broadley swapped one bohemian milieu—they worked for Beat poet Lawrence Ferlinghetti at San Francisco's City Lights bookstore—for another when they moved to the southern Willamette Valley in the early 1980s. Operating on a shoestring, the Broadleys had to let the wines speak for themselves, over time. More than 25 years down the line the wines do just that, eloquently. The now 5,300-case operation still handcrafts its in-demand wine, including the four estate Pinot bottlings and a range of others sourced from top vineyards in the valley.

BOTTLE TO TRY

● Reserve Pinot Noir / $$$

CRISTOM VINEYARDS

Cristom is a remarkable story of continuity: Winemaker Steve Doerner and vineyard manager Mark Feltz have been in place since owner Paul Gerrie bought the property in 1992. Why mess with success? The winery's Pinot Noirs—whole-cluster fermented with native yeasts—have been some of the state's most celebrated wines. Four relatively rare single-vineyard bottlings are all named for family matriarchs, but three often-outstanding blends also put you in the Cristom picture.

BOTTLES TO TRY
○ **Pinot Gris** / **$$**
● **Mt. Jefferson Cuvée Pinot Noir** / **$$**

EVENING LAND VINEYARDS

One of Oregon's—not to say the wine world's—bolder projects, Evening Land aims to create Burgundian wines (read: graceful and acid balanced) from three West Coast regions, including western Sonoma and Sta. Rita Hills. In Oregon, the operation boasts Burgundy legend Dominique Lafon as a consultant, and the superb Seven Springs Vineyard as a springboard. Though the White Label wines, like the Seven Springs Summum Chardonnay, are expensive, the Blue Label bottlings can be terrific deals.

> **WINE INTEL**
> Evening Land wines are now available not only in restaurants and shops, but also at the winery's new tasting room in downtown Dundee, next to the acclaimed Paulée restaurant.

BOTTLES TO TRY
○ **Seven Springs Vineyard Summum Chardonnay** / **$$$$**
● **Blue Label Pinot Noir** / **$$**

HAMACHER WINES

Eric Hamacher shook the Napa Valley dust off his boots, moved north, married into Oregon wine gentry (Luisa Ponzi) and helped found the Carlton Winemakers Studio, an ultra-green cooperative winery that hosts a small legion of artisan operations. Along the way he gained a reputation for lovely, layered Chardonnays and for Pinot Noirs of great refinement and balance. The wines are sourced from top growers, but the Hamachers are now planting their own vineyard in the Chehalem Mountains AVA.

BOTTLES TO TRY
○ **Hamacher Cuvée Forêts Diverses Chardonnay** / **$$$**
● **Hamacher Pinot Noir** / **$$$**

KEN WRIGHT CELLARS

Ken Wright has been one of Oregon Pinot Noir's leading citizens since 1986, not only as a producer (he also founded the Panther Creek and Tyrus Evan brands), but also as a mentor and a leader in helping to establish Oregon's AVAs. Most importantly for consumers, Wright has also maintained his position in the forefront of wine quality, turning out complex, stylish Pinots seemingly vintage in, vintage out. At the top of the line are the single-vineyard wines that typify his place-based philosophy, but the more affordable Willamette Valley blend can be a wonderful wine in its own right.

BOTTLES TO TRY
○ Pinot Blanc / $$
● Abbott Claim Vineyard Pinot Noir / $$$

LEMELSON VINEYARDS

Environmental lawyer Eric Lemelson uses a combination of high tech (a state-of-the-art winery) and low tech (all certified organic farming; natural winemaking) to produce his sought-after Pinot Noirs and some very well priced Pinot Gris and Riesling. Winemaker Anthony King, lured north from Acacia (see p. 169), produces most of these wines from Lemelson's seven estate vineyards, which are scattered across three Willamette Valley AVAs.

BOTTLES TO TRY
○ Tikka's Run Pinot Gris / $$
● Thea's Selection Pinot Noir / $$

OWEN ROE

David O'Reilly's wine endeavors are category defying. Based in Oregon, where he makes some fine Pinot Noir, he also gets high accolades for Washington-sourced Bordeaux-style wines—he operates on kind of a Yamhill–Yakima axis. Add to that the fact that the winery produces a number of high-end bottlings as well as a bevy of affordably priced wines, many of which are very fine bargains, and you see why some consumers get confused. But the quality level is generally strong across the Owen Roe portfolio, and occasionally it's outstanding.

BOTTLES TO TRY
○ DuBrul Vineyard Chardonnay / $$$
● Sharecropper's Pinot Noir / $$

REX HILL

One of Oregon's pioneering wineries back in 1982, Rex Hill caught a second wind in 2007 when the partners behind A to Z Wineworks (see p. 206) purchased the property. Among other things, the new owners are adamant about sustainable agriculture, and beyond: Rex Hill's own vineyards are now farmed biodynamically. A to Z winemaker Michael Davies has also bumped up the quality of the wines, which can be among Oregon's best. In addition to the often-superb fruit from its estate vineyards such as Jacob-Hart, the winery has long-term relationships with top growers like Shea.

BOTTLES TO TRY

○ **Old Vine Chardonnay** ╱ **$$$$**

● **Shea Pinot Noir** ╱ **$$$**

SCOTT PAUL WINES

Martha and Scott Paul Wright are so passionate about Pinot Noir that after producing their first vintage in 1999 (supervised by Pinot guru Greg LaFollette), they moved from Sonoma to the Willamette Valley to create their own boutique brand (and began importing artisan wines from Burgundy and Champagne). Based in downtown Carlton, they hired Eyrie Vineyards alum Kelley Fox (she also bottles estimable wines under her own name) to help craft their Burgundy-inspired wines. These wines have gone from strength to strength in the past several vintages.

BOTTLE TO TRY

● **Les Gourmandises Pinot Noir** ╱ **$$$**

ST. INNOCENT WINERY

Although St. Innocent makes a small amount of white wine, its hallmark is Pinot Noir—specifically, small-lot Pinots made by owner Mark Vlossak from an all-star roster of Willamette Valley sites, including his own Zenith Vineyard. The wines have gained a well-deserved following; their small production and high quality make them hard to find in stores (some even sell out as futures). Fortunately, Vlossak also fashions the often-delicious, larger-production Villages Cuvée, which blends fruit from young vines and several vineyards.

BOTTLES TO TRY

○ **Vitae Springs Vineyard Pinot Gris** ╱ **$$**

● **Villages Cuvée Pinot Noir** ╱ **$$**

WILLAMETTE VALLEY VINEYARDS

Founder and native Oregonian Jim Bernau bought a run-down plum orchard in 1983, cleared it himself and planted vines. Bernau and his partners eventually built Willamette Valley Vineyards into one of the state's largest producers, at around 90,000 cases. Though the single-vineyard Pinot Noir bottlings are expensive, the sweet spot for reds here is in the midrange, where you'll find many of the estate vineyard wines. WVV is also a prime source for white wines that overdeliver on quality for price.

BOTTLES TO TRY

○ **Riesling / $**
● **Estate Pinot Noir / $$$**

WITNESS TREE VINEYARD

Estate wines are the currency here: All of Witness Tree's Chardonnays and Pinots come from Dennis and Carolyn Devine's 100 acres in the Eola Hills near Salem. (The tree itself, still presiding over the vineyard, is an ancient oak that was used to mark a property boundary in 1854.) At their best, the wines here are stylish and graceful, with a lively underpinning of acidity.

BOTTLE TO TRY

● **Hanson Pinot Noir / $$$**

WASHINGTON STATE

CLAIM TO FAME

Once known chiefly for its value wines and terrific Riesling, Washington has built a reputation for complex reds that rival top California bottlings. Cheaper land and a lower profile mean that these ambitious wines often sell for much less than their more prestigious California counterparts. The industry is growing too: In the past decade, Washington has more than tripled its number of wineries and recently approved its 13th AVA.

REGIONS TO KNOW

COLUMBIA GORGE Scenic Columbia Gorge isn't better known for its wine in part because its output is hard to define. Encompassing both sides of the Columbia River east of Vancouver, the region is warmer and drier inland and cool and rainy toward the west: No wonder so many grape varieties are planted here.

COLUMBIA VALLEY This huge southeastern region covers a third of the state and grows 99 percent of its wine grapes; most other Washington AVAs (including Horse Heaven Hills and Walla Walla and Yakima valleys) are Columbia Valley subregions. Some 6,800 vineyard acres exist outside designated subzones. Its newest AVA is **ANCIENT LAKES,** a chilly, dry subregion northeast of Yakima.

HORSE HEAVEN HILLS Bordeaux-style reds and earthy, elegant Syrah are the stars of this southeast district, one of the state's premier wine regions.

LAKE CHELAN Approved in 2009, this newish AVA is defined by the influence of its eponymous 55-mile-long glacial lake in north-central Washington. Cool-climate varieties such as Riesling and Pinot Gris show terrific promise here.

WAHLUKE SLOPE Warm and dry, this up-and-coming district in south-central Washington is planted chiefly with heat-loving red grapes like Merlot, Cabernet and Syrah.

WALLA WALLA VALLEY Many of Washington's finest Cabernets come from this remote southeast region, which extends into Oregon. Merlot, Syrah and Chardonnay excel here as well.

YAKIMA VALLEY The state's oldest AVA, established in 1983, this district is a major source of Washington Chardonnay, but plantings of Merlot and Cabernet Sauvignon are widespread as well.

❦ KEY GRAPES: WHITE

CHARDONNAY Washington Chardonnays are typically lighter and more refreshing than California versions, thanks to a generally cooler growing season.

PINOT GRIS This white variety is on the rise—more than tripling in recent production. Most of it goes into large-production tank-aged wines made in a fresh, appley style.

RIESLING Washington growers produce slightly more Riesling—the state's signature white grape—than they do Cabernet. Cool nights and ideal growing conditions allow the grapes to be crafted into a range of styles from dry to sweet.

SAUVIGNON BLANC, VIOGNIER & GEWÜRZTRAMINER These aromatic white varieties do well in Washington's northern climate and represent a little more than 10 percent of the state's white grape production. Gewürztraminer tends to yield ripe and floral wines, usually in an off-dry style.

♣ KEY GRAPES: RED

CABERNET SAUVIGNON Washington's most planted red grape variety makes terrific wines up and down the price scale, its high-end cuvées competing with the world's best. Smooth textured and bold, they're more restrained than California's dense, riper-style offerings.

MERLOT Washington is arguably the country's best source of delicious Merlot; its top bottles have a distinctive, spicy complexity and seductive depth.

SYRAH Columbia Valley's Walla Walla Valley, Wahluke Slope, Yakima Valley and Red Mountain subregions provide ideal conditions for Syrah. The grape yields wines with a mix of peppery, earthy flavors and a firm structure that follows a classic style of this Rhône variety.

Producers/ Washington State

ÀMAURICE CELLARS

The Schafer family—fifth-generation Washingtonians with a legacy in the timber business—founded this winery in 2004 with the goal of being stewards of the land and a commitment to sustainable farming. Winemaker Anna, a Paul Hobbs protégé, brings her experience working in the Southern Hemisphere to produce one of Washington's top Malbecs, Amparo. The winery also has a sure hand with whites, including an elegant Viognier.

BOTTLES TO TRY
- ○ Columbia Valley Viognier / $$
- ● Amparo / $$$

BASEL CELLARS

Based in an impressive mansion near Walla Walla that has made it a wine-tourism destination, Basel Cellars bottles a boutique-level (5,000 to 7,000 cases) array of reds centered on Bordeaux varieties, including a popular Merlot and the winery's flagship Merriment blend. Winemaker Ned Morris, formerly of àMaurice and Canoe Ridge, pulls grapes from four estate vineyards around the Columbia Valley, including the certified sustainable Double River Ranch, to make his generous, palate-flattering reds.

BOTTLES TO TRY

○ **2901 White** / **$$**

● **Merriment** / **$$$**

BUTY WINERY

Nina Buty co-founded this boutique Walla Walla winery in 2000, and soon brought on board top-notch California-based consultant Zelma Long. Buty's reds focus on multivariety blends, including the sought-after Rediviva of the Stones, an unusual (outside Australia) combination of Cabernet Sauvignon and Syrah; the whites include an equally unusual unoaked Chardonnay. Winemaker Chris Dowsett emphasizes supple tannins and moderate alcohol levels, which lend the wine a particular finesse. A second label, Beast, with many one-time bottlings, allows Dowsett to continue to follow his curiosity and push his talent.

BOTTLES TO TRY

○ **Conner Lee Vineyard Chardonnay** / **$$$**

● **Rediviva of the Stones** / **$$$**

CADARETTA

The Middleton family released the first wines from its Walla Walla boutique operation in 2008, but the family has been in business in Washington since the 19th century (*Cadaretta* was the name of one of the family's timber schooners). The two wines in general release, the SBS Sauvignon Blanc–Sémillon and the Cabernet Sauvignon, have been widely praised in their first editions. Cadaretta also bottles smaller lots for members of its wine club.

BOTTLES TO TRY

○ **SBS** / **$$**

● **Cabernet Sauvignon** / **$$$**

CADENCE

This small-scale enterprise run out of Seattle was founded by a wine-loving couple who ditched legal and engineering careers to follow their hearts into the vineyards. Those they found in the Red Mountain area—Tapteil, Klipsun and Ciel du Cheval—are some of Washington's best, and their own tenderly planted Cara Mia vines may very well join them. Graceful Bordeaux-style reds are the ticket here, with all the flavor intensity of Red Mountain's site-stressed, small-berried grapes carrying through in each.

BOTTLE TO TRY

● Camerata ∕ $$$

CHATEAU STE. MICHELLE

Chateau Ste. Michelle, one of the many Ste. Michelle Wine Estates brands, is Washington's largest and most famous producer. Thanks to its visitors' facilities in suburban Seattle, it's also the most familiar name to wine tourists. Luckily for the state whose wines were so long almost synonymous with it, Chateau Ste. Michelle has for years been an innovator, a talent incubator, and a highly reliable label for good wine at a fair price.

BOTTLES TO TRY

○ Eroica Riesling ∕ $$

● Indian Wells Cabernet Sauvignon ∕ $$

COLUMBIA CREST

If Chateau Ste. Michelle's more price-conscious alter ego is seemingly ubiquitous in supermarkets, wine shops and restaurants, there is a reason for that: Very few large-production wineries in the world produce better wine consistently at such reasonable prices. Under longtime winemaker Ray Einberger, who passed the reins to protégé Juan Muñoz Oca in 2011, Columbia Crest has often punched above its weight, particularly with supple, aromatic Cabernet Sauvignons and Merlots as well as lovely, well-proportioned Chardonnays.

BOTTLES TO TRY

○ Grand Estates Chardonnay ∕ $

● Stone Tree Vineyard Merlot Reserve ∕ $$

DUSTED VALLEY

In 2003 sisters Cindy Braunel and Janet Johnson and their husbands followed their wine dreams out of northern Wisconsin all the way to Walla Walla, where they age their wines in Wisconsin oak barrels. They have made some complex, sophisticated and delicious wines in the early going; the Rhône-style Syrahs and blends have met with particular success. The main Dusted Valley line is produced in limited quantities and generally priced accordingly, but their Boomtown and Blind Boar wines offer a great value in easy-drinking wines. All three lines are sealed with screw-caps, in keeping with the winery's belief that these closures offer the best chance of ensuring a fresh wine.

BOTTLE TO TRY
- Rachis Syrah / $$$

EFESTE

A group of family members and friends established Efeste (pronounced as the letters *FST*, the initials of the founders' last names) in 2005 in Woodinville. Winemaker Peter Devison sources his grapes from vineyards around the Columbia Valley, but his cellar treatment—native yeasts, limited or no fining and filtering—emphasizes the individuality of each lot. The winery has had success with both Cabernet and Syrah, but it also puts out a well-regarded, well-priced Riesling that's well worth a look amid the big reds.

BOTTLES TO TRY
- ○ Evergreen Riesling / $$
- ● Big Papa Cabernet Sauvignon / $$$

K VINTNERS/CHARLES SMITH WINES

These two labels share an owner and winemaker, Charles Smith—a wild-haired, iconoclastic former sommelier who moved to Walla Walla after a stint overseas as a rock band manager. For all his flamboyance, Smith is a meticulous winemaker whose acclaimed K reds focus on minuscule lots of costly, typically full-throttle Syrahs, while his namesake brand turns out wines to drink now, with names like Kung Fu Girl Riesling and the Velvet Devil Merlot that reflect his joie de vivre.

BOTTLES TO TRY
- ○ K Viognier / $$
- ● K Syrah, Cougar Hills / $$$

MCCREA CELLARS

Doug McCrea was Washington's original Rhône Ranger back in 1988, with a number of state firsts (first Rhône blend, first Viognier, first Counoise). Having started with a modest patch of Grenache, McCrea now produces wines from 10 different Rhône grapes—yes, he's got your Picpoul—including some of the state's finest Syrahs. His vineyard sources include two of the state's best, Yakima's relatively cool Boushey (including McCrea's own Grand Côte vines) and Red Mountain's hot (in every respect) Ciel du Cheval.

BOTTLES TO TRY

○ **Viognier ⁄ $$**
● **Cuvée Orleans Syrah ⁄ $$$**

NORTHSTAR WINERY

Part of the Ste. Michelle Wine Estates portfolio, this Walla Walla winery was founded in the early 1990s with talented winemaker Jed Steele at the helm. Northstar's focus was on Merlot, which at the time looked to be Washington's up-and-coming grape. Fashion, in the shape of Cabernet and Syrah, has since moved on from Merlot, but Steele's successor, winemaker David Merfeld, continues to turn out some of the state's very best—a reminder of how wonderful the grape can be when given the star treatment usually accorded to Cabernet (which Northstar, not suprisingly, also handles very well).

BOTTLES TO TRY

○ **Stella Blanca Sémillon ⁄ $$**
● **Walla Walla Valley Merlot ⁄ $$$**

PACIFIC RIM

California Central Coast vintner Randall Grahm, of Bonny Doon fame, created this Riesling-focused brand partly to combat what he perceived to be an ocean of fat, oaky Chardonnays and partly for the sheer food-lovingness of Riesling itself, which, among other things, is a fine complement to many Asian cuisines. Winemaker Nicolas Quillé stayed on when the Mariani family (of New York–based Banfi Vintners) bought Pacific Rim in 2011 and continues to turn out tasty, value-priced Rieslings that range from dry to sweet.

BOTTLE TO TRY

○ **Dry Riesling ⁄ $**

RARITIES & COLLECTIBLES

CÔTE BONNEVILLE The Shiels family's DuBrul Vineyard in the Yakima Valley supplies grapes for some of the state's top wineries. But as the Shielses' acclaimed Côte Bonneville DuBrul Vineyard Bordeaux blend shows, no one knows DuBrul fruit like its owners.

MARK RYAN WINERY Mark Ryan McNeilly started out as a *garagiste* in the literal sense, making small batches of wine in friends' garages. He still doesn't produce oceans of wine, but his full-bore renditions of fruit from top vineyards, such as his prized Dead Horse Bordeaux blend, have earned him a cult following.

SHERIDAN VINEYARD Self-taught Yakima winemaker Scott Greer left a finance career to devote himself and his 76-acre hilltop estate to producing luscious reds, including collectors' wines such as the Block 1 Cabernet and the Singularity Syrah.

PURSUED BY BEAR

Yakima native and *Twin Peaks* star Kyle MacLachlan returned to his Washington roots with this label, and fortunately had the good sense to enlist star winemaker Eric Dunham (Dunham Cellars) in the enterprise. The winery's good-humored name refers to the famous Shakespearean stage direction, but the project's first four vintages of high-end Cabernet Sauvignon are more refined, supple and spicy than theatrically flamboyant.

BOTTLE TO TRY
- Cabernet Sauvignon / $$$$

REININGER

Onetime professional climbing guide Chuck Reininger caught a major case of the wine bug, and he and his wife, Tracy, began bottling their own back in 1997. With the help of much of Tracy's family, the winery has quietly risen to become one of Walla Walla's most esteemed producers, partly on the basis of the lesser-known (in France) Bordeaux grapes Carmenère and Malbec. The Reininger label is reserved for limited-production wines from Walla Walla; a fine second label, Helix, is for larger-production, somewhat lower priced bottlings from the broader Columbia Valley.

BOTTLES TO TRY
- ○ Helix Chardonnay / $$
- ● Pepper Bridge Vineyard Malbec / $$$

TAMARACK CELLARS

In 16 years, this family-owned winery tucked into a renovated firehouse in an abandoned U.S. Army airfield in Walla Walla has gone from zero to 20,000 cases. It has managed this partly by bottling some extraordinary wines from top vineyard sites like Ciel du Cheval, DuBrul and Sagemoor, and partly by offering a range of very realistically priced wines all the way down to a bargain Rosé of Mourvèdre. Check out the Firehouse Red, a kitchen-sink blend that combines up to 11 grapes and still remains harmonious.

BOTTLE TO TRY

● **Ciel du Cheval Vineyard Reserve** / **$$$**

WATERS WINERY

Guitarist Jamie Brown moved to Seattle for the grunge scene but found himself loving good wine as much as great music. Today he's one of Washington's rising stars, thanks to his insistence on lively acidity and grace in his small-production Walla Walla Valley–focused Rhône- and Bordeaux-style reds. Wines of Substance and 21 Grams—Brown's side projects with another emerging talent, Greg Harrington—have been insider hits, too.

BOTTLES TO TRY

○ **Prelude** / **$$**

● **Loess Syrah** / **$$$**

OTHER U.S. STATES

REGIONS TO KNOW

MICHIGAN Savvy Midwestern sommeliers have known for years what the rest of the country is just finding out: Michigan's Rieslings are some of the country's best (the grape is the most widely planted wine grape in the state). Top vineyards hug the shores of Lake Michigan, on the Old Mission and Leelanau peninsulas, where the lake effect moderates the northern climate. Other whites, such as Gewürztraminer and Pinot Gris, do well, too.

NEW YORK Though long since overshadowed by California, New York, with 320 wineries and more than 1,400 vineyards, nearly all of them boutique-size and family owned, vies with Washington for the rank of America's second-largest wine-producing state. The two major growing regions, Long Island and the Finger Lakes, are located at opposite ends of New York State, but both produce high-quality wine. First planted with international varieties 40 years ago, the Long Island wineries, easily accessible to Hamptons vacationers, are best known for fine examples of Sauvignon Blanc, Chardonnay, Merlot and Cabernet Franc, which manage to succeed in the uncertain, somewhat Bordeaux-like maritime climate. Upstate, while native *Vitis labrusca* and hybrid grapes are still widely grown, quality-minded vintners in the Finger Lakes region are turning out sophisticated and complex dry Rieslings, Gewürztraminers and Pinot Noirs.

THE SOUTHWEST Thanks to cooler temperatures in its high deserts, **ARIZONA** has emerged as a fine-wine producer. Full-bodied reds such as Syrah, Cabernet Sauvignon and Sangiovese are succeeding in high-altitude vineyards, and the state's number of wineries has skyrocketed to nearly 50 in recent years. **TEXAS,** too, is in the midst of a significant wine boom. It ranks fifth among the states in wine production and boasts 273 wineries. Its highest-quality wines—mostly those made from Cabernet Sauvignon, Merlot and Chardonnay—come from the Hill Country (a central district that's larger than the state of Maryland) and the High Plains, in the Panhandle. **COLORADO**'s rugged vineyards are some of the highest in the world. Bordeaux-inspired reds have become the state's signature pour, most of them produced in the Grand Valley AVA, while the West Elks region is gaining a solid reputation for cool-climate whites and reds. The most renowned of **NEW MEXICO**'s 40-odd wineries is Gruet, a family-owned producer of Champagne-style sparkling wine in North Albuquerque (see p. 288). Gruet's wonderfully tasty and low-priced wines have made it an increasingly widely available and delicious alternative to the big-name sparkling brands.

VIRGINIA Centuries after settlers planted vinifera grapes in Virginia in the early 1600s, the state has become a reliable source of well-made wines, especially aromatic Viognier, minty Cabernet Franc and lush Chardonnay, in addition to wines made with the native Norton grape variety. Investment has accelerated in recent years, with small-production winemaker-owners joined by ambitious newcomers such as Rutger de Vink and even the renowned teetotaler Donald Trump.

Producers/ Other U.S. States

BARBOURSVILLE VINEYARDS/Virginia

This winery near Charlottesville, Virginia, was once the 19th-century estate of the Barbour family, close friends and neighbors of Thomas Jefferson and James Madison. Italy's Zonin family bought the winery in 1976 and accomplished what Jefferson could not: making fine wine in this area (as many wineries do today). Barboursville produces a galaxy of bottlings from French- and Italian-descended grapes, most famously its high-end red Bordeaux blend Octagon.

BOTTLES TO TRY

○ **Philéo / $$**

● **Octagon / $$$**

CADUCEUS CELLARS/Arizona

Rock 'n' roller Maynard James Keenan, lead singer of Tool and A Perfect Circle, brings his intensity and willingness to experiment to this Arizona winery, which sources grapes from its own Merkin Vineyards as well as from around the state and into California and New Mexico. Among Keenan's successes are Primer Paso, a unique blend of Syrah and Malvasia Bianca, and Dos Ladrones, which combines Malvasia Bianca with Chardonnay.

BOTTLES TO TRY

○ **Dos Ladrones / $$$**

● **Primer Paso / $$$**

DUCHMAN FAMILY WINERY/Texas

Drs. Lisa and Stan Duchman put Driftwood, Texas (near Austin), on the wine map; their stone-clad villa is on many tourists' maps as well. The emphasis here is on the Italian-style wines the Duchmans love: Nero d'Avola, Dolcetto and Trebbiano. Most of the grapes are sourced from the higher, cooler vineyards of the High Plains AVA in the Texas Panhandle.

BOTTLES TO TRY

○ **Vermentino / $$**

● **Sangiovese / $$**

KESWICK VINEYARDS/Virginia

The dream project of expat Michiganders Al and Cindy Schornberg, who moved to Keswick, Virginia, just outside Charlottesville, this winery is rare in the U.S. for its emphasis on Viognier, the perfumed but tricky-to-grow white variety of France's Condrieu. The hybrid Norton, which has found a home in many Virginia vineyards, is its largest red planting, and the Schornbergs have also done very well with their Bordeaux-style blends.

BOTTLES TO TRY

○ **Les Vents d'Anges Viognier** / **$$**
● **Norton Reserve** / **$$**

LAMOREAUX LANDING/New York

Lamoreaux's striking postmodern–Greek Revivalish winery building is a familiar landmark to New York Finger Lakes wine tourists. The winery represents both a continuation of the Wagner family's winegrowing in this region (they were at it back in the 1940s) and a new day, since co-owner Mark Wagner makes his wines (except for a Vidal ice wine) with European-descended vinifera grapes. Though most famous for its Rieslings, Lamoreaux has also enjoyed success with red Bordeaux varieties like Cabernet Franc.

BOTTLES TO TRY

○ **Estate White** / **$**
● **Cabernet Franc** / **$**

MACARI VINEYARDS/New York

The Macari family has owned its 500-acre domain on New York's Long Island Sound for decades, but they put in wine grapes only in 1995. (The grapes share the estate with longhorn cattle, goats, donkeys and a roaming farmyard menagerie.) Joseph Macari, Jr., cultivates the land biodynamically and has it planted to a bewildering collection of grapes, from Bordeaux blending varieties to Grüner Veltliner and Viognier. Macari also sources Riesling upstate, from the Finger Lakes.

BOTTLES TO TRY

○ **Sauvignon Blanc** / **$$**
● **Cabernet Franc** / **$$$**

Australia

Wine Region

Here's one of the great mysteries of wine: Why do people think that a wine-producing country that is nearly *14 times* the size of France can produce only one type of wine? And yet, people do. They assume that all Australia has to offer is simple, affordable, juicy, jammy Shiraz. But, in fact, Australian wine is as varied as the Australian continent. There are the Clare Valley's laser-sharp dry Rieslings and the great Cabernets of Coonawarra; lemony Sémillons from the Hunter Valley that can age for decades; even a growing number of impressive, spicy Pinot Noirs from such cool-climate regions as the Mornington Peninsula and the Yarra Valley. And, of course, there is Shiraz, the country's No. 1 grape; Australia's dozens of widely varying regions all produce distinctive versions of this wine, from the world-class to the humble. And now is the time to try them.

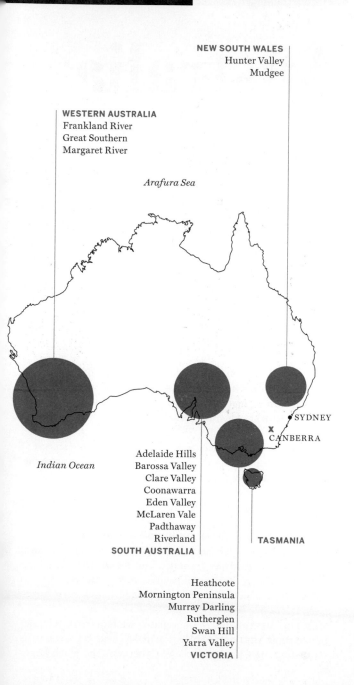

NEW SOUTH WALES
Hunter Valley
Mudgee

WESTERN AUSTRALIA
Frankland River
Great Southern
Margaret River

Arafura Sea

Indian Ocean

• SYDNEY

X
CANBERRA

Adelaide Hills
Barossa Valley
Clare Valley
Coonawarra
Eden Valley
McLaren Vale
Padthaway
Riverland
SOUTH AUSTRALIA

TASMANIA

Heathcote
Mornington Peninsula
Murray Darling
Rutherglen
Swan Hill
Yarra Valley
VICTORIA

Australia

REGIONS TO KNOW

SOUTH AUSTRALIA This area is home to the country's most acclaimed wine regions, among them the Shiraz-centric **BAROSSA VALLEY** and **MCLAREN VALE** and the cooler **CLARE** and **EDEN** valleys, which produce some of the country's greatest Rieslings. In **COONAWARRA,** iron-rich *terra rossa* soils yield stellar Cabernet Sauvignon, while the cool **ADELAIDE HILLS** produce crisp whites. Much of Australia's affordable, easy-drinking wine comes from **RIVERLAND,** the country's single largest wine-producing region.

NEW SOUTH WALES The best-known subzone of this eastern, coastal state is the **HUNTER VALLEY,** source of ageworthy Sémillon and plump, juicy Shiraz, as well as Cabernet and Chardonnay. The **MUDGEE** district produces richly fruited reds.

TASMANIA This bucolic island is an up-and-coming source of vivacious, cool-climate Riesling, Chardonnay and Pinot Noir, as well as sparkling wine.

VICTORIA The most exciting wines from Victoria are those from the coastal zones of this southeast state, where places like the **YARRA VALLEY** and the **MORNINGTON PENINSULA** are turning out refined Pinot Noir and Chardonnay. Warm northwestern zones such as **MURRAY DARLING** and **SWAN HILL** have long yielded plump, fruity reds and whites. **RUTHERGLEN** is Australia's source for high-quality fortified wine.

WESTERN AUSTRALIA On the isolated western coast, the celebrated **MARGARET RIVER** subregion makes some of the country's most stunning Chardonnays and Cabernets. The much larger

GREAT SOUTHERN produces a vast amount of wine, the best of which offers a crisp, focused liveliness. **FRANKLAND RIVER** and **MOUNT BARKER,** both part of Great Southern, are best known for racy, lime-inflected Rieslings and spicy Shiraz.

KEY GRAPES: WHITE

CHARDONNAY The country's dominant white grape is most easily found in multiregion blends made in a full-bodied, often lightly sweet style. But aside from these industrial bottlings, Australian Chardonnays are generally fresher and less sweet these days, and made with less oak. Look for examples from cooler regions, such as South Australia's Adelaide Hills, Victoria's Mornington Peninsula, Tasmania and especially Western Australia's Margaret River, which produces minerally, complex bottlings that can rival top Burgundies.

RIESLING The country's second most important high-quality white grape, Riesling here produces refreshing, dry wines with razor-sharp acidity. There are some ageworthy offerings from Clare and Eden valleys, Tasmania and Western Australia, while those from the Barossa Valley are riper and rounder.

SAUVIGNON BLANC Increasingly popular Sauvignon Blanc grows best in the country's coastal zones, where it retains its citrusy acidity. Styles range from grassy and tart to ripe and tropical. In Margaret River, it's commonly combined with Sémillon to create that region's Bordeaux-style blends.

SÉMILLON One reason wines made with this Bordeaux white grape are so underappreciated in the U.S. is that Australians keep most of the best bottles for themselves. Those from the Hunter Valley are bright when they are young and take on honeyed, nutty flavors as they age. Examples from the Barossa are more opulent and oak aged. Margaret River Sémillon hews to a style roughly between these extremes.

KEY GRAPES: RED

CABERNET SAUVIGNON In addition to the many straightforward, simple Cabernets made in Australia, there are a considerable number of complex, full-bodied bottlings; the finest are capable of extensive aging. Warmer areas tend to bring out plush berry and chocolate notes, whereas cooler-climate places such as the Margaret River region produce more-refined versions, with fresher, juicier flavors. Tiny Coonawarra yields some of the country's greatest Cabernets, which often show a eucalyptus note. Barossa Valley versions are bold, rich and ripe, and sometimes contain a touch of Shiraz.

GRENACHE & MOURVÈDRE These grapes—famous in France's Rhône Valley—thrive in many Australian regions. Grenache displays many of the same fruit-forward characteristics as Shiraz but with a lighter body, while Mourvèdre shows a smokier, spicier personality. Many vintners combine the two with Shiraz in blends labeled *GSM* (Grenache, Shiraz, Mourvèdre).

MERLOT Most Merlot in Australia is either used in blends or to make soft, simple wines. Yet at the high end there are small quantities of firmer, herb-inflected Merlots coming out of coastal areas like the Yarra Valley and Margaret River, and denser, riper versions from warmer inland regions like the Barossa.

PINOT NOIR Planted in several wine regions throughout Australia, Pinot Noir has succeeded mainly on the island of Tasmania and in Victoria's Yarra Valley and Mornington Peninsula, where cooler temperatures preserve its delicate fruit flavors, soft tannins and vibrant aromatics.

SHIRAZ Australia's leading red grape variety and signature wine is remarkably different from French Syrah (they are the same grape): Australian Shiraz has more-explosive berry flavors as well as spice and eucalyptus notes. Grown throughout the country, Shiraz is at its best in the Barossa Valley and McLaren Vale, in South Australia; the Hunter Valley, in New South Wales; and several Victoria regions. It is traditionally aged in American oak, which complements its jammy, ripe fruit flavors and adds to its affordability.

WINE TERMINOLOGY

Most Australian wine labels specify producer, region, vintage and grape. Blends tend to be named with the dominant grape listed first; sometimes only the initials are given, as in *GSM*, for Grenache, Shiraz, Mourvèdre.

Producers/ Australia

BROKENWOOD WINES

Iain Riggs is the king of Hunter Valley Shiraz. Brokenwood's winemaker began running its cellar in 1982, 12 years after the winery was founded by three lawyer friends (including the wine critic James Halliday). Riggs uses grapes from estate vineyards and purchased fruit from across New South Wales and beyond. His single-vineyard cuvées include the iconic Graveyard Shiraz; also look for his stunning multivineyard blends.

BOTTLES TO TRY

○ **Hunter Valley Sémillon** / **$$**
● **Graveyard Shiraz** / **$$$$**

CHÂTEAU TANUNDA

Marketing maven–turned–vintner John Geber purchased the then-derelict Château Tanunda on a whim in 1998 and thoroughly revived it. Noted winemaker Stuart Bourne joined in 2011, and the winery now turns out well-priced regional and site-specific wines from across the Barossa. The Cabernet and Shiraz offer classic Barossa brawn, tempered by restraint.

BOTTLES TO TRY

● **Grand Barossa Cabernet Sauvignon** / **$$**
● **Noble Baron Shiraz** / **$$$**

CLARENDON HILLS

Roman Bratasiuk is obsessed with the signature imprinted on a wine by its environment. At any given moment, this *terroir*-driven winemaker has 20 different cuvées from a single vintage aging in his cellar. Bratasiuk creates only single-variety wines, all from small plots of old vines in McLaren Vale's Clarendon Hills district. As a result, the Clarendon portfolio brilliantly illustrates the region's diversity. Top wines are famous for their hedonistic flavors (and astronomical cost).

BOTTLES TO TRY

● **Clarendon Grenache** / **$$$**
● **Astralis Syrah** / **$$$$**

CLONAKILLA

One of the great names in Australian wine, Clonakilla produces an iconic Shiraz-Viognier blend that's a reference point for Shiraz everywhere. It's made in small quantities from a vineyard outside Canberra first planted by a biochemist, John Kirk, as a side project in 1971. At the suggestion of his son Tim, and in the tradition of Rhône winemaking, the Kirks first co-fermented the two varieties together in 1992; the resulting blend kicked off a nationwide craze for the technique. Easier to find is Clonakilla's elegant, peppery Hilltops Shiraz.

BOTTLES TO TRY
- Hilltops Shiraz / $$
- Shiraz-Viognier / $$$$

CORIOLE VINEYARDS

This McLaren Vale label is known for two things: Its brilliant Lloyd Reserve Shiraz, which is one of Australia's most famous reds, and its groundbreaking work with Italian grapes. The Shiraz comes from a historic vineyard dating to 1919 that has belonged to the Lloyd family since 1967, when Hugh and Molly Lloyd purchased the estate and renamed it Coriole. Their son, Mark, and the current winemaker, Alex Sherrah, continue the winery's focus.

BOTTLES TO TRY
- Sangiovese-Shiraz / $
- Lloyd Reserve Shiraz / $$$

D'ARENBERG

Although it's more than a century old, this celebrated McLaren Vale producer is anything but stuffy. Founded by Joseph Osborn (a teetotaler), d'Arenberg is now run by his great-grandson Chester, who has helped maintain its status as one of the most inventive and vital producers in Australia. Osborn makes more than 50 wines, many with outlandish names such as the Broken Fishplate or the Wild Pixie. Despite their fanciful monikers, d'Arenberg's best wines, like the Dead Arm Shiraz, rank among Australia's finest.

BOTTLES TO TRY
- ○ The Hermit Crab Viognier-Marsanne / $
- The Laughing Magpie Shiraz-Viognier / $$
- The Dead Arm Shiraz / $$$

GIANT STEPS/INNOCENT BYSTANDER

Phil Sexton is one of Australia's premier cool-climate specialists. After selling his successful Margaret River winery, Devil's Lair, Sexton headed to Victoria's Yarra Valley. A jazz enthusiast, Sexton named his flagship venture Giant Steps after a John Coltrane album and as a reference to his big leap from western Australia to a cool part of the country's southeast coast. The *terroir*-driven label Giant Steps concentrates on mainstream varieties such as Pinot Noir and Chardonnay. Its affordable sister label, Innocent Bystander, offers terrific takes on Pinot Gris and Moscato.

BOTTLES TO TRY

○ **Innocent Bystander Pinot Gris** ⁄ **$$**
○ **Giant Steps Sexton Vineyard Chardonnay** ⁄ **$$$**

HENSCHKE

Few people are lucky enough to taste Henschke's legendary Hill of Grace Shiraz, because of both its price (about $500) and its scarcity. But this 146-year-old Eden Valley winery offers many wines that are less stratospherically expensive, yet still thoughtfully made. Henry's Seven is a supple, rich Rhône-inspired red blend; Keyneton Euphonium, a Shiraz-based blend, gives a taste of Henschke's polished, powerful style. The current winemaker, Stephen Henschke, descends from the estate's founders.

BOTTLES TO TRY

● **Henry's Seven** ⁄ **$$$**
● **Keyneton Euphonium** ⁄ **$$$**

JIM BARRY WINES

This world-renowned Clare Valley producer is a go-to name for all three of the region's signature varieties: Riesling, Shiraz and Cabernet Sauvignon. Its prominence comes both from its history—at more than a half-century old, it pioneered modern Clare Valley viticulture—and from the inarguable quality of its offerings. Winemaker Luke Steele brings an international résumé to the cellar, having worked at the iconic estates M. Chapoutier in the Rhône Valley (see p. 59) and Napa's Joseph Phelps Vineyards.

BOTTLES TO TRY

○ **The Lodge Hill Riesling** ⁄ **$$**
● **The Cover Drive Cabernet Sauvignon** ⁄ **$$**

JOHN DUVAL WINES

By the time the star winemaker John Duval left Penfolds (see p. 232) in 2002, after 29 years, he was overseeing a slew of different wines each year, many of them made in large quantities. Now, at his own boutique Barossa winery, he focuses his considerable talents on just four cuvées: two Shirazes (Eligo and Entity) and a pair of Rhône-style blends (one white, one red) under the Plexus label. The wines' rich, concentrated flavors are true to Barossa type, but their finesse makes them stand out from many of their peers.

BOTTLES TO TRY

○ **Plexus MRV / $$**
● **Entity / $$$**
● **Plexus SGM / $$$**

KAESLER

Formerly a globe-trotting consultant, the winemaker Reid Bosward advised vineyards worldwide before investing in his own estate. In 1999, Bosward teamed up with a Swiss banker, Edouard Peter, and a trio of wine-loving colleagues to acquire the Barossa's Kaesler Vineyards, home to 120-year-old vines. The combination of heirloom vines, financial resources and Bosward's vast experience adds up to thrilling wines, particularly for fans of high-octane reds.

BOTTLES TO TRY

● **The Bogan Shiraz / $$$**
● **Old Vine Shiraz / $$$**

KILIKANOON

Kilikanoon's definitive Clare Valley wines are the work of Kevin Mitchell, one of the founding partners of this relatively youthful estate. Starting in 1997 with about 2,000 cases of wine, Kilikanoon has grown into a midsize winery with a formidable reputation for producing steely, mineral-rich Rieslings and polished reds. Most acclaimed are Kilikanoon's Mort's Block Riesling and its powerhouse Shirazes from the Clare, Barossa and McLaren valleys.

BOTTLES TO TRY

○ **Mort's Block Riesling / $$**
● **Killerman's Run Shiraz / $$**
● **Oracle Shiraz / $$$$**

LEEUWIN ESTATE

In 1972, Robert Mondavi zeroed in on a cattle ranch in the remote Margaret River region and concluded that it could produce world-class wines. His analysis proved astute: On his advice, Leeuwin Estate's founders Denis and Tricia Horgan planted vines on their land in 1974 and went on to become one of Australia's most revered producers. Leeuwin's sleek, mineral-laden Art Series cuvées set the standard for Margaret River; Siblings bottlings are racy and elegant, and available at more wallet-friendly prices.

BOTTLES TO TRY

○ **Art Series Chardonnay** ∕ **$$$$**
● **Siblings Shiraz** ∕ **$$**

MITOLO

In record time, Mitolo became one of the most important names in McLaren Vale. The credit largely goes to Ben Glaetzer, whom Frank Mitolo hired in 2001, two years after taking his hobby winery commercial. Descended from a long line of Barossa Valley winemakers, Glaetzer immediately began turning out powerful, highly acclaimed reds, including the lush Serpico Cabernet, made from partially dried grapes, and the rich G.A.M. Shiraz. Second-label Jester is a smart value alternative.

BOTTLES TO TRY

● **Jester Shiraz** ∕ **$$**
● **G.A.M. Shiraz** ∕ **$$$**
● **Serpico Cabernet Sauvignon** ∕ **$$$**

PARINGA

South Australia's Riverland region churns out an ocean of affordable wine, some of which is industrial plonk and some that offers great everyday value. The wines from the family-owned Paringa estate belong to the latter category. Key to the brand's reasonable prices is its vast scale: Its owners, the Hickinbotham family, farm more than 1,800 acres of vineyards. Paringa's workhorse varieties are Shiraz, Cabernet and Merlot, which showcase the ripe, intense flavors typical of Riverland's warm climate.

BOTTLES TO TRY

● **Cabernet Sauvignon** ∕ **$**
● **Shiraz** ∕ **$**

PENFOLDS

Few wineries succeed as brilliantly as Penfolds in turning out both large-production everyday bottlings and rarified cuvées built for aging. The Shiraz-based Grange, Penfolds's top red, is Australia's greatest, most famous wine, with a cult following around the world. At the same time, Penfolds's affordable wines are reliable overachievers, like the inexpensive Koonunga Hill Shiraz-Cabernet. That emphasis on quality comes from an illustrious history (Penfolds has been in the Barossa since 1844) and the talent of its chief winemaker, Peter Gago.

BOTTLES TO TRY
- Koonunga Hill Shiraz-Cabernet / $
- Bin 28 Kalimna Shiraz / $$
- St. Henri Shiraz / $$$$

PENLEY ESTATE

The longtime Coonawarra winemaker Kym Tolley—a descendant of Penfolds's founder—started his own winery in 1988 after working at Penfolds for 15 years. While Australian reds have a reputation for going overboard with sweet fruit flavors, Tolley's all-estate-grown wines show balance and refinement, starting with entry-level offerings like the Hyland Shiraz and Condor, a smoky blend of Shiraz and Cabernet. Tolley's top wines can be hard to find but are worth seeking out as they showcase the complexity of Coonawarra *terroir*.

BOTTLES TO TRY
- Condor Shiraz-Cabernet / $$
- Phoenix Cabernet Sauvignon / $$

PETER LEHMANN WINES

Owned since 2003 by the Swiss entrepreneur Donald Hess, Peter Lehmann Wines has grown to become one of the Barossa's largest producers. The wines are labeled under a confusing variety of tiers and labels, but don't worry: A talented winemaking team and access to some of the region's oldest vines mean that it's hard to go wrong with this brand, especially when it comes to Shiraz.

BOTTLES TO TRY
- ○ Portrait Eden Valley Dry Riesling / $$
- Layers / $
- Stonewell Shiraz / $$$$

RARITIES & COLLECTIBLES

AP BIRKS WENDOUREE CELLARS Wendouree is the Greta Garbo of Australian wineries: legendary, elusive and internationally treasured. Wines from this Clare Valley icon have been made for the past four decades by owners Tony and Lita Brady, from vineyards first planted in 1892.

CHRIS RINGLAND The majestic Shirazes from this superstar prove that massive wines can be buoyant and balanced. Chris Ringland's namesake bottlings are incredibly scarce and crazy expensive and come chiefly from a single Barossa vineyard.

MOSS WOOD A bottle of the 1973 Moss Wood Cabernet Sauvignon sold for more than $2,000, breaking the record for a post-1970 Australian wine. Sourced from the winery's Margaret River estate, this eminent bottling is known for its longevity.

ROBERT OATLEY VINEYARDS

Bob Oatley made his fortune in coffee before turning his attention to wine in the late '60s, when he founded the wildly successful Rosemount brand. After selling Rosemount in 2001, Oatley doubled down on this namesake label with his son Sandy in 2006. The winery concentrates on regional specialties: two silky, bright Chardonnays from the Margaret River region and a Pinot Noir from Victoria's Mornington Peninsula, one of Australia's top spots for the grape.

BOTTLES TO TRY

○ **Finisterre Chardonnay** / $$
● **Signature Series Pinot Noir** / $$

RUSDEN

This boutique Barossa estate started small and has stayed small, despite high demand. That's because the Canute family crushes grapes from only their own 40-acre vineyard. Christian Canute joined his parents, Christine and Dennis, at the winery in 1997 and sparked Rusden's rise to fame. Christian's neo-traditionalist bent (he prefers old vines, handpicked grapes and unfiltered wines) results in polished cuvées like the acclaimed Black Guts Shiraz and Driftsand, a three-Rhône-variety red blend.

BOTTLES TO TRY

● **Driftsand** / $$
● **Black Guts Shiraz** / $$$$

SHAW & SMITH

Michael Hill Smith clearly relishes a challenge: Immediately after becoming the first Australian to achieve a Master of Wine degree, Hill Smith founded this Adelaide Hills label with his winemaking cousin, Martin Shaw. The duo owned neither vineyards nor winery, yet swiftly established a reputation for outstanding Sauvignon Blanc. Their rendition of that variety has become an Adelaide Hills benchmark, as has their M3 Chardonnay. But it's Shaw & Smith's coolly styled Shiraz and Pinot Noir that are revelatory, particularly for those who equate Australia with jammy fruit bombs.

BOTTLES TO TRY
○ **Sauvignon Blanc** / **$$**
● **Shiraz** / **$$$**

SHINGLEBACK

Winemaker John Davey had worked at some of Australia's biggest wine companies for more than a decade before creating his own brand with his brother Kym. They started with their family's McLaren Vale estate, first farmed by their grandfather in 1957, and have steadily built a stellar reputation for Shingleback. Their affordable Red Knot tier draws on vineyards from across McLaren Vale, while D Block focuses on specific plots in prime vineyards.

BOTTLES TO TRY
○ **Red Knot Chardonnay** / **$**
● **The Davey Estate Shiraz** / **$$**

THE STANDISH WINE COMPANY

The star winemaker Dan Standish fashions five tiny-production, old-vine Barossa Shirazes (and a mostly Shiraz blend, The Relic) that attract a cultlike following. The small, superconcentrated grapes from these elderly vines produce amazingly intense, complex wines. Just as key is Standish's minimalist approach in the winery, meaning that he resists techniques such as adding water and tannins, for example, and uses oak judiciously. The resulting wines display power and rare purity, and a kaleidoscopic mix of floral, mineral, fruit and savory flavors.

BOTTLES TO TRY
● **The Relic Shiraz-Viognier** / **$$$$**
● **The Standish Shiraz** / **$$$$**

TAHBILK

This Central Victoria winery is famous for its Marsanne, one of the two Rhône Valley varieties responsible for the legendary white wines of Hermitage. Tahbilk is also home to some of Australia's oldest vineyards, including a site that produces the winery's rare 1860 Vines Shiraz. Fortunately, Tahbilk also turns out a range of compelling wines in relatively greater abundance, all from estate vineyards in the lush Nagambie Lakes subregion. Its basic Marsanne is both affordable and ageworthy, and its reds are beautifully refined.

BOTTLES TO TRY

○ **Marsanne** / **$**

● **Shiraz** / **$$**

TIM ADAMS WINES

Riesling expert Tim Adams apprenticed under the legendary vintner Mick Knappstein at Clare Valley's Leasingham Winery before venturing out on his own in 1987. His namesake wines have proven him to be one of Australia's greatest cool-climate stylists. Adams brought his career full circle when he and his wife purchased Leasingham and much of its vineyards in 2011. Those vines have bolstered Adams's namesake wines, including the minerally, citrus-driven Riesling and a sleek Shiraz.

BOTTLES TO TRY

○ **Riesling** / **$$**

● **Shiraz** / **$$**

TORBRECK VINTNERS

Before becoming a winemaker, David Powell ditched an accounting career to go walkabout, an experience that involved a stint as a lumberjack in Scotland's Torbreck forest. Afterward, while working at the Barossa's Rockford estate, Powell picked up an obsession with very old vineyards—a passion he carried with him when he created Torbreck Vintners, named for the moody Scottish forest. Powell's top wines are brooding, phenomenally layered Barossa reds, like the famous (and expensive) RunRig. Other Torbreck wines, such as The Steading and Woodcutter's Shiraz, are more accessibly priced.

BOTTLES TO TRY

● **Woodcutter's Shiraz** / **$$**

● **Les Amis Grenache** / **$$$$**

TWO HANDS WINES

The "two hands" behind this ambitious, high-end *négociant* label are the owners, Michael Twelftree and Richard Mintz, who scour top wine regions for superlative vineyards, then convince their owners to sell them grapes. The label has become known for its showy, polished wines, chiefly Shiraz and Grenache, with a few oddballs like Moscato thrown in. Picture Series wines have goofy names and are the most affordable; Garden Series and Single Vineyard are a step up in price. The top cuvées are all named after Greek gods.

BOTTLES TO TRY
- ● Gnarly Dudes Shiraz / $$$
- ● Sexy Beast Cabernet Sauvignon / $$$

VASSE FELIX

The coolly refined Chardonnay and Cabernet from this pioneering Margaret River estate make a vivid contrast with wines from Australia's warmer regions. A Perth cardiologist, Tom Cullity, planted the original vineyard in 1967, and was the first to produce Margaret River wines. Since coming on board in 2006, the winemaker Virginia Willcock has dialed back the power of Vasse Felix's wines to gain brighter, more minerally flavors. Today the estate is producing its best bottles yet, with a multi-vineyard Chardonnay that's crisp yet creamy, and a generous, herb-edged Cabernet Sauvignon.

BOTTLES TO TRY
- ○ Chardonnay / $$
- ● Cabernet Sauvignon / $$$

WIRRA WIRRA VINEYARDS

The late Greg Trott and his cousin Roger revived this historic McLaren Vale winery in 1969. Greg was a prank-loving, cricket-playing winemaker, as was the man who founded Wirra Wirra in 1894, Robert Strangways Wigley. The wines, however, are very serious, offering classic McLaren Vale structure and, lately, an extra dollop of finesse, thanks to the ex-Petaluma winemaker and cool-climate specialist Paul Smith.

BOTTLES TO TRY
- ● Catapult Shiraz / $$
- ● Church Block Cabernet Sauvignon–Shiraz–Merlot / $$
- ● RSW Shiraz / $$$

WOLF BLASS

Chief winemaker Chris Hatcher has kept a steady hand in the cellar at this megawinery. For a time, Wolf Blass wines were hard to find in the U.S., but luckily new vintages are becoming more readily available. The winery's vast portfolio delivers great value wines (the Yellow Label Dry Riesling is a perennial steal) as well as ageworthy, finely crafted reds (the Black Label blend has won Australia's prestigious Jimmy Watson Memorial Trophy four times).

BOTTLES TO TRY

○ Yellow Label Dry Riesling / $

● Black Label Cabernet Sauvignon–Shiraz–Malbec / $$$$

YALUMBA

At 165 years, Yalumba is as old as the Australian wine industry and is still run by descendants of its founder. The current scion, Robert Hill Smith, constantly experiments with lesser-known grape varieties, from Vermentino to Viognier, although Shiraz and Cabernet Sauvignon remain the foundation of Yalumba's remarkable success. Highlights of the portfolio include The Signature, a powerful Cabernet-Shiraz blend that competes with cult bottlings twice its price, and the affordable Y Series Viognier, which is reliably silky, aromatic and succulent.

BOTTLES TO TRY

○ Y Series Viognier / $

● The Signature Cabernet Sauvignon–Shiraz / $$$

● The Octavius Shiraz / $$$$

YANGARRA ESTATE VINEYARD

Yangarra's winemaker, Peter Fraser, prizes finesse over power. Working with estate-grown grapes in McLaren Vale's comparatively cool climate, he crafts Yangarra's vibrant, well-balanced wines. Fraser works exclusively with fruit from a single biodynamically farmed vineyard south of Adelaide. Planted to Rhône varieties, it's home to a prized plot of 68-year-old Grenache that yields a consistently great Old Vine bottling. The winery's basic cuvées, like the spicy, herb-inflected Shiraz, have a subtlety that makes them especially food-friendly.

BOTTLES TO TRY

● Old Vine Grenache / $$

● Shiraz / $$

New Zealand

Wine Region

Contrary to what fans of Peter Jackson's movies might think, there are no hobbits in New Zealand. As compensation, though, there are an extraordinary number of really terrific wines. The country's crisp, sea-chilled breezes, lush green valleys and mostly long, cool summers make New Zealand a great source for Pinot Noir, Riesling and, to a lesser degree, Pinot Gris and Syrah, and it's one of the world's greatest spots to plant Sauvignon Blanc. In fact, the country essentially redefined people's idea of this grape starting in the 1980s, and it has since become New Zealand's signature variety. The rise of Sauvignon Blanc has been a great boon—it's the engine that powers the country's entire wine business—but it can also be a burden, as wine buyers often overlook the variety and ambition of New Zealand's wines.

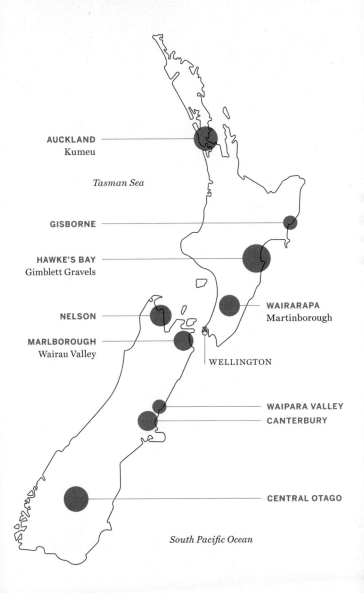

AUCKLAND
Kumeu

Tasman Sea

GISBORNE

HAWKE'S BAY
Gimblett Gravels

WAIRARAPA
Martinborough

NELSON

MARLBOROUGH
Wairau Valley

WELLINGTON

WAIPARA VALLEY

CANTERBURY

CENTRAL OTAGO

South Pacific Ocean

New Zealand

REGIONS TO KNOW

CENTRAL OTAGO In a rain-soaked country, this southern region's hot summers, cold winters and dry autumns make it unique—and perfect for growing voluptuous Pinot Noir. That variety has become synonymous with Central Otago, which routinely produces some of the country's best examples of the grape.

GISBORNE A white wine zone on the east coast of the North Island, Gisborne produces mostly creamy Chardonnay and a smattering of Pinot Gris, Gewürztraminer and Muscat.

HAWKE'S BAY One of the few spots warm enough to properly ripen heat-loving red grapes, this North Island region is the go-to zone for Merlot, Cabernet Sauvignon and Syrah, with the finest examples coming from the **GIMBLETT GRAVELS** area.

MARLBOROUGH Located on the northeast coast of the South Island, Marlborough is New Zealand's most important wine region, producing more than two-thirds of the country's Sauvignon Blanc and more than half its Pinot Noir, as well as juicy, fresh Chardonnays. The **WAIRAU VALLEY** is home to the majority of Marlborough's vineyards.

WAIPARA VALLEY & CANTERBURY These neighboring districts on the South Island both specialize in Pinot Noir. Canterbury's main white is Chardonnay, while Waipara grows aromatic varieties like Riesling, Sauvignon Blanc and Pinot Gris.

WAIRARAPA & MARTINBOROUGH The regions that originally staked New Zealand's claim to great Pinot Noir also turn out noteworthy Chardonnay and Pinot Gris.

❦ KEY GRAPES: WHITE

CHARDONNAY A trend toward less oak aging has improved New Zealand's Chardonnays, which showcase apple and citrus notes. Riper, oaked versions are now sharing shelf space with leaner, crisper styles.

PINOT GRIS, RIESLING & GEWÜRZTRAMINER Increasingly fashionable alternatives to the ubiquitous Sauvignon Blanc and Chardonnay, these Alsace grapes thrive in Waipara and Gisborne. New Zealand Rieslings tend to be made in an off-dry—i.e., lightly sweet—style, balanced by zesty acidity. Most of the country's Pinot Gris comes from the South Island, whose bottlings are leaner than those from North Island zones.

SAUVIGNON BLANC Few countries are as identified with a single grape as New Zealand is with Sauvignon Blanc. While the traditional style here is zingy and unoaked, with green pepper, lime and grapefruit notes, warmer vintages and a move toward more fruity wines have resulted in a wider array of styles. North Island Sauvignon Blancs tend to be riper and fruitier than those from Marlborough, the most prolific region for the grape.

❦ KEY GRAPES: RED

CABERNET SAUVIGNON & MERLOT One of the few spots in New Zealand warm enough for these reds is Hawke's Bay, on the North Island. Look for examples from its Gimblett Gravels subregion, where vintners make superb Bordeaux-style blends.

PINOT NOIR Vibrant acidity is a hallmark of New Zealand's most popular red. Cool regions like Marlborough offer tangy, berry-flavored versions, whereas Central Otago yields richer examples. Martinborough produces the North Island's best Pinots.

SYRAH Most of New Zealand is too cold for Syrah, but examples from Hawke's Bay's Gimblett Gravels subzone can be excellent, with seductive floral, spice and black-fruit notes.

WINE TERMINOLOGY

New Zealand labels generally list region, grape, vintage and, in some cases, vineyard name. The term *reserve* may be used to designate higher-quality wines but has no legal meaning.

Producers/
New Zealand

AMISFIELD WINE COMPANY

Amisfield's Pinot Noir grapes grow in the shadow of the Pisa Range, a rugged, often snow-capped mountain ridge in Central Otago. It's a remote region of cool, crystalline air and generous sunlight—qualities that seem almost palpable in Amisfield's two fragrant, structured Pinot Noirs. Purity and focus define these acclaimed reds, which are all the more remarkable for the winery's brief history; Amisfield crushed its first vintage in 2002.

BOTTLES TO TRY
- ● **Pinot Noir** / **$$$**
- ● **RKV Reserve Pinot Noir** / **$$$$**

ASTROLABE WINES

One of the odder strokes of bad luck in the wine industry hit Astrolabe when 4,000 cases of its zesty Sauvignon Blanc were lost in a shipwreck on New Zealand's Astrolabe reef. (Adding to the irony: An astrolabe is an ancient navigation instrument.) Simon Waghorn, his wife and a couple of friends created Astrolabe Wines when Waghorn was winemaker at the Whitehaven label. His talent is clear across Astrolabe's Marlborough-sourced range, including its juicy, overachieving Province bottlings.

BOTTLES TO TRY
- ○ **Province Sauvignon Blanc** / **$$**
- ● **Province Pinot Noir** / **$$**

BRANCOTT ESTATE

Brancott's basic Sauvignon Blanc is one of those reliable, widely available wines that's always delicious, regardless of vintage. Another plus: Its price goes down as easily as the tangy, grapefruit-tinged wine does. Brancott was the first to plant Sauvignon Blanc in Marlborough, in the early 1970s. Today it offers a cross section of varietals, but Sauvignon Blanc remains its strength.

BOTTLES TO TRY
- ○ **Sauvignon Blanc** / **$**
- ○ **Reserve Sauvignon Blanc** / **$$**

BURN COTTAGE VINEYARD

Take two *terroir*-obsessed, Midwestern wine importers (Marquis and Dianne Sauvage), add one of California's most revered Pinot Noir masters (Littorai's Ted Lemon), and a small sheep farm in Central Otago, and you have the beginnings of Burn Cottage Vineyard. The Sauvages released their first Pinots under the wryly named Cashburn label; in 2009, they bottled a few lots deemed good enough for the Burn Cottage Vineyard name. The wait paid off: The wine's savory complexity and gravitas puts it in New Zealand's top ranks. Burn Cottage's second wine, Cashburn, is no slouch, either.

BOTTLES TO TRY

- Cashburn Pinot Noir / $$
- Pinot Noir / $$$

CLOUDY BAY

It's rare that a single wine defines both a style and a country, but that's exactly what Cloudy Bay's iconic Marlborough Sauvignon Blanc did in the 1980s and '90s. Crisp, peppery and intense, it gained international fame and gave New Zealand a near-instant wine identity. Senior winemaker Tim Heath, who took over from the founding winemaker, Kevin Judd, has toned down Cloudy Bay's flamboyant herbaceousness in recent years. He even ferments a bit of the wine in barrels—just enough to take the edge off of its zippy acidity.

BOTTLE TO TRY

○ Sauvignon Blanc / $$

COOPERS CREEK VINEYARD

Star winemaker Kim Crawford (see p. 245) helped bring this family-owned Auckland winery to prominence in the 1990s with a string of award-winning wines. His successor, Simon Nunns, took over the cellar in 1998 and has indulged his experimental streak: With the support of owners Andrew and Cyndy Hendry, Nunns bottles 14 or so varietals each year, ranging from Arneis to Montepulciano. Coopers Creek's most reliable wines, though, remain its longtime strengths: bright, vibrant Chardonnay and Sauvignon Blanc.

BOTTLES TO TRY

○ Gisborne Chardonnay / $
○ Marlborough Sauvignon Blanc / $

CRAGGY RANGE

Arguably no winery better illustrates New Zealand's capability to produce world-class wine beyond Sauvignon Blanc than Craggy Range. This Hawke's Bay estate, a partnership between the Australian ex-billionaire Terry Peabody and the acclaimed Kiwi wine guru Steve Smith, produces one of New Zealand's greatest Syrahs, Le Sol, as well as some of its best examples of Chardonnay, Pinot Noir and Bordeaux-inspired reds. Of course, with a talent like Smith on board, it's no surprise that Craggy Range's Sauvignon Blancs are terrific, too.

BOTTLES TO TRY

○ **Kidnappers Vineyard Chardonnay ⁄ $$**

● **Le Sol ⁄ $$$$**

FELTON ROAD

Felton Road's minerally, dark-fruited Pinot Noirs have become standard-bearers for New Zealand versions of the grape. It's not just that they're complex and impeccably made; rather, with their effortless balance of lush New World fruit and savory strength, they're definitive expressions of Central Otago *terroir*. No place else produces Pinot Noir exactly like this. In fact, no two parcels on the Felton Road estate yield the same wine. That's why gifted winemaker Blair Walter bottles his best plots separately, like the famed Block 3 and Block 5 Pinots.

BOTTLES TO TRY

● **Bannockburn Pinot Noir ⁄ $$$**

● **Block 3 Pinot Noir ⁄ $$$$**

GREYWACKE

To Sauvignon Blanc fanatics, the name Kevin Judd is as well known as that of Cloudy Bay (see p. 243), the vaunted Marlborough winery that Judd helped make famous. Judd is a brilliant Sauvignon specialist who left Cloudy Bay to establish this boutique label in 2009. At Greywacke, he fashions Pinot Noir and small lots of Chardonnay, Riesling, Gewürztraminer and Pinot Gris. But Judd's hallmark wines are two exemplary Sauvignon Blancs: One is a stony, vibrant bottling; the other is fermented with wild yeasts.

BOTTLES TO TRY

○ **Sauvignon Blanc ⁄ $$**

○ **Wild Sauvignon ⁄ $$**

KIM CRAWFORD WINES

This well-known brand started in 1996 as a "virtual" winery: Founder Kim Crawford crushed Marlborough grapes in a rented facility while his wife, Erica, managed marketing out of their Auckland cottage. The Crawfords have moved on, but the label they founded has become incredibly successful. Under winemaker Anthony Walkenhorst, it turns out the best-selling New Zealand Sauvignon Blanc in the U.S. It's easy to grasp why: Ripe, bright and zesty, it's quintessential Marlborough.

WINE INTEL
Kim Crawford—the man, not the brand—recently introduced Loveblock, a line of organic wines. He crafts aromatic whites such as Sauvignon Blanc and Pinot Gris from Marlborough, and Pinot Noir from Central Otago.

BOTTLES TO TRY

○ Sauvignon Blanc / $$

○ Unoaked Chardonnay / $$

LAWSON'S DRY HILLS

Aromatic white wines, from crisply dry to sweet dessert versions, are the specialty of this family-run winery, located in Marlborough's Wairau Valley. Matriarch Barbara Lawson and her late husband, Ross, planted the first wine grapes on their farm in 1980—back when New Zealand's wine industry was in its infancy—and made their first wine in 1992. Lawson's signature variety is Gewürztraminer, which winemaker Marcus Wright fashions in a bright, ripe style that's reminiscent of Alsace. The tangy, citrusy Sauvignon Blanc is another good bet.

BOTTLES TO TRY

○ Gewürztraminer / $$

○ Sauvignon Blanc / $$

MATUA

Matua's founders Ross and Bill Spence were the first to plant Sauvignon Blanc in New Zealand, which is a bit like being the first people to plant tomatoes in Italy. Now one of New Zealand's largest brands, Matua has been on a roll lately, thanks to winemaker Nikolai St. George. An alumnus of Amisfield (see p. 242), one of Central Otago's top boutique estates, St. George joined Matua in 2008 and has refined its wines across the board.

BOTTLES TO TRY

○ Sauvignon Blanc / $

○ Paretai Sauvignon Blanc / $$

NAUTILUS ESTATE

This Marlborough estate was the first in New Zealand to build a facility customized entirely to Pinot Noir. Nautilus takes great pains with its flagship grape, including using only handpicked fruit and aging the wine in French oak barrels—which helps explain why its Pinot Noir regularly ranks among Marlborough's best. Just one other bottling from Nautilus gets wide distribution in the U.S.—its tangy, grapefruit-scented Sauvignon Blanc—meaning that you'll have to head to New Zealand to taste wines like its rare Grüner Veltliner.

BOTTLES TO TRY

○ Sauvignon Blanc / $$
● Pinot Noir / $$

NOBILO

Croatian immigrant Nick Nobilo came from a family that had been making wine for three centuries, so after he and wife Zuva arrived in New Zealand in the late 1930s, he planted grape vines as soon as he could. That small vineyard outside Auckland grew into one of the country's biggest wine brands. Nobilo's Marlborough Sauvignon Blanc offers classic Marlborough style, with a zesty balance of herb and citrus flavors. The Icon bottling is richer, with more tropical notes, and costs just a few dollars more.

BOTTLES TO TRY

○ Marlborough Sauvignon Blanc / $
○ Icon Sauvignon Blanc / $$

SAINT CLAIR FAMILY ESTATE

Marlborough vintners tend to be a Sauvignon-obsessed lot, but Saint Clair takes its passion further than most, with something like nine single-vineyard bottlings to choose from. The wines' small production can sometimes make them difficult to find, but never mind—the winery's entry-level Sauvignon Blanc, Vicar's Choice, is a fantastically citrusy, refreshing white that's made in much larger quantities. Consulting winemaker Matt Thomson has been the secret weapon behind Saint Clair since its first vintage in 1994; Hamish Clark steers the winery day-to-day.

BOTTLES TO TRY

○ Vicar's Choice Sauvignon Blanc / $$
○ Wairau Reserve Sauvignon Blanc / $$

SPY VALLEY WINES

Sure, Spy Valley grows Sauvignon Blanc (few Marlborough wineries don't), and its version is perfectly delicious. But anyone stuck in a Sauvignon rut should look to this midsize producer for alternatives, which include bright, richly styled Chardonnays, lithe Pinot Noirs, and aromatic whites such as Gewürztraminer, Pinot Gris and Riesling. Owners Bryan and Jan Johnson named their winery for a mysterious spy station located near their Marlborough estate.

BOTTLES TO TRY
○ **Sauvignon Blanc / $$**
● **Pinot Noir / $$**

WAIRAU RIVER WINES

Phil and Christine Rose faced skepticism from their neighbors when they planted some of the first vineyards along Marlborough's Wairau River in 1978. Today their estate is one of Wairau's most successful family wineries. Now run by their five children, Wairau River produces terrific estate-made Sauvignon Blanc and Pinot Noir. It's also among just a handful of carbon-neutral wineries in the country employing eco-friendly practices like water recycling and strict energy conservation.

BOTTLES TO TRY
○ **Sauvignon Blanc / $$**
● **Pinot Noir / $$**

Argentina

Wine Region

The words *wine* and *food* in Argentina inevitably bring two things to mind: Malbec and beef. By far, more Malbec is grown here than any other wine grape, and Argentineans are among the most beef-obsessed people in the world. That's not a bad thing. But what's surprising is how much more this South American country has to offer: Its top Chardonnays and Cabernets have the polish and poise to compete internationally, and its floral-edged Torrontés is a largely undiscovered gem. Meanwhile, the remote Patagonian wilderness has become the most unlikely source of impressive Pinot Noir—yet another good reason to start exploring the world of Argentine wine.

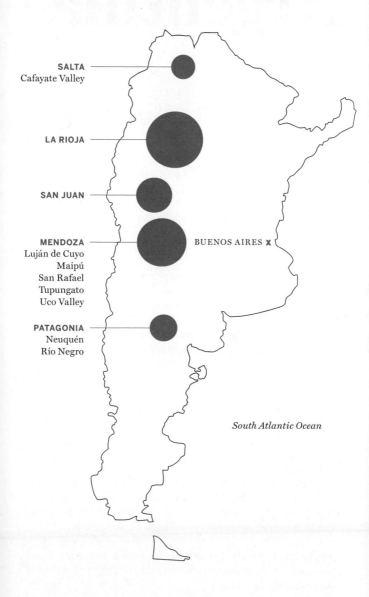

SALTA
Cafayate Valley

LA RIOJA

SAN JUAN

MENDOZA
Luján de Cuyo
Maipú
San Rafael
Tupungato
Uco Valley

BUENOS AIRES **X**

PATAGONIA
Neuquén
Río Negro

South Atlantic Ocean

Argentina

REGIONS TO KNOW

MENDOZA More than 80 percent of Argentina's wine comes from this vast west-central region. Of its major growing areas, **MAIPÚ**, **LUJÁN DE CUYO** and **SAN RAFAEL** are the oldest and best known. Newer, higher-altitude subzones such as the **UCO VALLEY** and its **TUPUNGATO** subregion, which lie at elevations of more than 3,200 feet, are gaining fame for their refined, cooler-climate reds and whites.

SALTA This isolated, mountainous province in northwestern Argentina boasts some of the world's highest-altitude vineyards; its **CAFAYATE VALLEY** is a source of refreshing white wines.

LA RIOJA & SAN JUAN These traditional wine regions have been moving gradually from bulk production to high-quality wine-making, especially in San Juan's cooler corners, which are gaining a reputation for Syrah.

PATAGONIA The world's most southerly vineyards have begun producing impressive wines from Pinot Noir and Malbec in this up-and-coming province.

🍇 KEY GRAPES: WHITE

CHARDONNAY Argentine Chardonnay ranges in style from crisp, lightly oaked and light-bodied to rich, full-bodied and creamy. Top wines have grown increasingly sophisticated, with many of the finest examples coming from high-altitude vines.

PINOT GRIS (PINOT GRIGIO), SÉMILLON & VIOGNIER Small amounts of these aromatic whites are finding a foothold in Argentina's cooler regions.

SAUVIGNON BLANC This crisp variety ripens easily in Argentina's sunny climate, yielding medium-bodied, melony whites. The best versions come from cooler climates, such as the Uco Valley and other high-altitude zones.

TORRONTÉS The country's signature white grape variety, Torrontés makes distinctive, refreshing wines that showcase crisp citrus flavors and exuberant floral aromas. For the best examples, look to Salta, a high-altitude province that has proven itself to be ideally suited to the grape.

🍇 KEY GRAPES: RED

BONARDA A staple in many Argentine vineyards and historically used in blends, Bonarda is a deeply colored red grape that's now being taken more seriously by winemakers: Polished, single-variety bottlings are joining rustic, cherry-inflected blends.

CABERNET SAUVIGNON Look for Cabernets from Mendoza, where sunny, arid days and cool nights result in wines packed with powerful cassis and a hint of bell pepper.

MALBEC While it yields tough, tannic wines in its native France, this grape becomes alluringly supple in Argentina, producing reds with peppery black-fruit notes.

PINOT NOIR Most of Argentina's wine regions are too warm to grow this thin-skinned grape. Patagonia has turned out to be ideal Pinot Noir territory, however, and examples from this remote region are velvety and aromatic.

SYRAH Argentinean vintners often blend Syrah with other red grapes, most often Malbec. But on its own Syrah can yield great wines full of dark, brooding fruit and spice.

WINE TERMINOLOGY

Most Argentine wine labels identify grape variety, the region where the grapes were grown, the producer's name and the vintage. Wineries are known as bodegas; the word *finca* refers to a particular vineyard or estate. Many wineries apply the designation *reserva* to their higher-quality bottlings, although this term has no legal meaning.

Producers/ Argentina

BODEGA CATENA ZAPATA

Led by the legendary vintner Nicolás Catena, this estate epitomizes Argentina's arrival as a fine-wine powerhouse. Inspired by visits to Napa Valley in the 1980s, Catena transformed his family's low-end wine business—and Argentine wine—with his ambitious, quality-driven offerings. Today his daughter Laura helps run the now iconic estate.

BOTTLES TO TRY
- Catena Cabernet Sauvignon / $$
- Alta Malbec / $$$

BODEGA COLOMÉ

Swiss-born wine entrepreneur Donald Hess and winemaker Thibaut Delmotte are pushing the boundaries of high-altitude winemaking in the remote Salta region. Hess's Colomé estate lies at elevations of up to about 10,000 feet, where chilly nights produce wines of rare freshness and purity. The Torrontés is a textbook rendition of the grape—floral, melony and crisp—and the basic Malbec is reliably vibrant and complex.

BOTTLES TO TRY
- ○ Torrontés / $
- Estate Malbec / $$

BODEGA DIAMANDES

Michèle and Alfred-Alexandre Bonnie, the owners of the Bordeaux *grand cru* Malartic-Lagravière, ventured into Mendoza with the creation of Bodega DiamAndes in 2005. The sleek new winery and vineyards are part of Clos de los Siete, the prestigious Uco Valley collective (see opposite). Silvio Alberto runs the cellar day-to-day, fashioning luscious, smoothly appealing reds.

BOTTLES TO TRY
- Perlita Malbec-Syrah / $
- Gran Reserva / $$$

CLOS DE LOS SIETE

When the French superstar winemaker Michel Rolland first visited Argentina to offer consulting advice, he was so impressed by the country's potential that he founded his own estate, with a handful of French investors as partners. Today Clos de los Siete encompasses four distinct wineries spread across 2,100 acres in the Uco Valley. Each partner contributes wine for a single, Rolland-made blend based on Malbec. With a velvety, luscious style, the wine is surprisingly affordable for such a high-profile venture.

BOTTLE TO TRY

● Clos de los Siete / $$

DOMINIO DEL PLATA WINERY

Winemaker extraordinaire Susana Balbo is as adept at making affordable, everyday wines as she is at fashioning tiny quantities of rarified reds. Her well-priced Crios line is a value hunter's dream, especially the peach-scented Torrontés. Both luscious and crisp, it's a reference point for the grape. At the high end, Balbo's famous Nosotros bottling comes from old-vine Malbec, much of it from Balbo's Dominio del Plata estate. Its voluptuous flavors and intense, ageworthy structure make it one of Argentina's benchmark reds.

BOTTLES TO TRY

○ Crios Torrontés / $

● Susana Balbo Malbec / $$

● Nosotros / $$$$

MENDEL

Roberto de la Mota made his name crafting superbly balanced and complex wines at the prestigious labels Terrazas de los Andes (owned by the luxury-goods giant LVMH) and Cheval des Andes. Mendel is de la Mota's personal project, a boutique estate focused with laserlike intensity on five small-lot wines: four reds and a Sémillon. De la Mota relies chiefly on very old vines planted in the gravelly soils of Luján de Cuyo, giving his wines fantastic depth. The supple Lunta bottling is both easy-drinking and easy on the wallet.

BOTTLES TO TRY

● Lunta Malbec / $$

● Unus Malbec / $$$

O FOURNIER

José Manuel Ortega Gil-Fournier got seriously into wine during his days as a high-rolling investment banker. That passion eventually became his profession, when the Spanish-born Ortega bought a 650-acre estate in the Uco Valley in 2000 and, not long after that, a second estate in Spain's Ribera del Duero. What's remarkable, given Ortega's newbie status, is how fantastic the wines are. Working out of a spaceship-esque winery plopped on a desert hilltop, the winemaker José Spisso fashions reds and whites that compete with the country's best across a range of prices.

BOTTLES TO TRY
- Urban Uco Malbec / $
- Alfa Crux / $$$

PASCUAL TOSO

The well-known California winemaker Paul Hobbs serves as consultant to this venerable winery, which turns out delicious, super reliable wines at amazingly low prices. The winery was founded in 1890 by its namesake, an immigrant from Italy's Piedmont region, and it is best known in Argentina as a maker of sparkling wine. But in the U.S., its red wines stand out, including a value Cabernet that's loaded with blackberry fruit and firm but velvety tannins, and a basic Malbec that has dark, rich fruit lifted by peppery notes.

BOTTLES TO TRY
- Cabernet Sauvignon / $
- Malbec / $

PULENTA ESTATE

An Argentine-wine mini dynasty of achievement and drive, the Pulenta family took over the megawinery Trapiche (see opposite) in 1971 and ran it for about 30 years. Brothers Eduardo and Hugo Pulenta founded this Mendoza winery in 2002, while their brother Carlos created the respected Vistalba label. Pulenta Estate's location in a relatively cool section of the Alto Agrelo area means that its reds maintain a spicy vibrancy and its whites are refreshingly crisp.

BOTTLES TO TRY
- La Flor Malbec / $
- XI Gran Cabernet Franc / $$$

RARITIES & COLLECTIBLES

BODEGA BRESSIA Walter Bressia spent 30 years making wine for some of Argentina's biggest brands, but at his boutique Mendoza estate he lavishes his attention on just a few hundred barrels a year. That focus shows in Conjuro, a stunning, three-variety red blend.

BODEGA NOEMÍA DE PATAGONIA This exciting estate, owned by Italian countess Noemi Marone Cinzano and run by Danish winemaker Hans Vinding-Diers, produces some of Argentina's best Malbecs from ancient vines in the remote Patagonian desert.

BODEGA POESÍA Hélène Garcin-Lévêque (of Pomerol's Clos L'Église) and her winemaking husband, Patrice, lend a Bordeaux touch to their Poesía cuvée, a beautifully polished, single-vineyard blend of Malbec and Cabernet.

TRAPICHE

In the foothills of the Andes in the Mendoza region, Trapiche has become one of Argentina's most ambitious wineries. Not long after its chief winemaker Daniel Pi took over a little more than a decade ago, Trapiche released an impressive collection of single-vineyard Malbecs that helped restore luster to the brand, which had been increasingly focused on value-driven wines. And while top bottles compete in quality with boutique labels, the estate remains a terrific source of everyday, affordable wines. Two great examples are the peppery Oak Cask Malbec and, at a small step up in price, the ebulliently fruity, grapey Broquel Bonarda.

BOTTLES TO TRY
- Broquel Bonarda / $
- Oak Cask Malbec / $

Chile

Wine Region

Given that Chile is only about 110 miles wide on average (albeit about 2,700 miles long), it's amazing that winemakers there keep discovering new—and exciting—regions for producing wine. The vineyards around Santiago have long been known for their inexpensive, appealing red wines, as well as for ambitious Cabernets that are on par with the world's best. Not that long ago, vivid, minerally Sauvignon Blancs started appearing from areas like San Antonio and Leyda, hard up against the cold Pacific Ocean; and in the past couple of years, Chilean winemakers have planted vines and produced wine—often terrific wine—in even cooler regions that had never been associated with grapes before, like the Elqui Valley in the north and Bío Bío in the south. All of this exploration has revealed a much more complex country than wine lovers may expect.

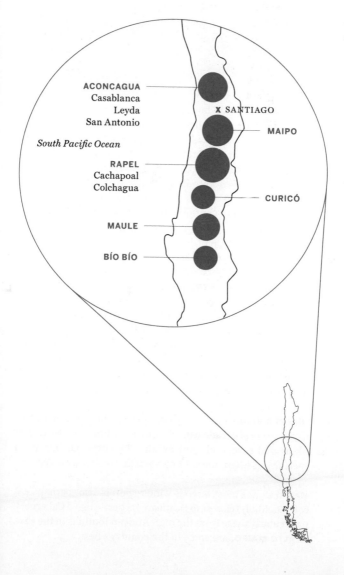

ACONCAGUA
Casablanca
Leyda
San Antonio

South Pacific Ocean

RAPEL
Cachapoal
Colchagua

MAULE

BÍO BÍO

X SANTIAGO

MAIPO

CURICÓ

Chile

REGIONS TO KNOW

ACONCAGUA Just an hour's drive from Santiago, Aconcagua includes a cluster of valleys that have achieved phenomenal success with crisp, cool-climate red and white varieties, chiefly Pinot Noir and Sauvignon Blanc. Look for wines from the **CASABLANCA** and coastal **SAN ANTONIO** subregions, as well as **LEYDA,** San Antonio's best-known zone.

BÍO BÍO This rainy, southern district is a stronghold of basic table wine. Recently, forward-looking vintners here have been creating exciting Pinot Noirs and aromatic whites such as Riesling and Gewürztraminer.

COSTA, ANDES & ENTRE CORDILLERAS While Chile's older appellations cluster around east–west gaps in its coastal mountain range, where chilly ocean winds pour into the central valley, these three new designations identify broad north–south swaths of Chile's coastal (Costa), Andean (Andes) and central (Entre Cordilleras) zones. Most of Chile's wines come from the Entre Cordilleras (between ranges) zone, which runs between the Coastal Range and the Andes.

LIMARÍ & ELQUI These northern districts burst out of obscurity in the past decade with stunning renditions of Sauvignon Blanc and savory, elegant Syrah. The latter has become a specialty of Elqui, the country's northernmost wine region.

MAIPO Chile's most famous wine region is also (perhaps not coincidentally) closest to Santiago. Its herb-tinged Cabernets, particularly those from the high Andean foothills to the east, in **ALTO MAIPO,** are some of the country's best.

MAULE Most of the wines coming from this relatively warm zone in south-central Chile are unremarkable, though exceptions are becoming more common, including some terrific old-vine Carignane and fruity, straightforward Merlot.

COLCHAGUA & CACHAPOAL Warmer temperatures help red wines flourish in the valleys south of Santiago, notably in Colchagua, where Cabernet Sauvignon vines dominate. Other heat-loving grapes such as Carmenère, Merlot and Syrah thrive in Colchagua as well. Some of the valley's most acclaimed cuvées come from its small, sheltered **APALTA** district. The Cachapoal zone, which like Colchagua is a subzone of the large **RAPEL** region, is also making increasingly ambitious reds.

❦ KEY GRAPES: WHITE

CHARDONNAY The cooler, ocean-influenced zones near the coast produce Chile's best Chardonnays.

SAUVIGNON BLANC This Bordeaux variety has become Chile's flagship white. Bright, fragrant Sauvignons come from regions up and down the coast, where cool breezes help develop its tangy citrus and grass flavors.

❦ KEY GRAPES: RED

CABERNET SAUVIGNON Cabernet is king in Chile. The country is supremely well-suited to the grape, which is why it's the most widely planted variety here and why a disproportionate number of the planet's greatest Cabernet bargains come from Chile. Offering savory notes and firm structure, in addition to exuberant fruit, the best Chilean Cabernets challenge premier California bottlings in quality.

CARMENÈRE Like Merlot, the grape for which it was long mistaken, Carmenère came to Chile from France's Bordeaux region. The confusion is understandable: Both varieties possess plummy fruit and fine-grained tannins, but Carmenère expresses an alluring spicy accent that's distinctively Chilean.

MERLOT Often combined with Cabernet Sauvignon or Carmenère grapes in blends, Chilean Merlot is typically juicy, supple and loaded with layers of ripe plum and black cherry.

PINOT NOIR Chilean Pinot Noirs have improved dramatically in recent years, though, as with Pinot everywhere, quality can be inconsistent. This famously finicky grape variety grows best in marginal climates with cooler temperatures, which in Chile means coastal zones like Casablanca, San Antonio and the latter's Leyda subzone, as well as the remote Bío Bío region.

SYRAH The Chilean wine industry's Francophile bent shows in its Syrahs, which at their best combine powerful dark fruit with cooler notes of pepper and violets, similar in many ways to renditions from France's Rhône Valley. Young plantings in districts like the Elqui and Limarí valleys are turning out impressive new wines from cool-climate vineyards.

WINE TERMINOLOGY

Chilean labels list the name of the winery (*viña*) or brand, grape variety and often a proprietary name for blends. Producers are increasingly using single-vineyard designations and adding the term *reserva* to top-quality wines. Introduced in 2011, the Costa, Andes and Entre Cordilleras geographical designations (see p. 258) are now appearing on wine labels.

Producers/ Chile

ALMAVIVA

Chilean powerhouse Concha y Toro and Bordeaux's esteemed Château Mouton Rothschild teamed up to create Almaviva, which is the name of both the label and the single ambitious wine produced under it each year. First created in 1996 and sourced in part from a legendary Maipo Valley vineyard called Puente Alto, the wine is a powerful, velvety red blend that's based on Cabernet Sauvignon, with smaller amounts of Carmenère and other Bordeaux varieties. With such resources and expertise behind it, it's no surprise that Almaviva consistently ranks among Chile's greatest reds.

BOTTLE TO TRY

● Almaviva / $$$$

ANTIYAL

After a fast-track career that included stints at Bordeaux's Château Margaux and Chile's Viña Carmen, star winemaker Álvaro Espinoza created his own label in 1996, focusing on just two wines. Antiyal is his flagship cuvée, a masterfully balanced Maipo Valley red fashioned from Carmenère, Cabernet Sauvignon and Syrah. Espinoza makes Kuyen, its baby brother, from the same organically farmed vineyards and varieties, but in different proportions.

BOTTLES TO TRY

- Kuyen / $$
- Antiyal / $$$

CONCHA Y TORO

The largest producer in Chile, Concha y Toro makes wine from every major grape in every major region of the country. Of its dizzying lineup—there are 12 sub-brands—the affordable Casillero del Diablo and mid-priced Marques de Casa Concha lines offer great value. The pricier Terrunyo tier highlights specific *terroirs*. Two world-class reds, the Don Melchor Cabernet Sauvignon and Carmín de Peumo Carmenère, top the portfolio.

BOTTLES TO TRY

- Casillero del Diablo Carmenère / $
- Terrunyo Pirque Vineyard Cabernet Sauvignon / $$$
- Don Melchor Cabernet Sauvignon / $$$$

DE MARTINO

The family-owned De Martino winery launched Chile's first carbon-neutral wine program in 2009 and has initiated a series of eco-friendly measures, including reducing gas emissions and measuring water usage. All of this makes environmentalists happy, but De Martino's terrific wines are reason enough to seek out this Maipo-based label. De Martino helped pioneer Carmenère grapes, and remains one of the most reliable producers of the variety. Under the winemaker Marcelo Retamal, the winery has also ventured into emerging zones: The ripe, juicy Legado Chardonnay, for example, comes from the Limarí Valley, where cooler temperatures temper the grape's lushness.

BOTTLES TO TRY

- ○ Legado Chardonnay Reserva / $
- Alto de Piedras Single Vineyard Carmenère / $$$

DOMUS AUREA

Ricardo and Isabel Peña never intended to become vintners. In the 1970s, they acquired a property on the outskirts of Santiago that was planted to old-vine Cabernet and sold the grapes. But demand for their stellar hillside fruit grew so clamorous that in 1995 the Peñas built their own winery. Their famous, powerful Domus Aurea red still comes from the same vineyard, as does its less costly sibling, the Peñalolen Cabernet Sauvignon. Value hunters should also look for the Peñalolen Sauvignon Blanc.

BOTTLES TO TRY
○ Peñalolen Sauvignon Blanc / $
● Domus Aurea / $$$

EMILIANA ORGANIC VINEYARDS

Emiliana is arguably Chile's most socially responsible winery, turning out terrific, eco-friendly wines from a carbon-neutral operation. Consultant Álvaro Espinoza (see Antiyal, p. 261) has been key to its success, helping Emiliana blaze a trail for organic and biodynamic farming. The vineyards operate on a vast scale, with more than 2,700 acres in five regions. The silky, black currant–tinged Coyam blend and zesty Natura Sauvignon Blanc are two consistently great picks.

WINE INTEL
A certified fair-trade winery, Emiliana returns part of its profits to its workers via scholarships and a microbusiness incubator. The employees learn to make honey, olive oil and other goods, which are sold at the winery.

BOTTLES TO TRY
○ Natura Sauvignon Blanc / $
● Coyam / $$$

LAPOSTOLLE

Lapostolle's Clos Apalta—a rich, Bordeaux-inspired blend—was one of the first wines to show that Chile could produce world-class reds. Alexandra Marnier-Lapostolle (as in Grand Marnier, the French liqueur) cofounded this Colchagua estate and imported a French winemaking team that includes the superstar consultant Michel Rolland and the winemaker Jacques Begarie. All wines come from organically farmed grapes.

BOTTLES TO TRY
● Casa Grand Selection Carmenère / $
● Cuvée Alexandre Merlot / $$
● Clos Apalta / $$$$

MONTES

The visionary winemaker Aurelio Montes was one of the first producers to realize the possibilities of Chile's hillside terrain and to exploit the Colchagua Valley's potential for Syrah. Montes also cultivates heat-loving Bordeaux red varieties in Colchagua, and Pinot Noir and white grapes in cooler regions like Zapallar. While most of Montes's wines are affordable bottlings designed for near-term drinking, his top cuvées—like the legendary, Cabernet-based Alpha M—compete with Chile's best.

BOTTLES TO TRY
- **Classic Series Cabernet Sauvignon / $**
- **Alpha M / $$$$**

ODFJELL VINEYARDS

The Norwegian shipping magnate Dan Odfjell purchased a large Maipo Valley estate partly to escape dreary winters in his homeland. He eventually asked his son Laurence, a Yale-trained architect, to design a winery, and convinced the famed American consultant Paul Hobbs to help mastermind the wines. Hobbs works with the Frenchman Arnaud Hereu to fashion Odfjell's classically styled, reasonably priced bottlings. In addition to Maipo fruit, the talented team draws on outstanding vineyards in Maule and Curicó and a cool site in Casablanca.

BOTTLES TO TRY
- ○ **Armador Sauvignon Blanc / $**
- **Orzada Carignane / $$**

SANTA RITA

Although Santa Rita is practically within the city limits of Santiago, this Maipo-based winery owns vineyards all over Chile. Founded in 1880, Santa Rita pioneered European grape varieties and became one of the country's biggest brands. Best known for its value bottlings, the winery also makes one of Chile's great Cabernets, the savory, iconic Casa Real. And despite its long history, Santa Rita continues to break new ground. Vineyards in emerging zones such as Limarí and Leyda are paying off with crisp whites and elegant reds.

BOTTLES TO TRY
- ○ **Medalla Real Chardonnay / $$**
- ○ **Medalla Real Sauvignon Blanc / $$**
- **Casa Real Cabernet Sauvignon / $$$$**

UNDURRAGA

Though it was founded more than 125 years ago, this mega-winery has gotten an infusion of ambition, cash and invention from its new owners, an investment group that purchased it in 2006. The most exciting of its projects is Terroir Hunter (T.H.), a series of new cuvées crafted by Rafael Urrejola. Previously the winemaker for Viña Leyda (see opposite), Urrejola scours Chile's diverse regions for great vineyards, then makes site-specific wines of compelling finesse.

BOTTLES TO TRY

○ **T.H. Lo Abarca Sauvignon Blanc / $$**
● **T.H. Alto Maipo Cabernet Sauvignon / $$**

VERAMONTE

The Huneeus family, Chilean natives who also own Napa's Quintessa, created this trailblazing estate, which pioneered cool-climate wines from the Casablanca Valley. There's another California connection at Veramonte: Its new wine-maker Rodrigo Soto spent six years heading up the cellar at Sonoma's respected Benziger label. Soto brings a boutique touch to one of Chile's most consistent producers of crisp, affordable Sauvignon Blanc and Chardonnay. Lately, Vera-monte's Pinot Noir has caught up to its whites, with a string of fragrant, gracefully fruity vintages.

BOTTLES TO TRY

○ **La Gloria Sauvignon Blanc / $**
● **Pinot Noir Reserva / $**

VIÑA FALERNIA

Falernia's Italian co-founder Giorgio Flessati pioneered wine-making in the remote, northerly Elqui Valley. With a number of observatories, Elqui attracts astronomers for the same reasons it attracts vintners: clear skies, boundless sunshine and crystalline-pure air. Throw in well-draining soil, snow-melt irrigation and huge temperature swings and you get the crisp, flavorful—and amazingly well priced—wines of Faler-nia. Its intense reserve Syrah offers an inky, spicy character that recalls the wines of France's Cornas appellation.

BOTTLES TO TRY

● **Carmenère-Syrah Reserva / $**
● **Syrah Reserva / $**

VIÑA LEYDA

Few wineries better demonstrate the fabulous potential of the coastal Leyda zone (and the larger San Antonio subregion) than this namesake label. Overcoming a total lack of water for irrigation (now delivered via a five-mile pipeline) and a cool growing season that makes grape-growing quite risky, Viña Leyda proved that the region could yield terrific wines. In the skilled hands of winemaker Viviana Navarrete, Leyda's sea-chilled vineyards yield refreshing, elegant Pinot Noir, spicy Syrah and some of the country's most thrillingly vibrant whites.

BOTTLES TO TRY
- ○ **Classic Sauvignon Blanc / $**
- ● **Las Brisas Pinot Noir / $$**

VIÑA VIK

After masterminding two of South America's most glamorous boutique hotels, Alex and Carrie Vik spent nearly a decade bringing their dream Chilean winery to fruition. They broke ground in 2006 on a 10,000-acre estate in the Apalta Valley, about two hours south of Santiago, and brought on board one of Chile's best-known winemakers, Patrick Valette. The estate's first commercial vintage, 2010, consisted of a single, powerful red blend (Cabernet Sauvignon, Carmenère, Cabernet Franc, Merlot and Syrah) that the Viks sell directly through the Vik.cl website.

BOTTLE TO TRY
- ● **VIK / $$$$**

South Africa/

Wine Region

South Africa is the only African wine-producing country of any note. Its primary wine region, the Cape, is stunningly gorgeous. And its wines have a style in between the ripe generosity of the New World and the more austere elegance of the Old World. Value hunters will find that South Africa abounds in overachieving white varietals, including fantastic old-vine Chenin Blancs and zippy Sauvignons. At the high end, collectors can look for Stellenbosch's Bordeaux-inspired reds; and *terroir*-driven idealists will discover a new generation of ambitious, minimalist young winemakers, most of whom can be found in the up-and-coming Swartland region. They're a great example of the potential of South Africa, and a fine reason to start drinking its varied, impressive wines right now.

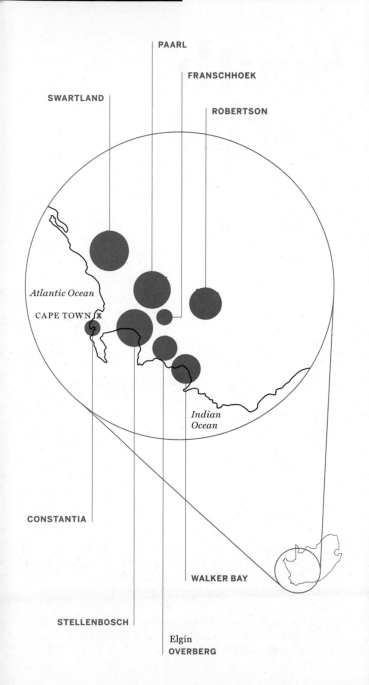

PAARL

FRANSCHHOEK

ROBERTSON

SWARTLAND

Atlantic Ocean

CAPE TOWN

Indian Ocean

CONSTANTIA

WALKER BAY

STELLENBOSCH

Elgin
OVERBERG

South Africa

REGIONS TO KNOW

STELLENBOSCH The heart of South African wine country, Stellenbosch produces many acclaimed bottles, mostly red (though good whites exist, too). Some of the best known are blends based on Cabernet Sauvignon and Merlot.

PAARL While large cooperative wineries dominate this region north of Stellenbosch, smaller, quality-focused producers are increasing; the **FRANSCHHOEK** subzone includes many prestige estates. Paarl's relatively warm climate means that red grapes—chiefly Cabernet, Shiraz, Pinotage and Merlot—thrive here.

CONSTANTIA Breezy, coastal Constantia started providing wines for thirsty Cape Towners centuries ago. Today Cape Town's suburbs stretch nearly to Constantia's vineyards, which specialize in cool-climate renditions of Sauvignon Blanc, Chardonnay and Pinot Noir.

OVERBERG Located where the Atlantic and Indian oceans meet, Overberg—especially its **ELGIN** subzone—is home to talented winemakers styling fresh, cool-climate wines.

SWARTLAND Old vines and unirrigated vineyards have made Swartland—formerly known for its fields of grain and rustic red wines—into a mecca for South Africa's *terroir*-hunting purists. They're making unusual blends and acclaimed bottlings from both red and white grapes, notably Shiraz and Chenin Blanc.

WALKER BAY Burgundy grape varieties—i.e., Pinot Noir and Chardonnay—do well in this sea-cooled zone on the Indian Ocean side of the Cape of Good Hope.

❧ KEY GRAPES: WHITE

CHENIN BLANC South Africa's most important white grape (also known here as Steen) yields wines ranging in style from zippy to lush, with more tropical flavors than exhibited by French Chenin Blancs.

SAUVIGNON BLANC & CHARDONNAY South African Sauvignon Blancs range from herbal and tart to exotically fruity, whereas Chardonnays often hew to a line midway between the ripe fruitiness of California bottlings and the leaner, mineral-driven French versions.

❧ KEY GRAPES: RED

CABERNET SAUVIGNON & SHIRAZ (SYRAH) Wines produced from these powerful grapes make South Africa's most convincing case for greatness. Cabernet Sauvignon is the country's dominant red variety, and plantings of Shiraz (also called Syrah here) have more than doubled in the past decade. These reds tend to split into two camps: Some South African winemakers aim for ripe, plush styles akin to California's and Australia's, while others make earthier, herb-inflected versions that evoke comparisons with French bottlings.

PINOTAGE Once South Africa's preeminent red grape, Pinotage—a crossing of Pinot Noir and Cinsaut—now ranks behind Cabernet and Shiraz in plantings. Pinotage's distinctively pungent, funky notes limit its appeal abroad, although a few vintners craft fruitier versions of the grape.

PINOT NOIR With an increase in plantings in cool-climate regions, Pinot Noir production is on the rise, though not much is exported yet to the U.S.

WINE TERMINOLOGY

South African winemakers use straightforward labels that list winery name, variety, region and vintage. Blends may be given proprietary names, and the varieties that went into them usually appear on the back label. Regional names are regulated by the Wine of Origin system, which recognizes official winegrowing areas. In descending order of size, they are geographical unit, region, district and ward.

Producers/ South Africa

BAYTEN

Finally, ordering the wines of this top-notch Constantia label is as easy as drinking them. Founded in 1769 as Buitenverwachting, the estate now goes by its shorter, local nickname, Bayten, in the U.S. Its vineyards are cooled by the winds of False Bay, an ideal location for yielding minerally, refreshing whites. Cellarmaster Hermann Kirschbaum and winemaker Brad Paton craft some of South Africa's best Sauvignon Blancs.

BOTTLES TO TRY

○ **Bayten Sauvignon Blanc** ⁄ **$**
○ **Beyond Sauvignon Blanc** ⁄ **$**

DE TOREN

De Toren founders Emil and Sonette den Dulk left Johannesburg's urban grind for the Polkadraai Hills, in Stellenbosch, where they transformed an old poultry abattoir into a modern winery. Made in a rich international style, their culty, Cabernet-based red, Fusion V, helped change perceptions of South African wine when it was released in 2001. The winery offers just one other wine, the Merlot-based Z.

BOTTLES TO TRY

● **Fusion V** ⁄ **$$$**
● **Z** ⁄ **$$$**

FAIRVIEW/GOATS DO ROAM

Few South African vintners have as much passion for Rhône varieties as Fairview's Charles Back, who named his value-driven Goats do Roam label in irreverent homage to Côtes-du-Rhône. But Back is serious about quality, and his high-end Fairview wines compete with the country's best. Beyond Rhône grapes, Back's bottlings cover the gamut from traditional (Chenin Blanc, Pinotage) to experimental (Tempranillo).

BOTTLES TO TRY

○ **Fairview Viognier** ⁄ **$$**
● **Goats do Roam Red** ⁄ **$**

GLENELLY

Bordeaux proprietress May-Eliane de Lencquesaing sold her Pauillac *grand cru claseé,* Château Pichon-Lalande, in 2007, but held on to Glenelly, her property on the Simonsberg Mountain. Bought in 2003, the 316-acre estate had never grown wine grapes but is now producing terrific reds and whites, among them Lady May, a Bordeaux-inspired flagship blend of Cabernet Sauvignon and Petit Verdot. Winemaker Luke O'Cuinneagain, whose résumé includes Napa's Screaming Eagle as well as the top South African estate (and Glenelly neighbor) Rustenberg, gets an assist from star consultant Adi Badenhorst.

BOTTLES TO TRY

○ **The Glass Collection Chardonnay / $$**

● **Lady May / $$$**

HAMILTON RUSSELL VINEYARDS

Hamilton Russell's wines compete with world-class whale watching as a compelling reason to visit the fishing village of Hermanus. Located on breezy Walker Bay, the area is home to some of the continent's southernmost vineyards. Cool-climate pioneer Tim Hamilton Russell gambled astutely on the region in the late 1970s; today his son Anthony fashions the winery's two benchmark, estate-grown cuvées, a Pinot Noir and a Chardonnay. Profits from Anthony's second label, Southern Right (named for a species of whale that frequents the bay), partly benefit conservation initiatives, some of them whale related.

BOTTLES TO TRY

○ **Southern Right Sauvignon Blanc / $**

● **Hamilton Russell Pinot Noir / $$$**

INDABA

One of the handful of South African labels that has relatively wide distribution in the U.S., Indaba is a reliable source for wines that consistently deliver straightforward pleasure at often single-digit prices. The juicy, fresh Chenin and Sauvignon Blancs are especially dependable. Another reason to like Indaba is that the brand donates a portion of its profits to support scholarships for disadvantaged students pursuing wine-related studies.

BOTTLES TO TRY

○ **Chenin Blanc / $**

○ **Sauvignon Blanc / $**

KANONKOP

Anyone who has been turned off Pinotage by a funky bottle or two should make a point to try Kanonkop's refined versions of the grape before coming to conclusions about South Africa's distinctive red variety. This Stellenbosch estate, which spreads across the lower slopes of the Simonsberg Mountain, turns out masterful Pinotage, thanks to winemaker Abrie Beeslaar and his predecessor, the legendary Beyers Truter. Old vines, deep know-how and a knack for finesse have made Kanonkop's wines a reference point for the finicky grape.

BOTTLES TO TRY
- **Paul Sauer / $$$**
- **Pinotage / $$$**

KEN FORRESTER VINEYARDS

Many of Ken Forrester's labels display the date 1689, the year the first winery was established on the land that eventually became his flagship vineyard. Forrester himself jumped into winemaking only in 1993, after a successful career as a restaurateur. Brilliant, old-vine Chenins turned Forrester into a poster boy for the variety, with the luscious FMC cuvée topping a portfolio that includes three other Chenin Blancs—all more food-friendly and much less expensive. The juicy Petit bottling offers value, though the layered Reserve is only a few dollars more.

BOTTLES TO TRY
- ○ **Petit Chenin Blanc / $**
- ○ **Reserve Chenin Blanc / $**

VILAFONTÉ

Legendary California winemaker Zelma Long (Simi, Mondavi) and her grape-guru husband, Phil Freese, created this pioneering label in 1996. Teaming up with Warwick Wine Estate's Mike Ratcliffe (see opposite), they planted 40 acres of Bordeaux varieties in the Paarl-Simonsberg area, a top zone for boldly structured reds. Long and her winemaker Martin Smith (an alumnus of Napa's Newton Vineyard) fashion two boutique cuvées: Series M, a Merlot-based blend, and Series C, based on Cabernet Sauvignon. The style is concentrated, rich and refined.

BOTTLES TO TRY
- **Series C / $$$**
- **Series M / $$$**

RARITIES & COLLECTIBLES

KLEIN CONSTANTIA VIN DE CONSTANCE This late-harvest white was one of the most famous wines of the 18th and 19th centuries—Napoleon even had it shipped to him in exile. Klein Constantia revived the style in the 1980s, making the wine from the original, 300-plus-year-old Muscat de Frontignan vineyards.

SADIE FAMILY Eben Sadie, the enfant terrible of South African wine, is known for his phenomenal old-vine Rhône blends and Chenin Blancs from Swartland. (He also made top-quality reds from Spain's Priorat region under the Terroir al Límit label.)

VERGELEGEN Established in 1700 and totally reinvented in the 1990s, this historic estate southeast of Cape Town produces a range of good wines, but its best and rarest is V, a world-class Bordeaux-style red.

WARWICK WINE ESTATE

Best known for its opulent Cabernet-based wines, Warwick Wine is the creation of a Canadian-born winemaker, Norma Ratcliffe. Her first vintages, using grapes planted on husband Stan Ratcliffe's family farm in Stellenbosch, helped pioneer South Africa's high-end, Bordeaux-inspired reds in the mid-1980s. Today, under the direction of Norma's son Mike, the winery's eight cuvées are still sourced from the same property, and production remains small. Among Warwick's best-known bottlings is Three Cape Ladies, a smoky, muscular blend of Cabernet Sauvignon, Syrah and Pinotage.

BOTTLES TO TRY

○ **Professor Black Sauvignon Blanc / $$**
● **Three Cape Ladies / $$**

Champagne & Other Sparkling Wines

Champagne goes with everything from scrambled eggs to a simple roast chicken dinner to birthdays to cruise-ship launches. This effervescent, complex wine pairs well with a vast variety of foods, thanks to its brisk acidity, modest alcohol and refreshing bubbles, so it's a shame that it isn't poured more often for everyday meals in addition to celebrations. Of course, the world of sparkling wine also includes Italy's affordable Proseccos and elegant Franciacortas; Spain's citrusy, earthy cavas; and from the U.S., Champagne equivalents at half the price. Anyone interested in food owes it to himself to explore all of these wines.

CHAMPAGNE

CLAIM TO FAME

The French went to court (and won) to keep wineries outside the Champagne region from labeling their sparkling wines as Champagne. But the word's enduring ubiquity as a casual synonym for any effervescent wine reflects the phenomenal success of Champagne: Few (if any) sparkling wines can match Champagne's best bottles in complexity and finesse. Chalk and limestone soils and a cool Atlantic climate—along with centuries of winemaking trial and error—mean these wines are in a category of their own, no matter how liberally the Champagne moniker is applied elsewhere.

REGIONS TO KNOW

AUBE A crucial source of fruit for large producers in the more prestigious districts of Reims and the Côte des Blancs, the Aube is located almost 70 miles southeast of central Champagne and has a slightly warmer climate and soil that is richer in clay. The grape variety of choice here is Pinot Noir, which represents most of the region's acreage. Increasingly, its top growers—chiefly located in the **CÔTE DES BAR,** the Aube's primary subregion—are vinifying their own wines rather then selling their grapes.

CÔTE DES BLANCS Chardonnay dominates this region, which lies south of the city of Epernay and produces wines renowned for freshness and delicacy. Its southernmost tip, called **CÔTE DE SÉZANNE,** also focuses on Chardonnay.

MONTAGNE DE REIMS This stretch of wooded hills and vineyards follows a mountain ridge south from Reims to Epernay and focuses primarily on Pinot Noir. Most of Champagne's *grand cru* vineyards for red grapes are found here.

VALLÉE DE LA MARNE Pinot Meunier is the main grape in Champagne's largest growing region. Encompassing the city of Epernay as well as land west of it, Vallée de la Marne is home to many acclaimed grower-producers, with the best vineyards located on sloping hillsides above the Marne River.

♛ KEY GRAPES: WHITE

CHARDONNAY Thanks to the Champagne region's cool climate and stony soil, its Chardonnay yields fresh, zesty whites. The variety accounts for less than a third of the region's vineyards. Most Champagnes are blends of Chardonnay, Pinot Noir and Pinot Meunier; blends based on Chardonnay offer citrusy mineral notes but are scarcer than those dominated by red grapes.

♛ KEY GRAPES: RED

PINOT MEUNIER This grape is prized for its ability to ripen early (a lifesaver for vintners in cooler vintages) and for its fruity, floral flavors, which round out a traditional Champagne blend.

PINOT NOIR Used to make both rosé and white wines, this black-skinned grape lends body, richness and bright berry tones to Champagne. Pinot Noir is the main grape of the Montagne de Reims and Aube subregions.

WINE TERMINOLOGY

BLANC DE BLANCS Most Champagnes are made from a blend of red and white varieties, but Blanc de Blancs (white from whites) cuvées are made entirely from white grapes—Chardonnay—and represent about 5 percent of all Champagne.

BLANC DE NOIRS These white Champagnes are produced using red grapes only (Pinot Noir and Pinot Meunier). To create the wine, the clear juice of red grapes gets drained from the skins before it gains any color. (Rosés are created by blending a bit of red wine into white sparkling wine or by leaving the red grape skins in the pressed juice for a short time to bleed in some color.)

DISGORGEMENT Fermenting sugar inside a bottle gives Champagne its fizz but also creates lees, a yeasty sediment. The disgorgement process removes the lees without losing the fizz. The disgorgement date is a key indicator of the age of a nonvintage wine, and of how long a vintage wine has aged on its lees.

DOSAGE The sugary syrup that is added to most Champagne after it is disgorged (see above). The dosage maintains the fill level of the bottle (some wine is lost during disgorgement) and adds some sweetness.

SWEETNESS LEVELS Bone-dry cuvées that had no dosage added after disgorgement (see opposite) are labeled **BRUT NATURE** (or *brut zéro, pas dosé* or *sans dosage*), *brut* meaning "dry." The second-driest of all Champagne styles, **EXTRA BRUT** wines are bright and zesty. The next category, brut, is the most widely produced style. **EXTRA SEC** bottlings are one step up from brut wines and have a hint of sweetness. Though translating as "semi-dry," **DEMI-SEC** wines are actually fairly sweet.

MÉTHODE CHAMPENOISE/MÉTHODE TRADITIONNELLE The most traditional and costly way to make sparkling wine is by causing a second fermentation in the bottle. That's done by adding sugar syrup and yeast. Only wines from Champagne made using this process may be labeled *méthode champenoise.*

PREMIER CRU Champagne ranks wines by the village from which they come. Forty-four villages, chiefly in the Montagne de Reims and the Côte des Blancs, have *premier cru* status.

GRAND CRU Seventeen Champagne villages rate high enough to call their wines *grand cru*, the most prestigious designation.

GRANDE MARQUE An unofficial term for large, traditional Champagne houses of high prestige.

TÊTE DE CUVÉE A Champagne house's top-tier bottling, usually sold under a proprietary name, such as Moët's Dom Pérignon.

GROWER CHAMPAGNE Champagnes made by vintners who bottle their own wines, rather than selling grapes to large producers. Instead of supplying fruit for enormous blends made to reflect a house style, grower-producers highlight the qualities imparted to wine by the particular plot where it was grown (its *terroir*).

NONVINTAGE/NV Most Champagnes are nonvintage, which means they are blends of wines from different vintages, a practice designed to maintain a consistent taste from year to year.

VINTAGE Producers make vintage Champagnes only in exceptional years; these wines are typically aged longer and priced higher than their nonvintage counterparts (see above).

Producers/ Champagne

BOLLINGER

Family-owned Bollinger produces luscious, full-bodied wines that are among some of the most long-lived in Champagne. Made predominately from Pinot Noir, the top cuvées get their toasty smoothness from fermentation in barrels, but even Bollinger's intro-level Special Cuvée sees some wood, which gives it rare structure for a basic brut.

BOTTLES TO TRY

○ R.D. Extra Brut / $$$$
○ Special Cuvée Brut NV / $$$$

> **WINE INTEL**
> At the Perching Bar, a stylish spot in a forest near Reims, visitors sip Bollinger (and other Champagnes) in a tree house while taking in the treetop views.

CHARLES HEIDSIECK

Of the three Champagne houses with the Heidsieck name, this Reims producer is the finest, though it's not the best known. The Brut Réserve represents the vast majority of the house's relatively small production and is an amazingly good value, thanks to the generous addition of older reserve wines to the blend. The strawberry-inflected Rosé Réserve is silky and intense.

BOTTLES TO TRY

○ Brut Réserve NV / $$$
● Rosé Réserve NV / $$$$

DIEBOLT-VALLOIS

One of Champagne's top boutique producers, Diebolt-Vallois is located in Cramant, a *grand cru* village in the Côte des Blancs. Jacques Diebolt, Nadia Vallois and their children together craft pure, precise Blanc de Blancs Champagnes; Tradition, a blend of three Champagne grapes; and a single rosé. The basic Blanc de Blancs outclasses similar wines that cost twice as much; its delicacy contrasts with the yeasty, layered Cuvée Prestige.

BOTTLES TO TRY

○ Brut Blanc de Blancs / $$$
○ Cuvée Prestige Brut Blanc de Blancs / $$$

FLEURY

Champagne Fleury is a granddaddy of grower Champagne, having been bottling estate-grown wines since 1929—about half a century before the craze for boutique Champagne began. It's also among the most important biodynamic growers in the region. Yet because it's located in the outlying Aube region, and because its output is comparatively small, it's still semi-obscure in the U.S. The Fleury family's gorgeous Pinot Noir–based cuvées combine bold, toasty fruit flavors and pinpoint acidity.

BOTTLES TO TRY

○ **Brut Blanc de Noirs NV / $$$**

● **Brut Rosé de Saignée NV / $$$**

LANSON

Lanson's house style—fresh and taut—is a point of pride for this ancient Champagne house, founded in 1760. Unlike most Champagnes, Lanson's don't go through a second fermentation to soften the wines' acidity. The basic Black Label bottling is an affordable introduction, and a good choice for fans of uncompromisingly tart, bracing bubbly. A big step up is the newer Extra Age cuvée: Created to honor the house's 250th anniversary, it's similarly pure but gets intensity from long-aged *grand cru* and *premier cru* wines.

BOTTLES TO TRY

○ **Brut Black Label NV / $$$**

○ **Brut Extra Age NV / $$$$**

LAURENT-PERRIER

Chardonnay reigns at Laurent-Perrier, which is one reason the wines of this *grande marque* (see p. 277) have become famous for their elegant, delicate style. Another is the lack of oak: All wines are fermented and aged in tanks, which contributes to their pure, mineral- and citrus-driven flavors. The exception to Chardonnay's dominance is Laurent-Perrier's famous rosé, a salmon-hued, berry-driven classic that's made entirely from Pinot Noir. At the high end, the Grand Siècle prestige cuvée blends top wines from three vintages, giving it impressively consistent quality.

BOTTLES TO TRY

○ **La Cuvée Grand Siècle / $$$$**

● **Cuvée Rosé NV / $$$$**

MOËT & CHANDON/DOM PÉRIGNON

Moët & Chandon bottled its first vintage Champagne in 1842, and has been choosy ever since, creating vintage-dated wines in just 70 of the ensuing years. The vintage bottlings—a white and a rosé—make up a tiny portion of its vast output. Moët is best known for the popular Brut Impérial—the best-selling Champagne worldwide—which is now drier and crisper than in years past. Moët's legendary tête de cuvée, the vintage-dated Dom Pérignon, became so successful that today it is its own brand, crafted by the winemaking genius Richard Geoffroy.

BOTTLES TO TRY
○ **Brut Impérial NV** ∕ **$$$**
○ **Dom Pérignon** ∕ **$$$$**

NICOLAS FEUILLATTE

The most popular Champagne brand in France as well as a top value bet, Nicolas Feuillatte is an upstart label created in 1976 by a jet-setting coffee baron and diplomat of the same name. Feuillatte promoted his brand among his glamorous friends, then sold it to Champagne's largest cooperative 10 years later. Sourcing from a vast network of some 5,000 growers, the co-op has kept quality high, and today Feuillatte's creamy, apple-scented nonvintage brut is France's best-selling Champagne. The Palmes d'Or Brut is a vintage-dated blend of Pinot Noir and Chardonnay that ages for at least nine years before release.

BOTTLES TO TRY
○ **Brut NV** ∕ **$$$**
○ **Palmes d'Or Brut** ∕ **$$$$**

PHILIPPE GONET

In 1990, siblings Pierre and Chantal Gonet were in their early 20s when, in a daunting step to fill their late father's shoes, they took over their family's small winery in Le Mesnil-sur-Oger. Channeling nearly two centuries of family tradition, the Gonets' estate-grown whites beautifully express the chalky minerality that defines top Blanc de Blancs, the signature wine of Le Mesnil. The superb Grande Réserve Brut blends three grape varieties from two vintages into a sleek, filigreed white.

BOTTLES TO TRY
○ **Brut Blanc de Blancs NV** ∕ **$$$**
○ **Grande Réserve Brut NV** ∕ **$$$$**

RARITIES & COLLECTIBLES

LARMANDIER-BERNIER Pierre and Sophie Larmandier's Côte des Blancs wines are some of Champagne's best. Firm and minerally in style, they can taste austere when young but mature into Champagnes of extraordinary complexity, purity and finesse.

ROSES DE JEANNE Cédric Bouchard has become one of Champagne's new stars by making stunning cuvées from the relatively unheralded Aube region. His single-vineyard, single-vintage varietal wines buck Champagne's tradition of blending, and with no dosage, aim for maximum *terroir* expression.

ULYSSE COLLIN A student of naturalist winemaker Anselme Selosse, Olivier Collin crushed his first vintage in 2004 from family vineyards once leased to Pommery. His scarce Champagnes have brought new luster to the emerging Sézanne region.

POL ROGER

It's not known if Sir Winston Churchill was thinking of Pol Roger when he said of Champagne, "In victory, you deserve it; in defeat, you need it." But the English statesman was a huge fan of this Epernay producer's wines—so much so that the Roger family named its prestige cuvée in Churchill's honor. Still family owned, Pol Roger makes good wines at every level, including its basic brut, White Foil, a vividly crisp yet creamy Champagne with complex fruit and toast notes.

BOTTLES TO TRY
- White Foil Brut NV / $$$
- Cuvée Sir Winston Churchill / $$$$

RENÉ GEOFFROY

The masterfully balanced wines of this culty Marne grower outperform their price at every level. Using only grapes from the family's own vineyards, René Geoffroy's son Jean-Baptiste fashions a range of exciting wines, including one of Champagne's best basic nonvintage cuvées, the chalky, vivid Expression. Unusually, the Geoffroys ferment many of their wines in large, old wooden vats (rather than tanks); the technique helps soften the wines without lending heavy, oaky flavors.

BOTTLES TO TRY
- Expression NV / $$$
- Premier Cru Brut Rosé de Saignée / $$$$

TAITTINGER

One of the few large Champagne houses that's still family-owned, Taittinger produces a range of elegant wines that remain oddly underrated. It's odd because the wines are terrific, defined by a sleek, minerally frame enriched by just enough creamy lushness to keep them from tasting austere. The entry-level Brut La Française is delicate and fine-boned. Prélude, a 50-50 blend of Pinot Noir and Chardonnay, adds body and intensity and makes a great alternative to Taittinger's pricey prestige cuvées.

BOTTLES TO TRY
○ Brut La Française NV / $$$
○ Prélude Grands Crus NV / $$$$

VEUVE CLICQUOT

The Clicquot Champagne house has been a smashing international success since as far back as the early 1800s, when it was led by Barbe Nicole Clicquot Ponsardin. Left a *veuve* (widow) at age 27, the entrepreneurial Ponsardin essentially invented modern Champagne, transforming it from a cloudy, gassy wine into a brilliantly clear, fine-bubbled elixir. The nonvintage brut is reliably bold, creamy and balanced. More complex (but not much more expensive) is Clicquot's nonvintage rosé; high rollers should seek out the splurgeworthy La Grande Dame cuvées.

BOTTLES TO TRY
○ La Grande Dame Brut / $$$$
● Brut Rosé NV / $$$$

OTHER SPARKLING WINES

REGIONS TO KNOW

FRANCE Beyond Champagne, France abounds with sparkling wines, most made with grapes typical of each region. Seven of the country's sparkling wine appellations—the largest is the Loire—are able to use the term *crémant* to indicate they are produced by the *méthode traditionnelle*. Wines labeled *brut* or *mousseux* may or may not have been made this way.

ITALY Italy's northern regions are the main source of the country's *spumante* (sparkling) wines. One of the best, very similar in taste to Champagne, comes from Lombardy's Franciacorta zone. Also noteworthy are Piedmont's flowery Moscato d'Asti and light red, berry-scented Brachetto d'Acqui. The Veneto's affordable and popular Proseccos are made using a process called the Charmat method, in which the wine undergoes its second fermentation in tanks rather than bottles. The effervescent liquid is then drained from its spent yeast and bottled.

SPAIN Long marketed as less expensive substitutes for Champagne, Spanish cavas by law must be made using traditional *méthode champenoise* techniques (see p. 277). Most cavas come from the Catalonia region near Barcelona and are based largely on the white Macabeo grape.

UNITED STATES The quality of American sparkling wines has been steadily improving. While the best bottlings still come from the cooler regions of Northern California—such as Carneros, Sonoma and the Anderson and Green valleys—Washington State, Oregon, New York and New Mexico are making a growing number of complex, vibrant sparklers.

Producers/Other Sparkling Wines

FRANCE
GRATIEN & MEYER

One of the top names in Loire Valley sparkling wine, Gratien & Meyer relies chiefly on Chenin Blanc for its white wines and Cabernet Franc for its reds. Those varieties, and the Loire Valley's cool growing season, give these wines their light body and crisp, vivacious snap—qualities that make them fantastic aperitifs and super-versatile with food. The wines undergo traditional, labor-intensive bottle fermentation, which lends complexity, and best of all, they sell for roughly half the price of an intro-level Champagne.

BOTTLES TO TRY

○ Saumur Brut / $$

● Saumur Brut Rosé / $$

LANGLOIS-CHATEAU

The Loire Valley produces more sparkling wine than any French region after Champagne, and its top *crémants*—like those of Langlois-Chateau—can offer amazing value. Bollinger, one of the most famous Champagne houses (see p. 278), acquired this respected producer in 1973. It ages its pear-inflected *crémant* on its lees for 24 months rather than the typical nine months, which helps give it unusual lushness. The rosé version is classic Loire: Composed entirely of Cabernet Franc, it offers light, delicate berry flavors.

BOTTLES TO TRY

○ **Brut Crémant de Loire NV / $$**
● **Brut Crémant de Loire Rosé NV / $$**

MAISON PARIGOT & RICHARD

Burgundy's *crémants* get little notice, and yet they're among the best sparkling wine bargains anywhere—as Parigot's wines demonstrate. Located in the Côte de Beaune (i.e., in prime Burgundy territory), Parigot is a family-owned winery run by the fifth generation of founder Emile Parigot's descendants. Current owner Gregory Georger fashions seven cuvées, all based on the same grapes as the wines from neighboring Champagne (Pinot Noir and Chardonnay), with a little Aligoté added to some.

BOTTLES TO TRY

○ **Crémant de Bourgogne Blanc de Blancs NV / $$**
● **Crémant Rosé / $$**

ITALY
ADAMI

Brothers Armando and Franco Adami inherited one of Prosecco's best vineyards, Giardino, a steeply terraced, vine-staked amphitheater that was recognized as the region's first official *cru* in 1920. It's the foundation of the Adami estate and the source of one of Italy's finest Proseccos, Vigneto Giardino. What's amazing is that this single-vineyard wine sells for around $20—proof that top Prosecco remains one of the world's great values. Other highlights include the Garbèl bottling: Drier than most Proseccos, it's a perfect warm-weather white or aperitif.

BOTTLES TO TRY

○ **Garbèl Prosecco Brut / $**
○ **Vigneto Giardino Prosecco / $$**

MIONETTO

This well-known label is a source of terrific Prosecco (and other sparkling wines) at equally terrific prices. One key to its success is location: Mionetto is in Valdobbiadene, the hilly Prosecco subregion where terraced vines yield the best grapes. Another important factor is the winery's close relationships with growers, many of whom have been supplying Mionetto with fruit for decades. In the large lineup, the brut bottling stands out: It's crisp, zesty and a perennial steal. For Moscato fans, Mionetto's graceful, lightly sweet (dolce) version is a go-to choice.

BOTTLES TO TRY

○ **Brut NV Prosecco** / **$**
○ **Moscato Dolce** / **$**

NINO FRANCO

Primo Franco, the third-generation owner and winemaker of this top-notch Prosecco producer, wanted to be an architect, but instead took over his family's *spumante* firm in 1982. Over the course of three decades, Franco transformed its winemaking and made vast improvements in grape-growing. The result of his efforts is some of Italy's best Proseccos. Ranging from sweet to bone-dry, they include Rustico, which has just a bare hint of sweetness, and the refined Grave di Stecca, made with grapes from an old vineyard partially enclosed by a park.

BOTTLES TO TRY

○ **Rustico Prosecco NV** / **$$**
○ **Grave di Stecca Prosecco** / **$$$**

SPAIN
AVINYÓ

Avinyó is the brand of the Esteve Nadal family, which owns four Penedès farms from which it harvests all the fruit it needs for its wines. Joan Esteve Nadal planted the oldest of the vineyards to traditional cava grapes 50-odd years ago, with the goal of making enough sparkling wine for himself and his friends. Today his three children manage an enterprise turning out enough stellar wine to supply many thousands of friends. The basic Brut Reserva is classic cava, with earthy citrus notes and a crisp finish.

BOTTLE TO TRY

○ **Brut Reserva Cava** / **$$**

FREIXENET

Propelled by the phenomenal success of its two flagship cavas, Carta Nevada and Cordon Negro, Freixenet has become an international powerhouse, with wineries all over the world. Created in 1861 by the marriage of members of the Ferrer and Sala families, Freixenet produced its first *méthode traditionnelle* sparkling wines in 1914. Still family-owned, it's a source for reliably delicious and well-priced cava. The pink-hued, berry-driven Elyssia Pinot Noir, for instance, delivers elegance beyond its price, while the ubiquitous, black-bottled Cordon Negro is fresh, tasty and balanced.

BOTTLES TO TRY

○ **Cordon Negro NV∕$**
● **Elyssia Pinot Noir Brut Cava NV∕$$**

RAVENTÓS I BLANC

The Raventós family tree doesn't just contain some cava experts—it includes the inventor. An ancestor traveling through Champagne brought the idea back to Spain, and in 1872 the now famous Cordoníu brand (and an entire industry) took off. Raventós i Blanc is the family's smaller project, crafting fine cava from estate grapes. Its two most consistent wines are the creamy, remarkably elegant L'Hereu Reserva Brut and an outstanding *rosado*, the de Nit Brut.

BOTTLES TO TRY

○ **L'Hereu Reserva Brut∕$$**
● **de Nit Brut Rosado∕$$**

UNITED STATES
ARGYLE WINERY

This pioneering winery released its first sparkling wines in 1987, when the idea of fine Champagne-style wines from Oregon raised more eyebrows than enthusiasm. Argyle's co-founder Rollin Soles persevered; today the winery's polished sparklers rank among the country's best. Made in six styles using traditional Champagne techniques and varieties, they are all vintage-dated. Soles's protégé Nate Klostermann has been in charge of the Argyle cellar since Soles stepped aside in 2013.

BOTTLES TO TRY

○ **Vintage Brut∕$$**
● **Vintage Brut Rosé∕$$$**

DOMAINE CARNEROS

Perched on a hill near a bucolic road leading to Napa Valley, Domaine Carneros's mansion-like headquarters evokes a French château. The allusion is intentional: The estate is an outpost of the illustrious Taittinger Champagne house (see p. 282). Established in 1987, Domaine Carneros produces some of California's best sparkling wines, all from the hand of longtime winemaker (and CEO) Eileen Crane. Organically farmed, estate-owned vineyards supply nearly all of the fruit for its wines, which include a crisp yet luscious rosé and Le Rêve, an elegant, dry Blanc de Blancs.

BOTTLES TO TRY

○ **Le Rêve Blanc de Blancs** / **$$$$**
● **Brut Rosé** / **$$$**

FLYING GOAT CELLARS

When he finally launched his own brand, winemaker Norm Yost named it after his kids: two highly acrobatic pet pygmy goats named Never and Epernay. Yost sources grapes for his four culty Goat Bubbles sparkling wines from well-known vineyards located in California's coastal Santa Barbara region. Produced in small lots using the *méthode champenoise,* the wines are hard to find at retail. But their coolly refined flavors make them worth seeking out.

BOTTLES TO TRY

○ **Goat Bubbles Blanc de Blanc** / **$$$**
● **Goat Bubbles Rosé** / **$$$**

GLORIA FERRER CAVES & VINEYARDS

Despite the abundance of still wine producers in California's cool Carneros zone in the mid-1980s, there were no sparkling houses in the region until Spanish wine maven José Ferrer (of the Freixenet wine empire, see opposite) established this estate in 1986. Ferrer named it after his wife, Gloria, and in short order the winery was turning out fantastic sparkling whites and rosés made chiefly from Pinot Noir. That grape takes the lead role in most Gloria Ferrer wines, from the berry-scented Sonoma Brut to the creamy, zesty Blanc de Noirs.

BOTTLES TO TRY

○ **Blanc de Noirs** / **$$**
○ **Sonoma Brut** / **$$**

GRUET WINERY

Central New Mexico's high desert grows more than amazing-looking cacti: It produces grapes for delicious sparkling wine, thanks to the pioneering Gruet family. Vintners in Champagne, the Gruets were on vacation in 1983 when they heard about a patch of experimental vines south of Albuquerque. Six years later, the Gruets debuted their first New Mexican sparkling wine. A favorite of sommeliers, the apple-and-citrus-driven basic brut and toasty Blanc de Noirs are among the best value sparkling wines made anywhere.

BOTTLES TO TRY
- **Brut NV / $**
- **Blanc de Noirs / $$**

J VINEYARDS & WINERY

The already terrific wines at this boutique Sonoma estate have gotten even better since owner Judy Jordan lured ex–La Crema talent Melissa Stackhouse on board. Jordan (whose father founded Sonoma's Jordan Vineyard) dedicated the winery almost from the start to producing Russian River sparkling wine using traditional Champagne methods. Though still wines have become more important over the years, the winery's flagship cuvée remains its yeasty, citrusy J Vintage Brut. Its luscious Late-Disgorged bottling benefits from extra aging on lees, giving it a toasty richness.

BOTTLES TO TRY
- **J Late-Disgorged Vintage Brut / $$$**
- **J Vintage Brut / $$$**

PIPER SONOMA

Although this Sonoma label has changed hands twice since its founding by Champagne's Piper-Heidsieck group, it's still a reliable source of tasty sparkling wine. Its two cuvées are made in Mendocino from Sonoma-grown grapes by longtime wine-maker Raphaël Brisbois. He enriches the Blanc de Blancs with reserve wines and ages it for 16 months on its lees. The succulent brut is based on Chardonnay, with Pinot Meunier and Pinot Noir playing minor roles.

BOTTLES TO TRY
- **Brut NV / $**
- **Blanc de Blancs NV / $$**

ROEDERER ESTATE

Famed Champagne producer Louis Roederer's estate in Northern California's cool and foggy Anderson Valley puts out some of America's top sparkling wines. Sticking closely to Champagne tradition, Roederer cuvées benefit from the addition of reserve wines, aged in French oak casks. The older wines lend depth and nuance beyond their price to the nonvintage brut and strawberry-scented rosé, and the vintage white and rosé L'Ermitage wines can rival true Champagne.

BOTTLES TO TRY

○ **Roederer Estate Brut NV / $$**
● **L'Ermitage by Roederer Estate / $$$**

SCHRAMSBERG VINEYARDS

Skeptics thought that Jack and Jamie Davies were crazy to purchase this dilapidated Napa Valley property in 1965 and convert it into a high-end sparkling wine estate. Just seven years later, President Richard Nixon served a Schramsberg Blanc de Blancs during his trip to China; today the wines are benchmarks of their type. The founders' son Hugh Davies continues to focus on quality, aging the wines in hillside caves that were dug in the 1870s. Made in a firm, refined style, Schramsberg's vintage Blanc de Blancs is consistently one of the best American all-Chardonnay sparklers.

BOTTLES TO TRY

○ **Vintage Blanc de Blancs / $$$**
● **Mirabelle Brut Rosé NV / $$**

Fortified & Dessert Wines

The most exciting news right now in fortified wines is sherry. Long maligned, almost universally (and mistakenly) thought of as always sweet, this complex, beautiful wine from southern Spain is an obsession of hip sommeliers. It has become commonplace to see at least a few terrific, artisan-produced sherries on wine lists at top restaurants. Other dessert wines (save for Moscato, which crowds supermarket shelves thanks to its adoption by rap stars) get less press but are no less worth investigating: from Italian *vin santos,* to Sauternes and Barsacs from Bordeaux, to the most storied of them all, vintage port from Portugal's Douro Valley.

FORTIFIED WINES

The practice of fortifying wines involves adding a neutral spirit before bottling. Traditional fortified wines include sherry, port, Madeira and Marsala, although variations abound. These wines have a higher alcohol content—usually 16 to 20 percent—than most unfortified wines. A fortified wine's style depends largely on when the spirit is added. Adding it during fermentation, as is the case with most port and Madeira, yields wines with a lot of natural grape sugar. When brandy is added after fermentation, the result can be drier, such as a fino sherry.

FORTIFIED WINES

SHERRY

CLAIM TO FAME

Made only in southern Spain's Jerez region, sherry gets stereotyped as an aperitif but is actually a vastly underrated food wine. Dry fino styles complement salty, savory dishes; sweeter olorosos are delicious with desserts. Sherry gains its distinctive taste from the Jerez area's chalky soils and, in most cases, from flor, a yeast that appears on the surface of the wine as it ferments. Flor helps give sherry its nutty, appley tones, while neutral spirit—added after fermentation—increases its alcohol and body.

KEY GRAPES

Sherry's chief grape variety is Palomino, though sweeter styles sometimes contain Pedro Ximénez or Moscatel. Except for a handful of rare, vintage-dated wines (called *añadas*), all sherries are blends of wines from different years, combined in a fractional blending system called solera. In it, small amounts of younger wines get blended into older wines, which in turn get blended into a set of even older wines, and so on. A typical bodega ages three to nine levels of wine at the same time. Because only a small portion of wine is removed from each barrel each year, the oldest level contains a blend of wines from decades— and sometimes more than a century—of different vintages. The blending and long aging result in consistent, complex sherries that come in two basic types, fino and oloroso, and a range of sweetness levels.

WINE TERMINOLOGY

FINO Dry, pale and delicate, with notes of green apple and straw, fino sherry ages under a protective blanket of flor. The yeast covers the surface of the wine as it ages, preventing it from oxidizing and keeping it fresh. Like white table wine, fino tastes best chilled and loses its appeal within a few days of opening.

AMONTILLADO This nutty sherry starts out as fino, then loses its flor and ages in barrel for many years (at least for high-quality versions). The resulting oxidation is what gives amontillados their darker color. The finest examples are dry; "medium" amontillado is sweeter, though not as sweet as most olorosos.

MANZANILLA A fino sherry made around the port city of Sanlúcar de Barrameda, this is racy and bone-dry. Its lighter alcohol and salty tang make it terrific with seafood or tapas.

OLOROSO Darker than finos and shading from dark gold to amber, olorosos are more highly fortified, which prevents the formation of flor. Exposure to oxygen darkens their color and creates nutty, earthy flavors. Most olorosos are sweet, though dry examples are usually high quality and worth seeking out.

PALO CORTADO With the freshness of an amontillado and the body and depth of an oloroso, this relatively rare sherry is exposed to oxygen as it ages. Some vintners create inexpensive shortcuts to the style by blending amontillado and oloroso.

PEDRO XIMÉNEZ (PX) Made from partially raisined grapes, this rich, viscous and ultra-dark sherry can stand in for dessert.

CREAM SHERRIES These sweet, often simple sherries are typically made from a blend of young sherries—usually oloroso—that are sweetened with partially fermented, fortified Pedro Ximénez wines. "Pale" versions are lighter in color and taste.

ALMACENISTA An *almacenista* is a small-scale sherry producer that doesn't grow grapes or bottle sherry but instead buys young wines, refines them in a solera system and sells finished wines to large producers. Some of the best sherries are released as small-lot bottlings bearing an *almacenista* family name.

VOS This term designates any sherry with a minimum average age of 20 years. Made in a smooth and complex style, these wines can be dark and intensely nutty. VOS stands for *Vinum Optimum Signatum,* a Latin phrase meaning "certified best wine," but the category is easier to remember as "very old sherry."

VORS Although this designation is reserved for sherries with a minimum average age of 30 years, some VORS (*Vinum Optimum Rare Signatum,* or "certified best rare wine") bottlings are much older. Most often used to boost the complexity of younger wines, VORS wines are increasingly bottled and sold on their own.

Producers/ Sherry

BODEGAS DIOS BACO

This stellar firm produces traditionally made sherries on a small scale. Though it has been around in one form or another since 1765, its modern history began in 1992, when the Páez Morilla family purchased the Dios Baco cellar, plus about 100 acres of vineyards. José Páez Morilla and his daughter Alejandra mastermind the wines, which consist of a brisk, salty manzanilla, a rich oloroso and an usually lush, almond-edged fino.

BOTTLES TO TRY
- Oloroso / $$
- Riá Pitá Manzanilla / $$

EQUIPO NAVAZOS

This cutting-edge label is not a sherry producer so much as a curator: Jesús Barquín, arguably the world's foremost sherry expert, noses out extraordinary, limited-edition wines from the best bodegas and bottles them by cask (*bota*) number. Originally available only to a private group of fellow sherry fanatics, they're now sold in the U.S., albeit in tiny quantities. But the wines' revelatory flavors make them well worth seeking out.

BOTTLES TO TRY
- La Bota de Manzanilla Pasada Capataz Rivas No. 30 / $$$$
- La Bota de Palo Cortado No. 34 / $$$$

SANDEMAN

A fortified-wine powerhouse, Sandeman has been selling sherry and port since 1790, the year Scotsman George Sandeman set up shop in London. Today it's owned by Portugal's Sogrape Vinhos, but a seventh-generation Sandeman descendant is still involved in running the company. The brand's signature image of a black-cloaked don adorns a range of basic sherries, but look especially for the stellar amontillados and rich, complex wines in the 20-year-old series.

BOTTLES TO TRY

○ **Don Fino** ╱ **$**

○ **Royal Esmeralda Aged 20 Years Fine Dry Amontillado** ╱ **$$$ (500 ml)**

FORTIFIED WINES

PORT

CLAIM TO FAME

Portugal's second-largest city, Oporto, gave its name to the country's emblematic wine. Ranging from light, juicy ruby ports to decadent, powerful vintage bottlings, port's lush fruit and sweetness make it the quintessential after-dinner drink. Experimental bartenders are discovering its versatility in cocktails, too, and in the process freshening up port's dusty image.

♣ KEY GRAPES

Port is a blended wine, made chiefly from five major red grapes (although more than 80 kinds are allowed). The most important of these is Touriga Nacional, with Touriga Franca, Tinto Cão, Tinta Barroca and Tinta Roriz (Tempranillo) valued for bringing qualities like fragrance, fruit, spice and tannins to the blend. Port comes in two main styles, ruby and tawny; the occasional white is made from a handful of mostly obscure local grapes.

WINE TERMINOLOGY

RUBY The most common style of port, ruby is a juicy, fruity blend of young wines. Ruby reserve ports are more complex, often bearing proprietary names such as Graham's Six Grapes. Late Bottled Vintage (LBV) ports are thick-textured, single-vintage rubies that have been aged four to six years in barrel and are drinkable upon release. The most famous rubies are vintage ports, which are made from grapes harvested in a single year; they spend only two years in cask and age primarily in bottle. Producers declare a vintage in only the best years, usually just two or three times a decade. Decadent vintage ports are big, black, densely flavored wines that age effortlessly for decades. Single-quinta (vineyard) vintage ports are made with grapes from one vineyard, usually in nondeclared vintages.

TAWNY Ready to drink on release and often served lightly chilled, tawny ports offer delicate, nutty aromas and notes of dried fruit. In theory, a tawny has been aged in wood longer than a ruby and has thus taken on a lighter, tawny hue. In reality, many inexpensive tawny ports are the same age as most rubies; they are just made with lighter wines. Aged tawny ports, however, are very different: Seductive and complex, they're made from blends of the highest-quality ports. They are released in 10-, 20-, 30- and 40-year-old versions, with the number referring to the average age of the blend's component wines.

WHITE Bright, citrusy white port is a terrific aperitif or summer drink, especially when it's served chilled with tonic or over ice.

Producers/ Port

CHURCHILL'S

While most port houses measure their history in centuries, Churchill's has existed for a mere 30 years or so. But its founder, John Graham, has impressive roots in port: His ancestors founded the venerable port company W. & J. Graham's. John Graham's winemaking style combines lush fruit with firm structure, as evidenced in the spicy, seductive Late Bottled Vintage. The Quinta da Gricha Vintage bottlings come from a pocket of old vines in the house's flagship vineyard of the same name.

BOTTLES TO TRY
- **Late Bottled Vintage / $$**
- **Quinta da Gricha Vintage / $$$$**

DELAFORCE

This nearly 150-year-old port producer has returned to form in recent years. Real Companhia Velha, its current owner, has been making port for more than two and a half centuries and is one of the largest vineyard owners in the Douro. It works with the Fladgate Partnership, the company behind several of the world's greatest port houses (Taylor's, Fonseca, Croft) to produce the Delaforce line, including the mellow, toffee-scented Curious and Ancient tawny. Delaforce's Late Bottled Vintage matures in wood for up to six years and is ready to drink.

BOTTLES TO TRY

- ● **Late Bottled Vintage** ∕ **$$**
- ● **Curious and Ancient 20 Years Old Tawny** ∕ **$$$**

DOW'S

One of the great names in wine (fortified or otherwise), Dow's produces benchmark ports of all sorts. Owned for the past half-century or so by the Symington family, Dow's style is drier and more austere than that of other Symington brands, such as Graham's or Warre's. Dow's vintage wines are legendary for their ability to improve with age, and the best are known to last effortlessly for more than a century. For years in which a vintage isn't declared, Dow's Senhora da Ribeira single-quinta (vineyard) vintage port makes a stellar alternative.

BOTTLES TO TRY

- ● **10 Year Old Tawny** ∕ **$$$**
- ● **Quinta Senhora da Ribeira Vintage** ∕ **$$$**

FONSECA

David Guimaraens must've been born under a lucky star: His first year as winemaker for his family's port house, 1994, turned out to be one of the 20th century's best vintages. The sixth-generation vintner produced a magnificent vintage port and hasn't faltered since. Fonseca's rich, full-bodied wines cover all of port's major bases; its 10 Year Old Tawny is creamy, nutty and lush. For a summery alternative to red port, try Fonseca's Siroco, which makes a refreshing cocktail over ice with a splash of tonic.

BOTTLES TO TRY

- ○ **Siroco/$$**
- ● **10 Year Old Tawny** ∕ **$$**
- ● **Vintage Port** ∕ **$$$$**

QUINTA DO VESUVIO

One of the great vineyards of the Upper Douro, Vesuvio is a remote, forbiddingly rugged estate that was planted in the early 1800s by the Ferreiras, one of the century's most prominent port families. Today it's owned by the Symingtons (Dow's, Graham's, Warre's), who've spent the past 25 years restoring the site to its former glory. Peter Symington and his son Charles fashion only vintage-dated port from the vineyard. Made from handpicked grapes crushed by foot, Quinta do Vesuvio ports offer powerful fruit flavors and a muscular structure.

BOTTLE TO TRY
- **Vintage Port ∕ $$$$**

RAMOS PINTO

Adriano Ramos Pinto founded this winery in 1880 (see p. 133), focusing on exports to Brazil. Now the estate is owned by the French Roederer Group, of Champagne fame, and its wines are masterminded by João Nicolau de Almeida. Together with his uncle, José Ramos Pinto Rosas, de Almeida helped revolutionize Douro winemaking in the 1970s and '80s by winnowing the Douro's many native grape varieties to the five best for port production. In the broad lineup, Ramos Pinto's velvety, complex tawny ports stand out.

BOTTLES TO TRY
- **Quinta de Ervamoira 10 Years Tawny ∕ $$$**
- **Quinta do Bom Retiro 20 Years Tawny ∕ $$$$**

DESSERT WINES

The longest-lived wines in the world are sweet. Legendary bottlings of Bordeaux's Sauternes wines and Hungary's Tokaji routinely outlive the people who made them, and offer luscious, honey-tinged flavors of incredible complexity (as well as price tags to match their prestige). But great sweet wines are made all over the world, often at affordable prices. Whether from California, Italy, Australia or elsewhere, they're characterized by ample sweet fruit and enough bright acidity to keep them from becoming cloying. That acidity also explains why "dessert wines" is a bit of a misnomer: Many of them make a terrific, and unjustly overlooked, match not only for desserts but also for savory foods, including foie gras and blue cheeses.

WINE TERMINOLOGY

BOTRYTIS Botrytized wines owe their unique taste to *Botrytis cinerea,* a mold ("noble rot") that concentrates the wine's sugars and adds smoke and truffle notes. The finest are Bordeaux's Sauternes, made of Sémillon, Sauvignon Blanc and Muscadelle. Superb examples come from Bordeaux's Barsac subregion, while nearby Loupiac and Cadillac yield less-costly versions. Loire Valley vintners make terrific botrytized sweet wines with Chenin Blanc; in Alsace, these wines are identified by the Sélection de Grains Nobles designation. German and Austrian vintners use mainly Riesling to craft sublime botrytized wines, labeled *Beerenauslese* (BA) or *Trockenbeerenauslese* (TBA), depending on sugar levels (see p. 138). California, Australia and South Africa also make botrytized wines, many of them terrific.

LATE HARVEST These wines rely on grapes harvested very late in the season, when they have developed extremely high sugar levels. The best-known bottlings come from Germany (marked *Auslese* or *Beerenauslese,* indicating progressively greater sweetness) and Alsace (where they're called Vendanges Tardives). California, Australia, South Africa, Chile and the Greek island of Samos make good versions, too.

ICE WINE/EISWEIN This wine is made by pressing grapes that had frozen on the vine, a process that yields very small amounts of sweet, concentrated juice. The finest ice wines are made from Riesling in Germany and Austria; many great examples also come from Canada.

PASSITO An Italian specialty, *passito* wines are made from grapes that have been dried before pressing. Tuscan vintners use Trebbiano and/or Malvasia to make the local version, *vin santo,* while Sicilian winemakers use the Zibibbo grape (a.k.a. Muscat of Alexandria) for their delicious *passito* wines.

DOUX This term refers to the sweetest wines produced in the Loire region as well as to sweet Champagnes and Vins Doux Naturels, the lightly fortified wines of Southern France (see opposite). Wines labeled *doux* often have an almost syrupy consistency.

MOELLEUX In the Loire, *moelleux* refers, in theory, to the less sweet of the region's two dessert-wine categories (the other being *doux*). Confusingly, though, there's no official sugar level used to define the category, and some producers use the term even on incredibly sweet bottlings. *Moelleux* wines often gain complexity and sweetness from botrytis (see opposite). The term is also used in other French regions to describe medium-sweet wines.

VIN DOUX NATUREL Fortified with brandy during the fermentation process, these wines are produced mainly in southern France. The two most noteworthy white examples are Muscat de Beaumes-de-Venise from the Rhône Valley and Muscat de Rivesaltes from the Roussillon region; Banyuls is the most famous red Vin Doux Naturel.

TOKAJI This distinctive wine is infused with a mash of *aszú*, or botrytis-affected grapes (see opposite). Produced mainly in Hungary, Tokaji is graded by the amount of *aszú* mash added to the base, on a scale measured by *puttonyos*—the more *puttonyos*, the more intense the wine. Every Tokaji tends to exhibit delicious ripe apricot, orange and almond notes, and high acidity.

Producers/ Dessert Wines

BLANDY'S MADEIRA

No other wine in the world can claim the extraordinary longevity of fine Madeira, which starts to reach its peak decades—even centuries—after most wines are finished. In fact, a few years ago, Blandy's poured a thrilling Bual wine from the year of its founding—1811—at tastings celebrating its 200th anniversary. Just as impressive, the company is still owned and run by descendants of its founder, John Blandy. Its intense vintage Malmsey is virtually indestructible; the far more affordable 10 year old is decadent, caramel inflected and ready to drink now.

BOTTLES TO TRY

○ Aged 10 Years Malmsey / $$$
○ Vintage Malmsey / $$$$

CHÂTEAU COUTET

Thomas Jefferson praised Château Coutet's Sauternes in 1787, by which time this important Bordeaux estate had already been producing wine for nearly a century and a half. Located in Barsac, the region's top commune, Château Coutet produces a flagship bottling that's classic Sauternes: a nectarlike elixir with honeyed citrus and stone-fruit flavors and racy acidity. Even more opulent is the rare Cuvée Madame, made in exceptional vintages from old-vine Sémillon. The estate's second wine, La Chartreuse de Coutet, is a fantastic, affordable alternative.

BOTTLES TO TRY
- La Chartreuse de Coutet / $$ (375 ml)
- Château Coutet / $$$$ (375 ml)
- Cuvée Madame / $$$$

CHÂTEAU D'YQUEM

Château d'Yquem occupies a rarified spot among fine wines. Made for three and a half centuries from a vineyard atop a low hill in Bordeaux's Sauternes district, Yquem is the most famous, collectible and expensive dessert wine in the world. A single bottle of the 1811 Yquem sold for $140,000 in 2012, and current vintages run about $400 for a mere half bottle—if you can find one. Sure, Yquem's prestige drives up its price. But it's inarguably a magnificent wine, with a stunning, saturated intensity and buoyant structure that give it rare longevity.

BOTTLE TO TRY
- Château d'Yquem / $$$$

DOLCE

The partners of Napa's acclaimed Far Niente winery started making this late-harvest Sémillon–Sauvignon Blanc dessert blend in 1985. Modeled on the great sweet wines of Sauternes, it became so successful that Far Niente spun it off as a separate brand, Dolce. Grapes come from a single Napa vineyard chosen for its rare propensity for developing *Botrytis cinerea* ("noble rot"; see p. 298). With its layers of silky, intense stone-fruit and citrus flavors, Dolce is one of California's finest sweet wines. Try it with creamy vanilla puddings, baked fruit desserts or lightly sweet soufflés.

BOTTLE TO TRY
- Dolce / $$$$ (375 ml)

LES CLOS DE PAULILLES

This is the largest single vineyard holding in the Banyuls, a region in southwest France known for sweet red wines. Based on the Grenache grape, Clos de Paulilles's vintage-dated Rimage is made much like fine port: Ultra-ripe fruit is harvested by hand, gently crushed and then fortified with spirits before all of the wine's sugars have fermented into alcohol. The result is a gently spicy, full-bodied red redolent of warm cherry and berry fruit. Its lusciousness makes it a terrific match for intense chocolate desserts; its obscurity makes it an equally terrific value.

BOTTLE TO TRY
- Banyuls Rimage ∕ $$ (375 ml)

WEINLAUBENHOF KRACHER

The brilliant dessert wines from this Austrian estate gained cult status under its late, great winemaker and resident genius, Alois Kracher, Jr. Working with family vineyards along Lake Neusiedl, near the Hungarian border, Kracher pioneered magnificent botrytized and ice wines from a variety of grapes, including Scheurebe, Welschriesling and Muskat Ottonel. Kracher's son Gerhard continues the tradition. Like his father, he helpfully numbers the wines according to concentration: The higher the number, the greater the wine's residual sugar in that vintage.

BOTTLES TO TRY
- ○ Cuvée Beerenauslese ∕ $$$ (375 ml)
- ○ Welschriesling Trockenbeerenauslese ∕ $$$$ (375 ml)

YALUMBA

Australia's oldest family-owned winery produces a bewildering array of terrific dry wines (see p. 237) and some of the continent's top sweet ones, too. Best known are Yalumba's tawny ports, which compete with Portugal's finest bottles in complexity. Made from a hodgepodge of varieties, including old-vine Shiraz, Grenache, Muscadelle and traditional Portuguese grapes, they're gorgeously refined. Its FSW8B Botrytis Viognier, meanwhile, is oddly named (it stands for Fine Sweet White, Lot 8B) and absolutely delicious: Silky and vibrant, it's a phenomenal value.

BOTTLES TO TRY
- ○ FSW8B Botrytis Viognier ∕ $$$ (375 ml)
- Museum Reserve Antique 21 Years Old Tawny Port ∕ $$$$ (375 ml)

Pairing

Wine & Food

These days the adage "White wine with fish and red with meat" seems to have been replaced with "Drink whatever you like with whatever you want." Both approaches have advantages, but neither is an absolute. The truth is that there is no one principle for creating perfect wine matches beyond the fact that you want to bring together dishes and wines that highlight each other's best qualities rather than obscure them. To help make delicious matches at home, the following pages provide five basic strategies for matching and tips for pairing based on the main course and cooking technique. The specific bottle recommendations are all from this guide.

WINE-PAIRING GUIDELINES

THINK ABOUT WEIGHT One simple approach to pairing wine and food is to match lighter dishes with lighter wines and richer dishes with richer wines. We all know that a fillet of sole seems "lighter" than braised beef short ribs. With wine, the best analogy is milk: We know that skim milk feels lighter than whole milk, and wine is similar. So, for instance, Cabernet Sauvignon or Amarone feels richer or heavier than a Beaujolais or a crisp rosé from Provence.

TART GOES WITH TART Acidic foods—like a green salad with a tangy vinaigrette—work best with similarly tart wines: a Sauvignon Blanc, say, or a Muscadet from France. It might seem as though a richer, weightier wine would be the answer, but the acidity in the food will make the wine taste bland.

CONSIDER SALT & FAT Two things to keep in mind about how your palate works: First, salt in food will make wine seem less sour, softening the edge in tart wines; and fat in a dish—whether it's a well-marbled steak or pasta with a cream sauce—will make red wines seem lighter and less tannic.

SPLIT THE DIFFERENCE In restaurants, a group of people will rarely order the same entrees; instead, someone will order fish, another person a steak, a third the pasta with duck ragù, and so on. In instances like this, go for a wine that follows a middle course—not too rich, not too light, not too tannic. For reds, Pinot Noir is a great option; for whites, choose an unoaked wine with good acidity, like a dry Riesling or a Pinot Gris from Oregon.

MOST OF ALL, DON'T WORRY Pairings are meant to be suggestions. Play around with possibilities and don't get caught up in absolutes. After all, Cabernet may go well with a cheeseburger, but if you don't like cheeseburgers, that doesn't matter at all.

Pairing Cheat Sheet

	DISH	BEST WINE MATCH
CHICKEN	STEAMED OR POACHED	Medium white or light red
CHICKEN	ROASTED OR SAUTÉED	Rich white or medium red
CHICKEN	CREAMY OR BUTTERY SAUCES	Rich white
CHICKEN	TANGY SAUCES MADE WITH CITRUS, VINEGAR, TOMATOES	Medium white
CHICKEN	EARTHY FLAVORS LIKE MUSHROOMS	Light or medium red
CHICKEN	HERBS	Light white
PORK	GRILLED OR SEARED, LEAN	Medium red
PORK	GRILLED OR SEARED, FATTY	Rich red
PORK	BRAISED OR STEWED	Rich red
PORK	SWEET SAUCES OR DRIED FRUIT	Medium white
PORK	SPICY INGREDIENTS	Medium white or light red
PORK	CURED OR BRINED	Medium white or rosé

GREAT VARIETIES	BOTTLE TO TRY
Chardonnay (unoaked), Gamay	Tormaresca Chardonnay / p. 103
Chardonnay, Marsanne, Tempranillo	Gallo Signature Series Chardonnay / p. 180
Chardonnay, Viognier	La Crema Sonoma Coast Chardonnay / p. 185
Verdicchio, Sauvignon Blanc	Domaine Pascal Jolivet Sancerre Blanc / p. 51
Pinot Noir, Cabernet Franc	Domaine Bruno Clair Les Longeroies Marsannay / p. 36
Pinot Grigio, Albariño, Vermentino	Pazo de Señoráns Albariño / p. 116
Sangiovese, Cabernet Franc	Lang & Reed North Coast Cabernet Franc / p. 186
Grenache blends, Merlot	Yangarra Estate Vineyard Old Vine Grenache / p. 237
Cabernet Sauvignon, Malbec	Bodega Colomé Estate Malbec / p. 252
Riesling, Pinot Gris (Alsace)	Hugel et Fils Pinot Gris / p. 23
Riesling (off-dry), Pinot Noir	A to Z Wineworks Pinot Noir / p. 206
Verdicchio, Sauvignon Blanc, rosé	Bonny Doon Vin Gris de Cigare / p. 172

DISH	BEST WINE MATCH
BEEF	
GRILLED OR SEARED STEAKS, CHOPS, BURGERS	Rich red
BRAISED OR STEWED	Rich red
SWEET SAUCES LIKE BARBECUE	Rich red
SPICY INGREDIENTS	Medium red
LAMB	
GRILLED OR ROASTED	Rich red
BRAISED OR STEWED	Rich red
SPICY INGREDIENTS	Light red
FISH	
GRILLED	Medium white, rosé or light red
ROASTED, BAKED OR SAUTÉED	Medium white or light red
FRIED	Light white or rosé
STEAMED	Light white
SPICY INGREDIENTS	Medium white
HERB SAUCES	Light or medium white
CITRUS SAUCES	Light or medium white
SHELLFISH, COOKED	Medium or rich white
SHELLFISH, RAW	Light white

GREAT VARIETIES	BOTTLE TO TRY
Cabernet Sauvignon, Malbec	Saddleback Cellars Napa Valley Cabernet Sauvignon / p. 196
Cabernet Sauvignon, Nebbiolo	Giacomo Borgogno & Figli Barolo / p. 73
Zinfandel, Grenache	Cameron Hughes Zin Your Face Zinfandel / p. 174
Tempranillo, Sangiovese	CVNE Viña Real Reserva / p. 111
Zinfandel, Grenache, Syrah	Qupé Bien Nacido Vineyard Syrah / p. 194
Syrah, Malbec, Cabernet Sauvignon	Buty Rediviva of the Stones / p. 213
Pinot Noir, Gamay, Dolcetto	Nautilus Estate Pinot Noir / p. 246
Chardonnay (unoaked), rosé, Pinot Noir	William Fèvre Champs Royaux Chablis / p. 43
Pinot Gris (Oregon), Gamay	Cristom Vineyards Pinot Gris / p. 207
Vermentino, rosé	Mas de Daumas Gassac Moulin de Gassac Guilhem Rosé / p. 65
Sauvignon Blanc	Spy Valley Sauvignon Blanc / p. 247
Riesling (off-dry)	S.A. Prüm Essence Riesling / p. 140
Arneis, Grüner Veltliner	Weingut Hirsch Veltliner #1 / p. 151
Pinot Grigio, Chenin Blanc	Alois Lageder Porer Pinot Grigio / p. 79
Chardonnay (unoaked), Grenache Blanc	Domaine Christian Moreau Père & Fils Chablis / p. 37
Muscadet, Albariño, Vinho Verde	Aveleda Alvarinho / p. 131

	DISH	BEST WINE MATCH
GAME	**VENISON**	Rich red
	DUCK OR GAME BIRDS, ROASTED OR PAN-ROASTED	Medium red
	DUCK OR GAME BIRDS, RAGÙ OR STEW	Medium or rich red
PASTA	**BUTTER OR OIL**	Medium white or rosé
	CREAMY, CHEESE SAUCES	Medium white or red
	TOMATO-BASED SAUCES	Medium red
	SPICY SAUCES	Medium white or light red
	MEAT SAUCES	Rich red
	FISH AND SEAFOOD SAUCES	Medium white
EGGS	**PLAIN OR WITH HERBS**	Sparkling
	WITH CHEESE (QUICHE)	Sparkling, medium white or rosé
SALADS	**TART DRESSINGS LIKE VINAIGRETTE**	Light white
	CREAMY DRESSINGS	Medium white
	PASTA & OTHER STARCHY SALADS	Rosé or light red

GREAT VARIETIES	BOTTLE TO TRY
Monastrell, Syrah	Bodegas Olivares Altos de la Hoya / p. 118
Pinot Noir	La Follette Manchester Ridge Pinot Noir / p. 185
Sangiovese, Touriga Nacional	Quinta do Vallado Touriga Nacional / p. 133
Pinot Blanc, Fiano di Avellino	Josmeyer Pinot Blanc / p. 23
Chardonnay (unoaked), Barbera	Michele Chiarlo Le Orme Barbera d'Asti / p. 74
Sangiovese	Fattoria Selvapiana Chianti Rufina / p. 89
Riesling (off-dry), Dolcetto	Poderi Luigi Einaudi Dolcetto di Dogliani / p. 75
Aglianico, Corvina	Terredora Aglianico / p. 102
Vermentino	Argiolas Costamolino Vermentino di Sardegna / p. 99
Champagne or other dry sparkling	Taittinger Brut La Française / p. 282
Champagne or other dry sparkling, Riesling (dry), rosé	Raventós i Blanc de Nit Brut Rosado / p. 286
Sauvignon Blanc, Vinho Verde	Greywacke Sauvignon Blanc / p. 244
Chenin Blanc, Pinot Gris	Hendry Vineyard Pinot Gris / p. 181
Rosé, Beaujolais	Domaine de la Mordorée La Dame Rousse Tavel / p. 57

Pairing

Recipes

Scallops with Grapefruit-Onion Salad & New Zealand Sauvignon Blanc

TOTAL: 25 MIN • 8 FIRST-COURSE SERVINGS

Tangy dressings and sauces won't overwhelm zippy white wines like Sauvignon Blanc, Vinho Verde from Portugal and Verdejo from Spain.

4   small Ruby Red grapefruits (about 2 pounds total)
3   tablespoons pickled cocktail onions
2   tablespoons packed flat-leaf parsley leaves
Freshly ground pepper
24 sea scallops (about 2 pounds)
Kosher salt
1   tablespoon extra-virgin olive oil, plus more for drizzling

1. Using a very sharp paring knife, peel the grapefruits, carefully removing all of the bitter white pith. Carefully cut in between the membranes to release the grapefruit sections into a bowl. Discard all but 1 tablespoon of grapefruit juice from the bowl. Stir in the pickled cocktail onions and parsley and season with pepper.

2. Pat the sea scallops dry and season them all over with salt. In a large nonstick skillet, heat the 1 tablespoon of olive oil until it is shimmering. Cook the scallops over moderately high heat, turning once, until they are browned and just cooked through, about 4 minutes total. Spoon the pickled-onion-and-grapefruit salad onto small plates and arrange the scallops around the salad. Drizzle with olive oil and serve at once.

MAKE AHEAD The recipe can be prepared through Step 1, covered and refrigerated for up to 2 hours.

Thai Green Salad with Duck Cracklings & German Riesling

TOTAL: 45 MIN • 8 SERVINGS

The slight sweetness of many Rieslings, Gewürztraminers and Vouvrays helps tame the heat of spicy Asian dishes.

- 8 duck confit legs—skin cut into fine strips, meat shredded (see Note)
- 1 tablespoon finely chopped peeled fresh ginger
- 1 large garlic clove, minced
- 1 serrano chile, seeded and minced
- 2 tablespoons light brown sugar
- 3 tablespoons Asian fish sauce
- 2 tablespoons fresh lime juice
- 1¼ pounds baby Bibb lettuce, leaves separated
- ½ cup mint leaves
- ½ cup cilantro leaves

1. In a large nonstick skillet, cook the duck skin over moderate heat until golden and crisp, about 8 minutes. Using a slotted spoon, transfer the cracklings to a plate. Pour off all but 2 tablespoons of the fat in the skillet and add the meat. Cook over moderate heat until tender and crispy in spots, about 7 minutes. Let cool slightly.

2. Meanwhile, in a mortar (or using a mini food processor), pound the ginger, garlic, chile and brown sugar to a coarse paste. Stir in the fish sauce, lime juice and 2 tablespoons of water.

3. In a large bowl, toss the lettuce with the mint, cilantro, duck, cracklings and dressing. Transfer to plates and serve.

NOTE Duck confit is available at many specialty markets and at dartagnan.com.

MAKE AHEAD The dressing can be refrigerated overnight.

Honeyed Fig Crostatas
& Moscato Dolce

ACTIVE: 45 MIN; TOTAL: 2 HR 45 MIN

8 SERVINGS

Slightly sweet sparkling wines such as Moscato dolce or demi-sec Champagne emphasize the fruit in the dessert, not the sugar.

2½ cups all-purpose flour
¼ cup plus 1 tablespoon sugar
Kosher salt
1½ sticks cold unsalted butter, cut into ½-inch pieces
¼ cup plus 3 tablespoons ice water
1½ pounds fresh green and purple figs,
      each cut into 6 wedges
5 teaspoons honey
1 teaspoon fresh lemon juice
¼ teaspoon thyme leaves, plus small sprigs for garnish
1 egg beaten with 1 tablespoon of water

1. In a food processor, pulse the flour, sugar and ½ teaspoon of salt. Add the butter and pulse until it is the size of peas. Add the ice water and pulse until the dough comes together. Pat the dough into a disk, wrap in plastic and refrigerate for 30 minutes.

2. On a lightly floured work surface, roll out the dough ⅛ inch thick. Cut out eight 5-inch rounds; reroll the scraps if needed. Transfer to a parchment-lined baking sheet and refrigerate for 30 minutes.

3. Preheat the oven to 375°. In a bowl, toss two-thirds of the figs with 3 teaspoons of the honey, the lemon juice, thyme leaves and a pinch of salt. Arrange the figs on the dough rounds, leaving a ½-inch border all around. Fold the edges over the figs and brush the dough with the egg wash. Refrigerate for 30 minutes.

4. Bake the crostatas for 35 minutes, until the crusts are golden. Let stand for 10 minutes.

5. Toss the remaining figs with the remaining 2 teaspoons of honey. Transfer the crostatas to plates, top with the figs and thyme sprigs and serve.

Leek-and-Pecorino Pizzas
& Oregon Pinot Noir

ACTIVE: 50 MIN; TOTAL: 1 HR 30 MIN
8 SERVINGS

Ingredients such as mushrooms and truffles taste great with Pinot Noir and Dolcetto, which are light-bodied but full of savory depth.

All-purpose flour, for dusting
1½ pounds pizza dough, cut into 8 pieces
¼ cup plus 2 tablespoons extra-virgin olive oil, plus more for brushing
2 large leeks, sliced ¼ inch thick
Salt and freshly ground black pepper
¾ pound ground lamb
32 cherry tomatoes, halved
¼ pound truffled pecorino cheese, thinly sliced

1. Preheat the oven to 500°. Heat a pizza stone on the bottom of the oven for 45 minutes. (Alternatively, heat a large inverted baking sheet on the bottom rack of the oven for 5 minutes.)
2. On a lightly floured work surface, roll out each piece of dough to a 7-inch round. Oil 3 large baking sheets and place the dough rounds on the sheets. Cover with plastic wrap and let rest for 15 minutes.
3. Meanwhile, in a large skillet, heat ¼ cup of the olive oil. Add the leeks, season with salt and pepper and cook over moderate heat until softened, about 8 minutes; transfer to a plate. Add the 2 tablespoons of olive oil to the skillet. Add the lamb, season with salt and pepper and cook until no pink remains, about 5 minutes.
4. Generously flour a pizza peel. Place a dough round on the peel and brush with olive oil. Top with some of the leeks, lamb, tomatoes and pecorino cheese. Slide the dough round onto the hot stone or baking sheet and bake for about 4 minutes, until bubbling and crisp. Repeat with the remaining ingredients and serve.

Pappardelle with Veal Ragù & Chianti Classico

ACTIVE: 30 MIN; TOTAL: 2 HR 45 MIN

8 SERVINGS

Foods and wines that have grown up together over the centuries are almost always a good fit.

3½ to 4 pounds boneless veal shoulder,
    cut into 3-inch chunks
Salt and freshly ground pepper
All-purpose flour, for dusting
 ½ cup extra-virgin olive oil
 1 large sweet onion, finely chopped
 4 garlic cloves, minced
1½ teaspoons ground coriander
1½ teaspoons ground fennel
1½ cups dry red wine
Two 28-ounce cans Italian whole tomatoes,
    drained and chopped
 4 cups chicken or veal stock
1½ tablespoons minced rosemary
 2 pounds fresh pappardelle
Freshly grated Parmigiano-Reggiano cheese

1. Season the veal with salt and pepper and dust with flour, tapping off the excess. In a large enameled cast-iron casserole, heat ¼ cup of the olive oil. Add the veal and cook over moderately high heat until browned all over, about 12 minutes. Transfer the veal to a plate.

2. Add the remaining ¼ cup of oil to the casserole. Stir in the onion, garlic, coriander and fennel and cook over low heat for 5 minutes. Add the wine and boil until reduced to ⅓ cup, 5 minutes. Add the tomatoes and cook over moderately high heat for 5 minutes. Add the stock and rosemary and bring to a boil. Add the veal, cover partially and cook over low heat until very tender, 2 hours.

3. Remove the meat and shred it. Boil the sauce until slightly reduced, about 10 minutes. Stir in the meat.

4. In a large pot of boiling salted water, cook the pappardelle until al dente. Drain and return to the pot. Add the ragù and toss over low heat until the pasta is coated. Serve with cheese at the table.

Grilled Hanger Steak with Garlic-Brandy Butter & Red Bordeaux

ACTIVE: 30 MIN; TOTAL: 50 MIN

4 SERVINGS

Bordeaux, Bordeaux-style blends and California Cabernet all go terrifically well with steaks or chops: Their tannins refresh the palate after each bite.

- 6 tablespoons unsalted butter, softened
- 3 tablespoons chopped parsley
- 2 medium garlic cloves, minced
- 1 tablespoon Cognac or other brandy

Salt and freshly ground pepper

- 3 tablespoons extra-virgin olive oil, plus more for brushing
- 3 large leeks, white and pale green parts only, sliced 1 inch thick
- 2 pounds trimmed hanger steaks

1. In a bowl, mash the butter with the parsley, garlic and Cognac; season with salt and pepper.

2. In a large skillet, heat the 3 tablespoons of olive oil. Add the leeks and season with salt. Cover and cook over moderately low heat, stirring occasionally, until tender, 10 minutes.

3. Light a grill or heat a grill pan. Brush the steaks with olive oil and season with salt and pepper. Grill over high heat, turning once, until nicely charred outside and medium-rare within, 5 to 6 minutes per side. Transfer the steaks to a carving board and let rest for 5 minutes. Slice the steaks across the grain and spread the garlic-brandy butter all over the meat, letting it melt in. Serve with the leeks.

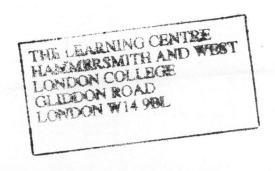

Index
of Producers